SPECULATION

SPECULATION

A Cultural History

from Aristotle to AI

GAYLE ROGERS

Columbia University Press
New York

Columbia University Press gratefully acknowledges the generous support for this book provided by a Publisher's Circle member.

Columbia University Press
Publishers Since 1893
New York   Chichester, West Sussex
cup.columbia.edu
Copyright © 2021 Columbia University Press
All rights reserved

Library of Congress Cataloging-in-Publication Data
Names: Rogers, Gayle, 1978– author.
Title: Speculation : a cultural history from Aristotle to AI / Gayle Rogers.
Description: New York : Columbia University Press, [2021] | Includes index.
Identifiers: LCCN 2020049429 (print) | LCCN 2020049430 (ebook) |
ISBN 9780231200202 (hardback) | ISBN 9780231200219 (trade paperback) |
ISBN 9780231553490 (ebook)
Subjects: LCSH: Speculation—History.
Classification: LCC HG6005 .R64 2021 (print) | LCC HG6005 (ebook) |
DDC 332.64/509—dc23
LC record available at https://lccn.loc.gov/2020049429
LC ebook record available at https://lccn.loc.gov/2020049430

COVER DESIGN: Milenda Nan Ok Lee
COVER IMAGE: Aliaksandr Mazurkevich © Alamy

CONTENTS

INTRODUCTION 1

1 THE MIRROR AND THE WATCHTOWER 9

2 EXPERIMENTING ON THOUGHT 38

3 GAMBLING ON A WORD 65

4 AMERICA THE SPECULATIVE 91

5 SPECULITIS, OR THE TECHNOLOGIES OF PROPHECY 115

6 THE LADY SPECULATOR 142

CONCLUSION: SPECULATIVE RISKS, INHUMAN IMAGINATIONS 172

Acknowledgments 185
Notes 189
Index 249

INTRODUCTION

*It is difficult to say which is the most remarkable—
the survival through the centuries of the feeling
against speculation or the survival of
speculation in the face of this feeling.*
—THE OUTLOOK (1917)

The world gives us imperfect and incomplete information for forecasting the future. We look for signs, we read everything around us, but we can never know with complete certainty what tomorrow will bring. One familiar story of modernity is that humans used to rely on primitive tools like divination and augury to guess what tomorrow might look like, but that scientific methods, hard evidence, and data-driven prediction now give us a greater degree of confidence. And yet, despite all our faith in our purported advances and innovations, we have never stopped *speculating*. We may tell ourselves not to conjure hypothetical scenarios supported by little evidence, but we constantly project what tomorrow will be like for ourselves, our families, and our societies, even when we have little plausible certainty. In fact, we encourage speculation as a mode of contemplative creativity, hoping that those among us who dream the impossible will envision a new future, much as speculative-fiction writers do. Some of us take the high-risk gambles on stocks or commodities that we also call speculations, spinning dreams of future wealth from the thinnest of current evidence. And even though such speculators are often demonized, we rebrand them as *visionaries*, *angel investors*, or *disruptors* when they build the futures that we come to inhabit. We'll never be able to foresee the future even with the best evidence, of course, and so, to guard against its uncertainties and its unknown risks, we buy insurance policies, which feel routine and natural to us—but even these are part of speculation's controversial history in modern finance capitalism.

Speculation might seem to coexist, if not thrive, in multiple ways within our otherwise scientifically verifiable present, just as we accept that some amount of randomness and luck will factor into our futures. But the 2500-year history of what we have termed *speculation* in its interconnected forms tells a more complex story. This story is full of bitter contests, protracted debates, and polemical redefinitions in the transition from antiquity to the medieval era, in the Protestant Reformation, in the emergence of contemporary capitalism, in the language of women's socioeconomics, and at many other crucial sites and moments. Speculation's history ranges from bubbles and frauds to the scientific revolution and dreams of technological futurity, and from the heights of divinity to the seedy underworlds of dice games in alleys. Its path into the present has been anything but simple and fluid. Whether it was Francis Bacon laboring to integrate speculation into his groundbreaking methods, Jane Austen rewriting speculative marriage markets, or any number of commentators claiming that addictive "speculative manias" had paralyzed their societies, an astounding number of figures over time modified this concept in order to stake their claims about the nature of provisional knowledge and its real-world effects. And yet we understand little about the threats that speculation has presented to orders of knowledge, political structures, and economic and informational complexes.

The reason speculation has mattered so much to so many is the remarkable role it has played in how we create—and potentially destroy—the future. Speculation provides the language and conceptualization by which we produce contingent knowledge, ideas, abstractions, risks, and even money and material gains, all of which radically shape our individual and collective futures. The roots of speculation's force lie not in the parts of the visible world we believe we can know fully, here and now, but in an interaction between the information our eyes process in the present and the scenarios we then envision for the future. In his *Dictionary of the English Language* (1755), Samuel Johnson felicitously captured *speculation* as our capacity "to look through with the mind."[1] Our visual perceptions are somehow insufficient, so we use our proverbial mind's eye to generate further insights, always adamant that what we see must *mean* more than what it presents on the surface. The stakes and contexts of that process have changed dramatically over time, informed by everything from religion to computers, but this fundamental premise of speculation has remained mostly constant. As we convert visual impressions into conjectural ideas, today's risks and contingencies become either tomorrow's empirical facts and concrete realities, or its failures and misses, the detritus of our collective imaginations. Distinct from reasoning, inferring, learning, gambling, guessing, risking, forecasting, investing, and many other related practices and concepts, speculation has been determinant to the debates that mediate between the seen and the unseen, the material and the immaterial, the concrete and the abstract.

This book is not a history of speculations; it is a history of how and why the single term *speculation* has been redefined, expanded, and dynamically varied over time: coming to name a "mania," strains of gambling, a genre of popular fiction, and so much more. Speculation is a certain kind of thinking and acting: a charged and unruly (and sometimes unscrupulous) "cognitive provisionality," rather than more rational and deliberate planning, knowing, and constructing.[2] The concept draws its specific energy from the premodern world of irrational reckoning and risk-taking, origins that we can still discern today. Speculation challenges the knowable, predictable modern world, finding it insufficient, just as it has ever done for visual impressions. As speculators become outsiders, threats, wayward dreamers of all types—philosophical, financial, scientific—the story of speculation intensifies around the nature of the concept itself, what it signifies and what its potency and danger entail. Everywhere it has gone, it has carried hints of being unnatural, corrupt, unverifiable, and somehow errant; therein lies both the source of its power for many thinkers over time, and its peril for many more. In fact, centuries ago, speculative thoughts were often called "chimeras," after the fantastical, fire-breathing lion-goat-snake. Far from innocuous flashes of insight, they were considered so fanciful as to be unnatural and impossible, and therefore menacing; we still use the word *chimera* to mean an illusory, unrealistic plan, a creature of the imagination. When we look back and claim that figures like Leonardo da Vinci or Ada Lovelace were prophetic, we point to the parts of their futuristic thought that eventually came into being, typically leaving aside the stray ends and paths, the wildness and disorder that brought them there. What has interested me all along about speculation, though, was *not* what came into being or did not—the results that justified or discredited the speculation—but rather the process. More specifically, the similarities among versions of that process, from omens to algorithms, despite the broad variety of implementations along the way, enchanted me. This book returns to the battles over the ways of knowing and learning and risking that speculation has prompted, as we all "look through with the mind." Each rearticulation of speculation, whether translations of Aristotle or modern stock markets, has been a claim for the authority to shape the future—how we talk about the future, how we characterize it, plan for it, produce facts about it, and more. The question of who can speculate, and how, and with what means, with what terms and instruments, is a question of how we read the world in constantly evolving ways, with endless reciprocity between concept and activities. But how did all these battles, and all speculation's many hazards, become so naturalized and even familiarized across modern history?

The story of this concept begins, as I did, with little more than the word itself, and with the tools of philological and rhetorical history. Speculation's odyssey from biblical and Greek philosophical sources, through Roman philosophy, and into medieval theological and scholastic writing, all before Chaucer brings it into Middle English, was not the smooth process that an etymological dictionary might seem to evince. We will see it raised up by classical philosophers, only to be castigated as "idle" by the Calvinists and severely narrowed; recuperated in the experimental culture and natural philosophy of the scientific revolution, then aligned with the risky "projects" that marked the new financial revolution, and finally brought to bear on the discourses of vulnerability in contemporary American life. In between, Adam Smith places it at the center of his theory and vocabulary of capitalism, and it is variously seen as a fevered, ravaging disease (even without any relation to money), or as a serene manner of abstract and contemplative cognition. Even when speculation becomes accelerated by the invention of the stock ticker, or when it becomes a keyword for social critique in the hands of women writers and contemporary activists concerned about global capitalism or algorithmic biases, we find its unusual adventure through history marked by the curiously pivotal role it plays as a concept that enters major debates from the side doors. The connective threads in speculation's story are most often insights—discoveries, challenging new ideas, expositions of boldly transformative concepts—invested in this term precisely because of its hypothetical, ungrounded, constantly protean connotations.

Like a habitual speculator myself, I could not let go of this concept once I began to unpack its history, which I saw constellated all across cultural history. Speculation has been in both productive and antagonistic relationships with a number of concepts and practices that intellectual historians of all stripes have recently plotted, including risk (Jonathan Levy), prediction (Jamie L. Pietruska), gambling (Ann Fabian, David G. Schwartz), luck (T. J. Jackson Lears), chance (Ian Hacking, Gerda Reith), failure (Scott Sandage), imagination (J. M. Cocking), and hoaxes (Kevin Young).[3] And speculation's own discrete affective and regulatory aspects since the late 1800s have been traced, too (Urs Stäheli and Stuart Banner, respectively).[4] When we combine all these studies with histories of factuality and experimentation in science, hope and wonder in religion, finance and futures markets, and a host of concepts like abstraction, fortune, superstition, and anticipation, we can see a clearer picture of what speculation's story weaves together on many levels. Speculation has been a means—to borrow a phrase from Raymond Williams that speaks to *speculation*'s etymological roots in vision—"not only of discussing but at another level of seeing many of our central experiences."[5] The present book's coordinated macro and micro methodologies operate as a version of what David Armitage calls a "history *in* ideas," by which I mean to signal the ways that I work through the terms that past figures used to understand novelty and change around them, and to construct their narratives of futurity in reciprocating thought, language, and practices.[6] Or, given that the term *speculation* has actually signified "idea" and "category of thought" over time, this book is something more like a metahistory in ideas. In philosophical history, for instance, the division between the "speculative" and the "practical" has provided categorical structure for centuries of thinkers. This conceptual history is also infused with a mode of philology indebted to Williams and buttressed by deep explorations of cultural archives. There is no single neat line to trace here, no originary moment like there is with words like *robot* or *quark*, and the internal tensions among the many senses of *speculation* are essential to the story.[7] I proceed instead by tracing the footprints of its history in a wealth of diverse sources, including economic reports, poems, political tracts, newspapers, philosophical writings, card-game manuals, plays, speeches, letters, novels, magazines, and other media—a method of "serial contextualism" that follows speculation's unusual journey, whether it takes us to the founding of America or the bursting of the South Sea Bubble.[8] And this allows us to see unexpected connections along the way, such as how the genre of speculative fiction draws from not only technological inventions but also the emergence of modern credit instruments.

The fascinating, untold stories of speculation's past, in short, also lie in the large-scale conceptual and ideological change that occurred *through* this term, often in its linguistic transformations and extensions. What we have used *speculation* to name and describe has been greatly consequential. For Williams, language is not a secondary reflection of social and historical processes or realities; rather, it molds and reconfigures them. Historical change occurs "*within* language," just as human "problems of meaning and of relationships" are constituted and expressed by the dynamism of language itself.[9] The change within and around *speculation* (as a word) has been spectacular, and it has functioned much as the kind of keyword Williams denoted, gaining value and purchase by proliferations of meaning, whether as a term in political critique or as a translational entity.[10] Speculation has even had the power, in the discursive histories of several fields, to assemble and bind together other concepts—to organize and taxonomize other terms, to build frameworks. Think of the way speculation's predominant modern financial sense has formed itself around an array of what is *not* "investment," for example; or how, in the past, it gathered together a host of other terms for ideation. Similarly, historians past and present have used it to classify the zeitgeist of entire periods.[11] Future president Woodrow Wilson exhibited this propensity when he wrote, on the brink of a new century, "We live for our own age—an age like Shakespeare's, when an old world is passing away, a new world coming in—an age of speculation and every new adventure of the mind; a full stage, an intricate plot, a universal play of passion, an outcome no man can foresee."[12]

Perhaps it is jarring to read that this otherwise capricious and discredited concept has had such explanatory and coordinating power. The adjectives that commonly precede it, after all, paint a different picture: *idle, mere, empty, vain, abstruse*. In fact, when speculation is *pure*, it's somehow even worse. In the past five centuries, it was *naked, corrupting, fantastical, seductive, fruitless, indolent, profane, carnal*, and *cabalistic*. We often hear people saying that "I don't want to speculate," or "that's just speculation," and we regularly condemn speculators, who cast implausible, seemingly contagious moneymaking schemes into the future; their risk-taking can create untold amounts of collateral damage. But speculation deserves our attention, as its history will show. In 1780, the satirical poet Christopher Anstey lamented in his *Speculation; or, A Defence of Mankind* that this "poor Word" had been mistreated, devalued, debased, and robbed of its inherent value, just like a speculator might swindle an unwitting investor of honest money (see chapter 3).[13] The term, which had no financial connotations until the 1700s, has itself seemed to rise and fall in moral valuation and in practical usage like a volatile speculative stock. But the moment is ripe to purchase it, as it were, not only when we confront an increasingly bleak future or must argue for the veracity of what used to be accepted as stable methodologies for demonstrating facts. Financial gambles are never purely about the money; contemplation is never a purely theoretical matter. The distances between our various speculative means of future-making across the centuries, be they algorithms or fortune-telling, mental wandering or fevered gambling, forecasting models or intuitive guesses, are startlingly short. The story of speculation's conflicts and revisions reminds us why our mind's eye, even when accused of being idle, and especially when seeming to direct us far from the path of reason, has always powerfully organized our future orientations.

1

THE MIRROR AND THE WATCHTOWER

> *The other evill extremitie whereof wee must
> likewyze beware, is speculation.*
> —JOHN CALVIN, *SERMONS* (1577)

The story of speculation's arrival in English looks simple and straightforward enough on its face: the Latin *speculatio* becomes the Old French *speculacïon*, which Chaucer brings over as *speculacioun*, in the late 1300s. But when we start to follow this linguistic path more closely, we find a web of textual references, cosmological schemas, and sharp disagreements on matters of perception that date back to Greek philosophy. We also find here the story of speculation's journey as a central yet constantly embattled concept from antiquity through to the early modern era. In fact, just one slight but telling hesitation on a point of translation in a landmark text from early Christianity, St. Augustine's *De trinitate* (ca. 400–428), signals the vast, world-shaping consequences of linguistic transmission that this first chapter will unfold. Augustine is commenting on Paul's famous passage in 2 Corinthians 3:18 (King James Version), "But we all, with open face beholding as in a glass the glory of the Lord, are changed into the same image from glory to glory, even as by the Spirit of the Lord." Paul's Greek term for "beholding as in a glass" is *katoptrizō* (from κατοπτρίζειν), to look downward and contemplatively view a reflected image. Augustine notes that the Latin Vulgate translates this conceptually loaded word as *speculantes*. But he immediately pivots and explains the translation itself:

> "Beholding as in a glass," [Paul] has said, *i.e.* seeing by means of a glass, not looking from a watch-tower: an ambiguity that does not exist in the Greek language, whence the apostolic epistles have been rendered into Latin. For in Greek, a glass, in which the images of things are visible, is wholly distinct in the sound of the word also from a watch-tower, from the height of which we command a more distant view. And it is quite plain that the apostle, in using the word "speculantes" in respect to the glory of the Lord, meant it to come from "speculum," not from "specula."[1]

We might wonder why Augustine—whose Greek was known to be shaky—lingers so carefully on this distinction between the Latin *speculum* (reflecting glass or mirror) and *specula* (watchtower), beyond their similar sounds. He is right that the sonic tension is no accident, and there is much more to the potential confusion between these two words than a mere mistranslation might imply. Paul's very directions to his fellow humans about how to find God and how to understand themselves in relation to God rest on this precise translation.

Augustine is highlighting two prominent and integral terms in theology, epistemology, and natural philosophy that help us see why *speculation* came to carry such historical weight once it came to English, and how its classical and medieval linguistic history set it on a course for its splintered modern conceptual life. *Speculum* and *speculatio* carried with them entire worldviews concerning whether the created world before us is a mirror (*speculum*) that reflects God, or whether we should look for evidence of God's glory by "command[ing] a more distant view" (from a *specula*). A multitude of philosophers, theologians, and writers came to invest such importance in these words, in ways that still resonate today. We can see this primarily through the roles Boethius, Geoffrey Chaucer, and John Calvin played in multilinguistic networks of translation and renovation, leading to what is now modern English discourse. The broad historical terrain and contexts around these figures, who were surrounded by even more translators, publishers, and readers, constantly redirected their interventions as they gave speculation its contours, too. Many lesser-known and now-forgotten figures helped make the battle for cultural authority in the meaning and proper course of speculation a long-range, widespread contest for interpreting the interrelationships among vision, cognition, materiality, and spirit among Christians especially.

The origins of speculation lie at the other extreme from the frenzied gambling that we'll encounter in later chapters; speculation begins, rather, as meditative reflection and wisdom. As a means of accessing divine truths, *speculation* becomes a highly flexible term that rises in valuation—like the assets it will later describe—in the mind of Boethius. The categories he builds around speculation will provide the framework for much of what will follow in the concept's history: namely, the nature of speculation as a mental activity or habit, its relationship to "practice," its moral valences, and its tensions with cognate terms in multiple languages. Its stakes grow, and its linguistic capacities and applications grow too, across the medieval era. By the sixteenth century, though, a great inversion is witnessed, in which speculation is roundly condemned, narrowed as a concept and iterated linguistically into a pigeonhole by Calvinists set on diminishing its abstracting power as anything but access to the divine. It is now inert, useless, and idle. It points to futurity in important ways that remain mostly abstract and otherworldly or figurative. To understand how this history ironically prepares speculation for its next major roles in the histories of knowledge creation within science, empiricism, and economics, we need to follow its curious path out of antiquity and into the sermons, poems, and translations that carried it across centuries of entwined epistemological, linguistic, and moral debates.

SIGHT AND INSIGHT

The linguistic and theological traditions that Augustine highlights arose from the consequences of a particular semantic distinction between *sight* and *insight*. *Speculation* belongs to one of the more complicated and far-reaching word families that Greek and Latin spawned well beyond their own porous borders. It would take another book just to chart the transformations of variations in those two tongues, but a particular developmental pattern clarifies the critical concepts at stake here. The Greek root *-skop* led to words such as σκοπέω (*skopéō*), to look, behold, watch, observe. *-Skop* then underwent a metathesis, or reversal of consonant positions, in order to become the Latin root *-spec*, as in *specere* (to see, to observe). (That metathesis adds to the proliferation here: the Greek stem *-skop* yielded a number of related derivatives ranging from *microscope* to *skeptic*.) The Latin *spectare* then added the sense of "to test, to consider," giving us *inspect*, *prospect*, *respect*, and many more. Within this word family, we have the myriad acts of comprehension that our eyes can initiate. These begin with what we might loosely call first-order visual impressions, or plain and pure sight, then lead to sight at a layer or level of distance, in which we contemplate or reflect upon what we have seen.[2] Our modern senses of *specter* and *spectral* highlight the recurring impression that something more, perhaps even something ghostly, lies behind or somehow haunts the phenomena our eyes take in.

As Augustine signaled, two polyvalent Latin words within this family, *speculum* and *specula*, both rich in metaphor and figuration, would be conjoined for centuries, and they captured a set of tensions that we will see across many contexts. A *speculum* is a mirror, looking glass, or reflective surface (and also, a copy or imitation).[3] To look in a mirror is to use the reflections of the here and now in order to look *inward*, to reflect upon oneself and one's life. A *specula*, by contrast, is a watchtower or lookout, and also a ray or glimmer of hope. To look from a watchtower is to look *outward* and *forward*, toward the unknown, toward the hypothetical future, away from one's most immediate surroundings. From *specula* we then have one more crucial transformation that will bear on *speculation* most directly in its purely linguistic lineage: the verb *speculari*, which indicates "to examine, explore, spy, look out," emerged in Latin, and from it comes our keyword *speculatio*, which means "a consideration or examination, a scrutiny: a measured analysis of an external object and/or scenario."[4] And finally, continuing this thread into extended territory, a *speculator* in Latin was a guardian or bishop, one who watches over; and it then came to mean an executioner—one who oversees a death.[5]

Among the many terms that -*skop* and -*spec* generated, *speculum* and *speculatio* became powerful keywords in early Christianity, impossible to separate from one another. They address the matter around us, how we perceive it, and how we use our faculties of contemplation, imagination, and reason to interpret what our eyes see. Our vision is imperfect; the objects we perceive in the world are imperfect and decay over time; and our minds can distort what our eyes take in. In short, how do we gain higher knowledge—wisdom, universal truths, insight into the divine mind—through what we perceive in this world? These issues have marked a dividing line between Aristotelianism and Platonism, between theories of immanence and transcendence, and between empiricism and rationalism more generally. And Augustine demonstrates how they had come to bear on early Christianity directly at the intersection of theology, language, and translation.

We can start to see the roots of the intellectual formation of speculation in this world. First and foremost, the *speculum* concept offered a means of imagining humanity's assessment of its relation to its own creation by God. Most famously, in his first letter to the Corinthians (13:12), Paul gives a line that most modern readers know through the King James translation: "For now we see through a glass, darkly; but then face to face." His Greek word for "glass" is *esoptrou* (ἐσόπτρου), a reflective surface, likely a burnished or polished metal, some type of lens, or perhaps a honed clear stone.[6] In the Latin Vulgate, this line becomes "Videmus nunc per speculum in ænigmate: tunc autem facie ad faciem," with *speculum*, as above, indicating similarly a reflective surface, or specular reflection.[7] This world is but a poorly reflected image; at the time, mirrors were typically low-quality objects compared to the clarity familiar to us in the present. Paul is conveying a scene of imperfection, like the distorted or hazy reflection on the surface of a shiny bronze object. Yet as we saw above, we can still behold God's glory in this mirror, and in this line of thought, our faulty vision now is still on a path toward seeing and experiencing divinity fully in the afterlife. Thus, despite their internal differences in Greek, Paul's two distinct terms for beholding reflections (*katoptrizō* and *esoptrou*) are brought together in Latin by *speculum*, not by any of the *-opt* derivatives. In Romans 1:20, Paul added that the "invisible things" (ἀόρατα [aorata], or *invisibilia*, in Latin) of God, such as God's eternity and divine nature, are knowable and comprehensible in the created world around us. The question is *how* we are to discover God—the *right* modes of perceiving and knowing. *Speculum* became an expansive concept for Augustine's theology and his explication of the nature of the soul and of God's creation. He even titled one of his works *Speculum*, indicating the "mirror of scripture." For all their shortcomings, mirrors attracted theologians and philosophers as a means of framing the relationship between perceiving human eyes and what exists beyond our sight.

The qualities and dispositions captured by the associations of the concept of *speculatio*, on the other hand, were less attractive. As Augustine explained, "From whence is speculation? To see from a distance, this is speculation" (*Unde speculatio? Longe videre, hoc est speculatio*).[8] This kind of speculation has a place in human perception and thought, and it has power and potential, but in a different way than the *speculum* tradition. For Augustine as for others, *visio* instead signified direct and present sight; *speculatio* was less clear, removed, more mediated. We can see this concretely in two discrete translations by St. Jerome. He used *visio* to translate the Hebrew "Jerusalem" as "sight of peace," whereas *specula* translated "Zion."[9] Zion is the hill *outside* Jerusalem from which one can see the Holy Land, as if from a watchtower. Thus, terms like *visio intellectualis* denoted in early Christianity a surer mode of what we would now call (with another visual metaphor) "insight" into divine and eternal knowledge. Similarly, speculative vision is distinct from other things our minds do, like knowing, studying, and deciding. That is to say, as conceptual terms, neither *speculum* nor *speculatio* could promise perfect clarity in vision and contemplation, and they constantly pointed to each other and to a host of related terms for optic insight. Yet as these traditions of thought were forming, *speculatio* was the more contingent, hypothetical, and provisional term, and its role in Christian and, more broadly, early Western thought seemed hardly secure going forward.

BOETHIUS AND THE FORTUNES OF *SPECULATIO*

But around a century after Augustine, *speculatio* found a zealous and successful advocate in Boethius, who would not only elevate it above the *speculum* tradition but also situate this conjectural, mediated term at the apex of human thought. Boethius's influence on the history of speculation as a concept in intellectual history, and on *speculatio* as a particular term in linguistic history (as it is very much alive in modern English), is difficult to overstate. For him, it becomes nothing less than a connection to the divine mind, a discovery of higher, immutable truths and futures. It represents abstract thinking of the most complex order and contemplation of one's nature. But to understand how he accomplished such a dramatic feat for this otherwise less prestigious term, we need to understand his own position as a philosopher, translator, and writer—and that begins with another scene of translation as conceptual transformation, this time through his engagement with Aristotle.

Though he was mostly a Neoplatonist, Boethius actually used his many translations of and commentaries on Aristotle to craft his vision of *speculatio*. Aristotle had posited three categories, or spheres, of human life: *poiēsis* (making), *praxis* (doing), and *theōria* (thinking or knowing). Aristotle saw each of his three spheres working together to produce the well-rounded, insightful human, as in his concept of *phronēsis*, or practical wisdom. In his *Nicomachean Ethics* he elevated *theōria*, helping to inaugurate the long-standing veneration of the theoretical life (*bios theōrētikos*) over the practical life (*bios praktikos*). The immaterial nature of *theōria* here is a good thing—though that will change markedly over time. The common translations of these terms into Latin gave us what Hannah Arendt would characterize as the growing antagonism between the contemplative life (*vita contemplativa*) and the active life (*vita activa*) in Western history.[10] These two main spheres of human activity, of contemplation and action—growing from but not corresponding exactly to Aristotle's three spheres above—were translated into divisions of knowledge, such as theoretical and practical sciences.

Then, in the third century CE, the important Neoplatonist Porphyry of Tyre attempted to reconcile certain ideas in Aristotle and Plato—with the latter having similarly exalted *theōria*. Porphyry's guide to the fields of Aristotelian logic, divisions, and categories, *Isagōgē* (Εἰσαγωγή, "Introduction"), became a well-known commentary in the centuries that followed. Porphyry writes in the very first line of his *Isagōgē* that he will give an overview of Aristotle's categories for the purposes of making definitions and divisions. He refers to the terms and fields in Aristotle (genus, difference, species, and so on) collectively in Greek as "*tēs toutōn theōrias*" [τῆς τούτων θεωρίας], or a useful "consideration of things." But by the early 500s, the Greek language was waning in the Latin West, so Boethius decided to produce both commentaries on *Isagōgē* and a new Latin translation of it.[11] Boethius's texts would become a major source of the transmission of Aristotle's philosophical logic at least into the 1500s.[12]

In his translation, Boethius renders the phrase glossed above as "a consideration of things" as "rerum speculatione," or "the speculation of subjects," marking a turning point in which he translates *theōria* with *speculatio*.[13] In his commentary on the text, he adds that there are "two species" of philosophy, "one which is called theoretical, the other practical; that is, speculative and active" (*species vero duae, una quae theoretica dicitur, altera quae practica, id est speculativa et activa*).[14] Boethius is performing something of a double translation: he first gives the Latin cognates (*theoretica* and *practica*), then retranslates them into his preferred Latin terms.[15] Boethius's doubling of Latin -*spec* words (*species* and *speculativa*) is one of many plays on this word family that exist in multiple languages. In this same text, for example, he even speaks of the truth of "speculation and thinking" (*speculationum cogitationumque*), and he thereafter avoids forms of the Latin *theoria* and *practica* altogether.[16]

Speculatio would hold the same honored place for Boethius that *theōria* did for Plato and Aristotle. Moving away from its literal roots in visual perception and toward its metaphorical power of insight, Boethius's translational redescription initiates a major turn in speculation's history. But we should have seen this coming from him: the term is all over his work. In his earlier, influential work *De institutione musica* (ca. 510s), Boethius employed forms of *speculativa* dozens of times and created a division between *musica speculativa* and *musica practica* that defined musicology for centuries.[17] He makes a similar substitution in one of the section titles in his treatise: *De ordine theorematum, id est speculationum* (On the order of theorems—that is, speculations).[18] And Boethius—born just after the fall of the *Imperium Romanum*—perhaps cheekily proclaims that the true musician operates in the "empire [or sovereignty] of speculation" [*imperio speculationis*].[19] We even see in his *De trinitate* that he used the address *speculemur* ("let us speculate") to open considerations of theoretical questions.[20] A search of Latin databases shows that he used the term far more than his contemporaries (with Cassiodorus a distant second) and that Augustine employed it much more than the other church fathers did. Boethius later became so closely identified with *speculatio* that the stalwart Lewis and Short dictionary of Latin would give for its second sense of *speculatio* ("a contemplation, speculation") two emblematic quotations from Boethius's *De consolatione philosophiae*.

Boethius planned to translate all of Aristotle's works "that I can lay hands on."[21] Though he never finished, we can see, in some of his extant translations, evidence of his plan to press *speculatio* firmly onto multiple forms of *theōria*. Early in the first book of his translation of Aristotle's *Topics*, Boethius translates both *theōria* and *theōrēma* as *speculatio*, while *contemplatio/contemplari* is nowhere to be found in this translation.[22] In other words, he was banking his reputation and his authority as a translator and conduit of Greek thought on this revision and amplification of *speculatio*, which was then a fairly new word in the corpus of Latin. In a period when very few actual translations of Plato and Aristotle were circulating in the Latin West, Boethius shifted the vocabulary for understanding both Aristotle and philosophical logic more generally.[23] He laid claim to an interpretation of speculation as a means to shape knowledge and human behavior itself.

In Boethius's interpretation, *speculatio* (plural: *speculationes*) is not to be denigrated as removed, distant vision; on the contrary, it is supreme, abstract knowledge and insight, and one cannot reach it purely through observation of empirical phenomena. Nor is speculation here some abstruse vagary about the future. It *is* how we think and form ideas; it modulates epistemologically between visible and invisible worlds, between human and divine knowing, helping us see figuratively beyond what we can see physically. The division between "speculative" and "practical" that Boethius helped rewrite would remain prominent in theology and philosophy well into the 1800s, too. His other preferred term—*activa* instead of *practica*—did not gain similar traction, but we can see here that the adjective that will later be most used to impugn speculation—*idle*—is already framed in this sense of speculation as *in*active.

We can see the drama of Boethius's linguistic, philosophical, and translational work play out in his most famous text, *De consolatione philosophiae*—which also forms the bridge to Chaucer's work to bring the term into English, in his translation *Boece*. This brief history of *speculatio*'s rise shines a light on the famous opening scene of Boethius's final, introspective text, composed as he awaited execution. In the *Consolation of Philosophy*, Philosophy personified comes to visit Boethius the author. She wears a robe that has a Greek Π (pi) embroidered at its "lower edge" and Θ (theta) "at the neck of the garment." Between the two letters is a ladder, "whose rungs allowed ascent from the lower letter to the higher."

But the path between those letters—the path from practical (pi, for *praktikē*) to theoretical (theta, for *theōrētikē*) philosophy—was difficult to discern, for "the robe had been ripped by the violent hands of certain individuals."[24] The Greek letters represent the very terms that Boethius had changed to *activa* and *speculativa*, respectively. The scene

FIGURE 1.1 Lady Philosophy visits Boethius as he awaits execution.

FIGURE 1.2 Detail from figure 1.1. The Greek letters pi and theta on Lady Philosophy's tattered robe, respectively representing *praktikē* and *theōrētikē*, which Boethius translates as *activa* and *speculativa*.

> Boethius, *De consolatione philosophiae*, fol. 4r. Paris, ca. 1465. The Morgan Library and Museum. MS M.222. Purchased by J. Pierpont Morgan (1837–1913) in 1905.

functions, then, like a self-referential intertext for Boethius as he opens what would become, from the 800s through the early modern era, arguably the only text in the philosophical tradition that had dependably broad university and lay readership.[25] The Greek terms *praktikē* and *theōrētikē* never appear in the text, and their Latin cognates *practica* and *theoria* are likewise absent—they are, rather, like untranslated ghosts in the text that implicitly speak to Boethius's own legacy as a translator of Greek for Latin readers.

Using his own text as a metaconceptual history and commentary, Boethius then saves the first appearance of his beloved term *speculatio* until the fourth of the *Consolation*'s five books. He says to Philosophy, "Lady, you are our guide to the true light, and your earlier injunctions have clearly emerged as both divine considered in themselves [*sui speculatione divina*], but beyond dispute by reason of your arguments."[26] *Speculatio* is now paired with *divina*; setting aside the long debates about the nature of Boethius's faith, we can see the term is reaching to the otherworldly, even while Boethius still frames it syntactically here as impersonal, with speculation considered in itself.[27] This changes in book 5, when Boethius is addressing the question of free will and chance. Philosophy tells him that the divine mind possesses perfect judgment and will, but that "human souls are freer when they keep themselves in speculation of the divine mind [*mentis divinae speculatione*], and are less free when they pass into bodily form—and even less free still when they are fettered in earthly limbs."[28] *Speculatio* reaches its summit here for Boethius: it is our line to divine cognition, a contemplation of abstract truths apart from our mortal coils. Speculation helps our minds and their powers depart from the quotidian phenomenal world and thus to discover ultimate truths, comprehended from a promontory of thought. It is *more* than a mirror (*speculum*): it is a route toward the divine that escapes and surpasses the very material world that it first ponders. Its mediation and distance are now part and parcel of its potential.

The *Consolation* is very much what would later be termed a *speculative* text: it looks inward and outward at questions of epistemology, and it considers the contingencies of fate and fortune, most famously emblematized in its Wheel of Fortune. In Boethius's thought, speculation is a power and a faculty that depends on one's ability to abstract the past, present, and especially the future, in concert with one's active life. This ascent toward wisdom is also a higher calling for the philosopher and for the devout religious individual, against the inhibiting confines of our earthly forms. In book 4, Boethius in fact claims that as God "gazes out from his high vantage-point of Providence [*providentiae specula*], he recognizes what is appropriate for each human being, and invests each of them with what is appropriate."[29] Here, the *specula* ("high vantage-point," or watchtower/turret), enables *providence*—from *pro-* and *video*, that is, seeing into the future. This language underscores one of the primary themes in the *Consolation* through which divine foreknowledge and fate operate. Boethius later adds that one who studies God and contemplates his ways is a *divini speculator*, a contemplator or speculator of the divine, even if he clearly never *sees* God.[30]

Boethius set *speculatio* on a remarkable course that was amplified by his own legacy as a figure widely read as an interpreter of Aristotle, and as a transitional figure in the Latin West's Christian thought, all the way through the medieval era. *Speculatio* has both the Boethian amplification of *theōria* and the early Christian provisionality to it, all contained in the translation, philosophy, theology, and wordplay through which he cast a long shadow over the Middle Ages.

SPECULATION, CONTEMPLATION, MIRRORING THE WORLD

Speculatio's course, however, was not a singular, uncontested path. Nor was the concept unquestioned or somehow completely purified by way of Boethius's outsize influence. Rather, a long line of medieval commentators, scholastics, and students would now have to grapple with how and why Boethius had magnified this particular term. As they sought to explain the divine, they needed to reinterpret, comment upon, and reconfigure their own authority around the legacy of Boethius's projection of speculation. In order for us to understand *speculatio*'s eventual transition into English as *speculation*, we need to sketch briefly the intellectual stakes of the terms with which it was circulating, for it was hardly a neutral term for Chaucer to eventually translate. On the one hand, Gillian Rosemary Evans credits the study of Boethius's texts with providing a critical vocabulary for "the awakening of interest in the nature of abstract thought in the first half of the twelfth century."[31] Here, "*Speculatio* is abstract thought, purposeful, investigative thought which is governed by consciously-held principles concerning 'appropriate methods and apposite modes of speech.'"[32] The term for this mode of thought was "speculative theology." There was no universal agreement among figures including Peter Lombard, Hugh of Saint Victor, and Richard of Saint Victor as to precisely what speculative theology implied in the realms of observation, reflection, meditation, and insight.[33] But its proponents aimed to distinguish it by arguing that its end was knowledge itself, and not the applied, often didactic form of understanding that practical theology offered.[34] Boethius's divisions of thought also helped name medieval fields of inquiry and study, such as *scientia speculativa* and *scientia practica*, and *musica speculativa* and *musica practica*.

On the other hand, while *speculatio* was finding robust conceptual purchase and growing in its implications, it was seen by plenty of theologians as "cold and unemotional," a clear step down on the ladder proceeding toward the divine from the practice of *contemplatio*, which "could be taught and discussed in the classroom," Evans explains.[35] Richard of St. Victor saw the mind as "moving from *speculatio* to *contemplatio* and, finally, in the suspended awe of contemplative vision, gazing into the beauty of the divine nature."[36] Richard writes that "although *contemplatio* and *speculatio* are usually juxtaposed and in this way often obscure and cover the proper nature of the meaning of scripture, nevertheless we more suitably and more precisely indicate *speculatio* when we perceive through a mirror, but *contemplatio* when we see the truth in its purity without any covering and veil of shadows."[37] For Aquinas, *contemplatio* is thinking of God as such; *speculatio* is thinking of God *through* the material world.[38] Here and elsewhere, *contemplatio* (and, later, *contemplation*, in English) most often emerged without the associations of mirrors, distance, and reflections that kept *speculatio* from signaling for some theologians the level of insight that Boethius had imagined for it.[39]

Moreover, in the same moment, a resurgence of the *speculum* tradition arrived in the medieval tradition of speculum literature, or reflections (mirrors) on a topic, often intended as encyclopedic works that could lead to better contemplation of God. The *Speculum virginum* (ca. 1140), for instance, outlines what Sara Ritchey characterizes as a "unique role for women contemplating the presence of God" through the material world by "urg[ing] the act of speculation as a form of meditation."[40] The *speculum* tradition came to include works like William of Saint-Thierry's *Speculum fidei* (ca. 1142–1144), Vincent of Beauvais's *Speculum maius* (ca. 1240–1260), and Ranulph Higden's *Speculum curatorum* (ca. 1350). William Durand (Guillaume Durand) was known by the appellation "Doctor Speculator" and authored the much-read *Speculum iudiciale* in 1271, and many texts arrived in the *Specula principum* line too. Henry Osborn Taylor adds that "the thirteenth century had a weakness for the word 'Speculum,' and the idea it carried of a mirror or compendium of all human knowledge."[41]

Within the high-medieval synthesis of Aristotelian, Platonic, and Christian philosophical systems, the lines between the traditions of *speculatio* and *speculum* became blurrier; they actually blended into each other to a degree in the 1200s and 1300s.[42] *Speculatio* now recouped some of its roots in visual perception, for instance, and started to expand its implications around what *speculum* had previously signaled—but, at the same time, *speculum* was also taking on elements of *speculatio*.[43] That is, with the revised Aristotelian elevation of empirical observation, the study of the visible world was more fully integrated into theories of insight into the divine than Boethius had proposed. Not simply the many intervening centuries between Boethius and Chaucer, but even the most recent century before Chaucer's translation itself, brought about shifts in thought and language that repositioned *speculatio* once again: it was now both a powerful and identifiably Boethian concept *and* a broadly reformed theological topic and practice. *Speculatio*'s strong association with *theōria* had weakened by the 1300s, and instead, new contexts of vernacular languages, poetic invention, and translational creativity across multiple contexts would give it yet another new life, as *speculation*.

CHAUCER'S *BOECE* AND THE ROOTS OF *SPECULACIOUN*

Even once *speculation* had begun its life in English, in the late 1300s, its terminological, conceptual, and etymological relationships with Latin and with Romance tongues continued—indeed, grew and evolved—over the next three hundred years. Chaucer navigated among these linguistic circuits, and among the theological debates about *speculatio/ speculum/contemplatio* and their implications for lay people. Thus his new word, *speculacioun*, needed to differentiate itself within a multilingual context of late medieval Latin, French, and English in which forms of *speculatio* also circulated, and in which *contemplacioun* was already a word in Middle English (in Chaucer's own texts, even).[44] And because *speculacioun* was not a completely foreign word to bring over into English, we need to sketch out some of its linguistic contexts in order to understand better how Chaucer's term functioned, and why he looked specifically to Boethius, rather than to his ecclesiastical contemporaries, as his specific source for it.

Chaucer's *speculacioun* came into English—if we can provisionally label the process as such—already having several relatives in use in other local languages. We could say that Latin dominated in theology, scholasticism, and learning; French in courts and aristocratic speech; and English among lower classes and spoken vernaculars.[45] Chaucer, like most members of the mercantile, clerical, and aristocratic classes in England at the time, would have grown up reading, writing, and conducting business in Latin and Anglo-Norman (a dialectal branch of Old French), even if his mother tongue was one of the dialects of Middle English. His reading audience for his *Boece* likely knew these languages as well. (Here we must note, too, that our modern concept of translation is mostly anachronistic.) Which is to say, Chaucer was not bringing an ancient text from an abstruse, unknown language to the common folk—and translations of the *Consolation* already existed in several tongues.

Because of these various familiarities and his contexts, Chaucer had substantial inventive leeway, and as a translator, he was at times staunchly literal, at other times highly figurative; his methods were a blend of scholarship, ingenuity, and stylistic flair.[46] He took Latin adjectives that became French nouns and made them back into adjectives, and so on. And Middle English was still emerging among myriad linguistic pressures from all the new contacts with other tongues, including those of the British Isles, modern France, and northern Europe. It was not a fixed or autonomous tongue, it had no royal academy policing its borders or producing official dictionaries, and it was a minor literary language in England. All this allowed Chaucer the space to develop hundreds of new words, some of which now strike us as significant and complex—like *universe*—and others that seem somewhat banal, like *trench*.

Around 1380, Chaucer began creating a version of the *Consolation* in the English vernacular that he would shape forcefully for posterity, and we can plot what he is doing with *speculatio* on both a linguistic and a conceptual level.[47] In a clear nod to the structure of his source text, Chaucer also follows Boethius's strategy of suppressing *speculatio* until late in the *Consolation* by way of a gloss he gives in the opening scene. He explains that sewn in the hem of Philosophy's robe, there is a "Grekissch P (that signifyeth the lif actif); and aboven that lettre, in the heieste bordure, a Grekyssh T (that signifyeth the lif contemplatif). And bytwien thise two lettres ther were seyn degrees nobly ywrought in manere of laddres, by whiche degrees men myghten clymben fro the nethereste lettre to the uppereste."[48] Here, with the theological debates mentioned above as context, he substitutes "contemplatif" for the *theōria* signified by the Greek theta, holding his version of *speculatio* until later, just as Boethius had, and not employing "contemplatif" again in the text. Similarly, in book 4, part 1, of the *Consolation*, he renders Boethius's first use of *speculatione divina* as "devyne lookynge."[49]

Chaucer builds up and expands the visual-insight sense of *lookynge* throughout his *Boece*, and so, by the time he comes to book 5, he is ready to bring over a new word—one that does not have an Old French precedent.[50] He writes, "But the soules of men moten nedes be more fre whan thei loken hem in the speculacioun or lokynge of the devyne thought; and lasse fre whan thei slyden into the bodyes; and yit lasse free whan thei bin gadred togidre and comprehended in erthli membres."[51] *Speculacioun* here is an Anglicized word that bore resemblance to, competed with, and was influenced by both the Latin *speculatio* (in both theological and secular texts) and words like *spéculer* and *speculacion* in Old and Middle French and in Anglo-Norman, and likely other terms that are lost to the historical record.[52]

The first clue as to Chaucer's work here—and a hint that this is more than just code-switching, for instance—comes in his hedging: Chaucer immediately adds an explanatory prepositional phrase ("or lokynge" [looking], which also plays sonically on "loken" [lock] just before it), knowing his readers may or may not grasp his sense of this new term by context. His move is similar to Boethius's intralingual retranslation in Latin, and it strengthens his identification with Boethius through the term. But *speculacioun* was somehow meant to be more than just *lokynge*, which itself signaled insight and foresight, just like *beholding* did: it is profound, serious contemplation—of God, of the heavens, of one's place within a cosmological schema, as in Boethius. (And, not by coincidence, Chaucer coins another word at this same moment, in his *Troilus and Criseyde*: "future.")

Chaucer has developed *speculacioun* by way of context, through his explorations and extensions of *lokynge* in the text. Speculation matters for Chaucer, as it did for Boethius, because it extends *lokynge* figuratively across the spectrum of comprehension at a distance and through mediation. But Chaucer now seeks to *revitalize* its etymological roots in vision through the more recent medieval developments.[53] To use speculation this way was to invoke both the *speculatio* tradition and the etymological connections to *speculum*. *Speculacioun* is an updated Boethian term, circulating alongside *speculatio* and *speculum* and having accrued new value from theological debates.

And yet, as far as we can see, Chaucer didn't use the word again in any of his works, and as late as the 1800s, it was absent from Stratmann and Bradley's *Middle-English Dictionary*. Even in book 5, part 6, of his *Boece*, Chaucer translates *divini speculator* as "byholdere of the devyne thought."[54] And Chaucer's own precedent in translation did not hold universally: John Walton will retranslate the "divine speculation" passage around 1410 as "devyne speculacioun,"[55] but Queen Elizabeth in 1593 would choose "contemplation of Godes will."[56] Chaucer's *speculacioun* was telling and consequential in modern hindsight, but the term did not solidify here. Instead, Chaucer let loose a provocation in language and in thought, one that reached—for the curious—from Aristotle to Aquinas to the heterogeneous English of the moment. And again, we must widen the scope of the paths that we follow both philologically and conceptually in order to understand how *speculation* became a fixture in English across the 1400–1600s, and was set on a collision course with its former companion, *practice*.

WHEN THINKING BECOMES IDLE

Speculation came to signal an even broader and more internally diverse form of visual perception, one combined with higher-order comprehension and contemplation, than perhaps Chaucer had foreseen. Its conceptual life grew as its many senses in English proliferated rapidly: by 1550, there were no fewer than seven, with some having come directly from Latin and others through routes still unclear.[57] In this proliferation, we start to see a phenomenon that will recur throughout the rest of this book: the wide-ranging and polymorphous applications of *speculation* as a concept-word. It quickly becomes apparent that one can bend the term for almost any purpose and thereby coin new senses along the way, all the while retaining the term's attachments to its roots in *speculatio* and its associated traditions. Some writers, for instance, followed Chaucer pretty closely: the scholastic Reginald Pecock's *Reule of Crysten Religioun* (ca. 1443) attempted to align *speculacioun* with other terms as he opened paths for the "contemplatijf lijf" through the love of God and of one's neighbors.[58] Similarly, in the 1470s, a translation of a book by French writer Christine de Pizan speaks of a man who "chase to lefe solitaryly for to be out of noyse and stryffe whiche letteth gret speculacion," while other texts from the late 1400s use *speculacioun* to indicate the kinds of divine contemplation that were still being measured in contemporaneous Latin ecclesiastical texts.[59] Yet around the same time, in a different domain, a text on the liberal arts referred to a truth "proeved in the speculacioun of Euclide," meaning theoretical knowledge of mathematics.[60]

Two important translational resources from this period give a sense of where speculation now began to assemble its meanings. In 1538 came the scholar Thomas Elyot's influential Latin-to-English *Dictionary*. In it, Elyot first lists several variations on the term: *speculatio* is "a beholdynge," now generalized and not specific to religious or scholastic discourse; *specula* is a "high hylle or towre, whereon thynges can be espied far of"; a *speculator* is "an espyall in warres"; and so on.[61] (*Contemplatio* is "a beholdynge," too.) But perhaps more telling of the work that *speculation* was doing in English lies in his other entries. His translation of the Latin *theorema* is simply the Boethian "speculation"; for *theoria*, he gives "speculation, understandyn"; *astrologia* is "the speculation of astronomie"; while *meteoria* is "speculation in high thynges." Speculation points to lofty, abstract thinking whose place in the sciences and mathematics we'll consider fully in the next chapter. Later, John Florio's Italian-to-English *A World of Words* (1598) employs similar translations: *speculatione* is "speculation, contemplation, watching or spying," *speculatore* is "a speculator, contemplator, a watcher ... a considerer," and *theorema* is "a theorem, a speculation, any axiom or undoubted truth of an arte, but particularly that which respecteth speculation more then practise."[62] One text from a few decades later even discusses "contemplative speculation."[63]

Amid this welter of new senses of *speculation*, however, one certain strong sense of the word in English became entrenched and threatened to overwhelm all other senses—much as the financial sense of *speculation* will do in the late 1800s. The speculative/practical division in Latin came to English more or less intact and through cognates, and the senses of each side of that division had been modified in the debates over the contemplative and active lives. But where long traditions of thinkers had seen these two as complementary parts, *practice* emerged in the postmedieval era as *speculation*'s full-fledged antagonist. Over time, especially across literary and theological texts of the 1400s and into the 1500s, we start to see an opposition taking hold: speculation is *not* practice. That is, in a pattern that continues to this day, in which *speculation* is often made legible by contrast with *investment*, *speculation* was redefined and often condemned by way of contrast.

Here, contentions over the value and morality of *speculation* weigh heavily on the term's very implications for basic questions of perception and comprehension. This crucial turn amplified speculation's shift away from the observation of material existence and toward pure, abstract thought. This process has deep roots in English, even if the speculation/practice battles are not as pronounced until later. John Wycliffe, a tireless propagator of the Middle English vernacular, noted in a sermon in the late 1300s that Peter's "cunnyng was not speculatif, of gemetrie, ne oþer sciencis, but practik, put in dede, how men shulde lyve by Goddis lawe."[64] That is, the path of right living under God's law lies in practice and deeds, not in theoretical knowledge.[65] The same schism that we saw in Latin is apparent in English, and *speculative* emerged as an important adjectival modifier here: there are speculative sciences, speculative theology, speculative grammars, speculative astronomy, speculative physics, and much more, all focusing on abstract, unprovable knowledge. Across the 1500s, the pairing of *speculation* and *practice* (in phrases such as "both in practik and speculation" and "in speculation as also in practyse") became a common shorthand for "in thought and in deed," "in every way," in all human endeavors—whereas a cognate pairing such as "in contemplation and in action" is very rare.[66] Edmund Bunny's *Booke of Christian Exercise* (1584), for instance, discusses when Solomon did "speaketh not of speculation, but of his own proofe and practise."[67] An ideal in which "the speculation and practise, reason and the worke concurre and ioyne together" seemed linguistically in place as an aspiration, at least in theory, much like what Boethius and Aristotle had envisioned.[68] But it was also apparent that speculation was becoming the lesser of the pair.

Soon, speculation began to suffer and become associated with abstruse, wasteful thinking, far from things like applied knowledge and daily good works. And this particular transition in the history of speculation both overwhelms the foregoing proliferation of senses and narrows them down to a largely focalized one. John Calvin was the surprising figure to influence the development of a term in the English language—though perhaps, given the contexts of French and Latin discussed above, he was not as much an outsider to these contexts as modern language divisions might suggest. When Calvin's works reached England in 1561 and stimulated multiple movements and protracted debates, the incipient Reformation would push *speculation* to the margins, this time as dangerously close to sins of curiosity, vanity, and waste. Martin Luther had already forcefully railed against speculation; continuing a line of thought going back at least as far as Augustine's warning against *vana curiositas*, Luther placed speculation near the sin of *curiositas*.[69] Calvin, via his first English translators, goes even further: he has no patience for those "ydle men, who occup[y] ... them selves more in the speculation or beholdyng of such thynges then in doynge of them."[70] The same is true for those who "doe but tryfle with vaine speculations."[71] For Calvin, "The knowledge of God standeth not in bare speculacion, but draweth with it the worshipping of him."[72] In a sermon published in England in 1577, Calvin names speculation in particular as an "evill extremetie" that misguides "many fantasticall folke."[73]

In his *Institutes of the Christian Religion* (Latin, 1559; French, 1560; English, 1561), *speculation* becomes a fixed term for Calvin to characterize pointless cognitive labor—especially the scholasticism in monasteries and in late medieval high theology. Thomas Aquinas's famous speculations about how many angels can cohabitate in one space stood as a prime example of such an extreme. Calvin denounces early in *Institutes* those who see God as inactive and inert, and "doe but tryfle with vaine speculations [later translations read "cold speculations" and "frigid speculations"]," and imagine a God who "only delyte[s] him self wyth ydlenesse, having no care of the world."[74] He amplifies Augustine's skepticism toward the projective, abstracting nature of *speculatio* and reads it onto the mental exercises of his theological opponents. And he further condemns the "arte of brawlyng whiche these men [Sophists and Logicians] call Speculative Divinitie, they woulde beleve that nothyng lesse is doone than any disputation had of God."[75] He even takes exception to Augustine's view, in telling language: "For that speculative devise [*speculatio*] of Augustine is not sounde, where he saith that the soule is a glasse [*speculum*] of the Trinitie, because that there are in it understandyng, will, and memorie."[76] Arguably worse still, in Calvin's mind, "speculating" ran counter to understanding what was already predestined, for "fortune and chaunce are heathen mens wordes, wyth the signification wherof the mindes of the godly ought not to be occupied," he declared, and thus humans should not let their affairs be "tossed up and downe with the rashe will of Fortune."[77]

Calvin seals this critique of speculation, and articulates the Protestant line, by declaring that it is most often "idle" and "vain" precisely because it is not a guide or a path toward God.[78] Even *speculation*'s intimation of a highly contingent futurity would have likely made it an unappealing term for the Calvinist reading of a preordained order. *Contemplation* and its variants, by contrast, are almost always positive and aspirational for Calvin, as something more circumscribed, knowable, orderly, and allowable. *Contemplation* fits his schema in ways that *speculation* does not. Moreover, Calvin's work in England was circulating in the three principal tongues that Chaucer was working across when he reshaped *speculacioun*: Latin, French, and English. Calvin composed in Latin and translated himself into French. In Latin, he attacked "vacua et meteorica speculatione, inani speculatione, otiosa speculatione, vanas speculationes," and so on. Such adjectives may well have reminded his readers of the opening of the Bible, where Genesis 1:2 has, "Terra autem erat inanis et vacua" (The earth was without form, and void). The French versions are also full of such phrases: "spéculations inutiles," "vaines spéculations," "spéculation extravagante," and many more.[79] By contrast, Calvin seems to give a robust embrace to the power of *speculum* in Christianity. The world is a mirror, he writes; we are "spectators" of it, and Christ is a mirror of the elect (*speculum electionis*). Therefore, the world is to be interpreted *actively* for signs and knowledge of God in its reflections and representations.[80]

In fact, the phrase still very much in currency today—"idle speculation"—was virtually coined by Calvinists in English translation. This occurred in part because Calvin would become the most printed and reprinted author in England in this era.[81] We can even pinpoint this, and it's worth doing so because of the intellectual imprint it left on speculation. Keeping in mind that our records are partial and the range of available dates within them is incomplete, we can see quite clearly in our largest database of texts from this era, Early English Books Online (EEBO), the pattern of an identifying phrase strongly associated with Calvinism. The first use of "idle speculation" ("ydle speculacion") comes from another Calvinist reformer, John Knox, who in 1560 argues that God's thought is never "idle speculation."[82] The following year, the translation of Calvin's *Institutes* appears and provides the next occurrence: God himself demonstrates that "knowledge by practise is wythoute doute more certayne and perfecte than any idle speculacion."[83] The next three citations come from translations of Calvin, too—and, not by coincidence, the reformist preacher and translator John Tomkys and Calvin's disciple Theodore Beza then account for the following two citations. Other preachers—also mostly Calvinists—pick it up across the 1590s. *Idle*, from a Germanic word meaning "empty," becomes a telling critical epithet for the ardent Calvinist Philip Sidney, then, as in *Astrophil and Stella* (1591), where he pairs it with "vain."[84] By the time of *Henry V* (ca. 1599), we find Shakespeare employing the phrase "idle speculation." Sermons and theological texts of the early 1600s are full of protestations against "idle speculation" and the "idle speculation[s] of our fantasticke brayne[s]."[85] By the mid-1650s, uses of "idle speculation" abound well beyond Calvinist circuits.

Mixing curiosity with inutile and unproductive thought, *speculation* fell from "divine" to "idle," from the foundations of knowledge to the sinful deviance from the kind of right thinking that guides right action. To be idle, in Calvinist terms, is to breach one's vocation; to be vain is to breach humility. In Calvin's words, "In readyng of Scripture we continually rest upon the searchyng and studying of suche thynges as pertaine to edification, and not geve our selves to curiositie or study of thynges unprofitable."[86] Curiosity, for Calvin, is often qualified as speculation is: it is "vayne," "mere," and "foolish," and he dismisses a conjecture by noting that his "speculation is but of mere and hungry curiositie."[87] And *imagination* is often surrounded by the same adjectives. The sonic overlap of *idle* and *idol* helped buttress the place of the former term in the religious discursive sphere. (Henry VIII warned clergy in 1538 about the "feigned images" that embodied "that most detestable sin of idolatry."[88]) For Calvin, the "wit of man is . . . a continual worship of idols"—or, as this line became better known in later translations, "the human mind is . . . a perpetual forge of idols."[89] We even find phrases like "idle Idols" in Thomas Becon's *A Comfortable Epistle* (1542).[90] Speculation participated in these misleading forgeries, these false images of the mind, whereas the *speculum*—if conceptually detached from speculation and properly segregated—could lead reflectively toward the right comprehension of the divinely created world. In the two centuries since Chaucer, speculation had grown and spread diversely, but this predominantly narrow and condemned sense of it now marked a low point in its semantic journey, so distant from the heights of Boethian imagination. And with the concurrent rise of *practice* in early modern discourse, the inversion in intellectual history was nearly complete.

THE TRIUMPH OF PRACTICE

While speculation still had a place in philosophy and theology, and still could be *divine*, *sweet*, or *high*, Calvin set in motion a vicious set of attacks on it that neither Boethius nor Chaucer could have imagined—*idle*, *vayne*, and *meer*, not to mention *bare*, *dangerous*, *barren*, *aerial*, *heartlesse*, and *cold*. Calvin and his followers' arguments were not entirely new, of course—countless figures in church history had condemned undirected cognition and laziness or sloth—but Calvin gave *speculation* a fresh charge that would stay with it for centuries. The philosophical point was visible in the model of Protestant sermons, which sought to leave congregants with applicable knowledge for daily life and to warn them against inert speculation.[91] Protestants, especially in England and the American colonies, took great pride in and fashioned crucial parts of their identities around differentiating themselves from Catholics by way of their phobic antipathy toward wasted labor, including wasted mental labor, a thread that Max Weber would later single out. Puritan biographer Samuel Clarke summed it up in praising the life of Calvin, who spent his life "wholly imploying himself to shew, that the life of Christianity did not so much consist in vain speculation as in practise."[92] The Westminster Confession of Faith (1646) contained a preface noting that the work of faith was "not a brain-knowledge, a mere speculation."[93]

At bottom, then, *idle* and *vain* were not simply modifiers of *speculation* for Calvin and the sermonizers who followed him; they were almost redundant, given the men's hostility toward speculation of any type. The split between speculation and practice becomes a hierarchy that pushes the older tension with *speculum* into the background and brings *practice* more clearly into the foreground. "The end of speculation is practice," as Presbyterian minister Richard Steele put it: speculation is only valuable if it leads to right action.[94] When it is removed or detached from practice, we find that, as the pastor John Davis warned, "To pretend to advance knowledge onely, without practice would be *vaine speculation*."[95] Another clergyman argued that "meer speculation without practice" is "but vaine and fruitlesse."[96] Here we are starting to see, too, what will eventually be articulated as the ontological grounds of the condemnations of financial speculation. The seed of the notion is that one should labor or practice for one's gains, not simply cast upon fortune for them.[97]

Thus it was that among the first statutes enacted in the Virginia Colony in 1619 were a series that, in succession, forbade blasphemy and swearing, "dicing, carding, and Idle gaming," and drunkenness; another grouped together anyone who "shall take the name of God in vain or shall play at Cards or dice."[98] Idleness was linked to playing with fortune, to speculating on chance rather than working naturally. Instead, Puritans and Benedictines alike agreed on the innate value of working with one's hands, reaping what one sows by natural processes, and understanding faith as empty when pursued only as a theoretical topic. Biblical lessons were reinterpreted through this sense of *speculation*: a 1610 tract warned, for instance, that "it is a meere *Idea*, speculation and fancy, to sow sparingly, and yet expect to reape plentifully."[99] "Truly this is no vaine speculation, nor unprofitable to man," reads the translation of Pierre de La Primaudaye's *The French Academie* (1586), with a hint of financial connotations.[100]

If speculation was the opposite, and not the complement, of practice, then it seemed to be something entirely different than the ancients had

envisioned, and to have lost the thread that the medieval theologians and Chaucer alike had cultivated even in skepticism. Calvin, the champion of "knowledge by practise," held that "Job sheweth that he is not a speculative teacher, but a true practicioner of the things that he speaketh, that is to say, of Gods judgements."[101] Indeed, the Presbyterian minister Daniel Mace found this *opposition* of speculation and practice so useful just over a century later that in his 1729 translation of the New Testament, he changed the well-known verse James 2:18. The King James version reads, "Yea, a man may say, Thou hast faith, and I have works: shew me thy faith without thy works, and I will shew thee my faith by my works." In Mace's version, we find: "It will be said, 'you have a speculative faith, but mine is practical. Where is your faith, if no effects appear?' As for me, my actions will vouch for my faith."[102] By the time of his *Dictionary* in the mid-1700s, Samuel Johnson specifically opposed "speculative knowledge" to "practical *skill*"; "practical" means "not merely speculative," while "theoretical" is equivalent to "speculative . . . not practical."[103] A title from 1831 later put it succinctly by asserting *The Superiority of Practice to Speculation*.

But before we assume that speculation would be unilaterally condemned and its conceptual range blunted, we should consider one more wrinkle in this complex relationship. As we have seen, speculative philosophy remained an established, respected realm of knowledge and cognition, despite all the flags around it. The long-standing ideal of complementarity between the speculative and the practical had not fully disappeared. In fact, Jonathan Edwards wrote that "there is a difference between having a right speculative notion of the doctrines contained in the word of God, and having a due sense of them in the heart. In the former consists the speculative or natural knowledge of the things of divinity; in the latter consists the spiritual or practical knowledge of them."[104] In other words, Edwards sees promise and purpose in speculation as a mode of natural philosophy—which we'll treat at length in the next chapter. And thus, for him, a "speculative knowledge of [divinity], without a spiritual knowledge, is in vain and to no purpose," but "a speculative knowledge" still has "infinite importance," because "without it we can have no spiritual or practical knowledge."[105]

John Wesley, too, warned against "a barely notional or speculative faith," in 1771.[106]

The matter, more precisely, was once again the *right kind* of speculation—the same questions of value and measurement, proportion in living, modes of abstraction and foresight, relationships between sight and insight, that have marked speculation's conceptual history from antiquity to this point. We *can* find God through speculation, and we *can* see our own futures, and even commune with abstract knowledge and with earthly insights alike, but we need to direct our speculations properly, not turn ourselves over to their powers. The matter of how we speculate, and who controls those speculations—and when and why—becomes paramount in Protestant thought. We know this because, by the same token, *practice* at this time could be errant, dangerous, and devious, too: to *practice*, and often *practice on*, meant in the sixteenth century to connive, to draw up nefarious schemes or to plot trickery. Practice could cut both ways and was not quite the concept championed without qualification that some accounts of scientific modernity, for example, seem directed at establishing. Speculation was not buried, and its opponent was hardly invincible. Rather, Calvin and his followers wounded it, brought it down from its Boethian, Chaucerian, and sometime-Catholic perches. Its path from Greek to Latin to English, with other languages pressuring it along the way, saw it both amplified and battered: what allowed it simply to become a word in English also made it a vitally embattled concept in Western intellectual history.

Over these first episodes in its history, speculation served a number of critical functions, whether it was capturing a mode of access to wisdom or standing in for a sense of immaterial cognition that stood opposed to purportedly right activity—including thought itself as activity. The writers and thinkers we have treated all needed to get *speculatio*/*speculacioun*/*speculation* right, they felt: to clarify it, expand it, elevate it, denigrate it, or otherwise modify the version of experience that it named. They could not let it remain idle in the conceptual fields in which they intervened, whether as philosophers, theologians, poets, translators, moralists, or playwrights. And even as *speculation* was rigorously modified by condemnatory adjectives, the implication is clear: if speculation itself did not have such potency, there would be no need to modify it. If the habits of thought deemed speculative were not so tempting and pervasive—if not inevitable—there would be no need to warn against them so stridently. What we're seeing, and what we'll pick up in the next chapter, is that speculation has an unlikely and less apparent creative potential that the conditions of knowledge production in the early modern period will soon dramatically renovate.

2

EXPERIMENTING ON THOUGHT

Opera enim meditamur, non speculationes.
[For we pursue works, not speculations.]
—FRANCIS BACON, *PARASCEVE AD HISTORIAM NATURALEM ET EXPERIMENTALEM* (1620)

The futures that speculation projected prior to the seventeenth century were most often abstract, hypothetical, and envisioned. But beginning in the early 1600s, a set of interconnected revolutions brought these futures closer to earth and into material existence in ways that radically reshaped speculation. What we now call the scientific revolution—the transformation of natural philosophy—and the entwined changes in early modern capitalism, political thought, theology, and philosophy staged a reckoning for speculation. The futures that one speculated might only be as far away as the result of an experiment, or the rise or fall of a financial gamble. With moral and religious concerns thus pushed to the background, speculation was granted a new potentiality, with its emergent sense of "the conjectural anticipation of something" animated by empirical observation.[1] Speculation had new life—and a new relationship to practice—in a world that was breaking fresh ground in the production and creation of knowledge itself.

We are familiar now with the profound conceptual labor that terms like *experience, experiment, evidence, sign,* and *nature* performed in the early modern era across many fields and domains that seem mostly discrete and autonomous in their contemporary formations. *Speculation* and *practice* played pivotal yet largely unacknowledged roles, too, in the common discourses and the conceptual habitus in formation here. Whether in Calvinism's influence on the early generations of the English Royal Society, in Isaac Newton's service as Master of the Mint, or in John Locke's interventions in parliamentary debates over coinage, we can see how such vocabulary addressed overlapping, urgent questions of innate properties or the nature of *value* as a category. Within those fields, given a reference point in the future and thus a narrative plot in the space-time of the new science especially, *speculation* could be retroactively validated as predictive, prophetic—the farthest thing from unprovable and inert. It became the forecast of knowledge, of future truth, leading to the question of whether it is *useful* truth. It followed a controversial and circuitous path from the realm of airy hypothesis toward factual production, so that empiricist philosophers, too, had to grapple with the realization that some truths still are known "only by speculation." Meanwhile, investors in new joint-stock companies gazed upon bubbles in which hard money seemed to be mysteriously appearing from speculative ideas of future wealth alone. From Francis Bacon's works to the South Sea Bubble, and with great range in between, the figures in this chapter, including Joseph Addison, Daniel Defoe, Jonathan Swift, and many others, gave speculation new meaning, new methods, new instruments, and new insights, even while remaining skeptical of activities now tied to the concept.[2]

Speculation was so contentious not because of its idleness or potential sinfulness, but because of its potentially disruptive power in the circuits of early modern capitalism and natural philosophy, tied to risk, use, and failure. It did not fit neatly or easily in the vocabulary of any movement or revolution, yet it becomes part of the debates about the future of governments, about "projects" and the value of public investments, and about the means by which knowledge purportedly advances through contemplation, anticipation, projection, observation, and action. As speculation becomes very busy with many time-bound processes, it gains new interest and value for traders, novelists, politicians, journalists, experimenters, philosophers, and crooks alike.

IDOL SPECULATION?

The figure at the foundation of the new science, Francis Bacon, inherited from Calvinism the prevailing senses of *speculation* and *speculationes* as "idle" and "inert." Like Calvin and Chaucer, Bacon played a decisive role in redirecting the intellectual course of speculation, though through very different—and less linguistically focused—means. At first, like Calvin before him, Bacon constantly attacked philosophical and scholastic idleness and focused on the "signatures" of the eternal divine mind that could be found in the "mirror" of the contingent, natural world. Like Calvin, he also believed that God could be discovered in the creations of the phenomenal world, and he concluded that the aim of empirical science was to understand and reveal that divine presence by way of experiment. And also like Calvin, he famously sought to purge the mind's "idols" and to offer an approach to scientific inquiry freed from internal biases, even calling the concept of "Fortune" (which Calvin detested) a "fiction . . . arising from vain and false speculations."[3] Bacon came to disagree with plenty of the theology of Calvin and his followers, not the least on the value of curiosity, but like those before him (even back to Paul) he was searching for signs of God in the Book of Nature, "looking through with his mind," as it were. Discovering and properly interpreting those signs would help restore the sanctity of humanity, too.

Bacon's project grows from theological-naturalist concerns; it's therefore unsurprising, given the contexts we have studied, to find him initially suspicious of, and even hostile to, speculation. Untestable, theoretical speculation, after all, apparently had no ready-made role to play in a burgeoning world of knowledge created by way of applied experiments and observations. Speculation therefore risked ending up like "sloth," little more than a niche sin mentioned mostly to warn against it, far from the power that figures like Boethius had seen in it. Bacon's terminology was inconsistent—he composed sometimes in English, sometimes in Latin (and often with revisions between editions)—so he doesn't have the fixed attention to *speculation* that Boethius or Calvin did, but we can see a pattern, especially since most of the translations were fairly straightforward (*mere speculativae*, for example, becomes "merely speculative").[4] Bacon proclaimed that he did not seek "to call Philosophy down from heaven to converse upon the earth," but to help philosophy "reject vaine speculations" and "to preserve and augment whatsoever is solide and fruitfull" in human thought.[5] He likewise warned in a combined English-Latin against "the vanitie of curious *speculatiōs*."[6] Natural history done correctly, he believed, would further show that "Natures subtilty far exceeds the subtilty of our Sense, or that of our Understanding; so that the delicate meditations of Mankind, their speculations and inventions are but foolish things, if they were narrowly searched into."[7]

This all seems fitting for Bacon: speculative truths, the philosophical traditions held, could only be proved deductively or abstractly, by proposing theorems or reasoning logically—not by collecting sensory data from the material world. One rarely, if ever, "speculated" upon a certain plant or mineral. Even to speculate upon heavenly bodies meant to consider them in astrological, often mystical terms, not as objects whose motions or physical properties were to be studied. Speculation was now for a bygone world, not the present one and its new implements. But as he constantly exhorted, natural philosophers should focus on "things themselves," in order to move beyond an old model of "the inquisition of Nature" in which thinkers of the past "adored the deceiving and deformed Images, which the unequall mirrour of their owne minds, or a few received Authors or principles, did represent unto them."[8] A distortion in our minds, as inadequate mirrors, he argues, has so skewed human vision that we cannot see clearly, literally or metaphorically.[9]

Against his "idols"—where imagination, opinion, and ideology have run wild and overtaken our capacities of dispassionate observation and reasoned inference—Bacon proposed speculation's more stable cousin, contemplation, as a means to wipe clean the mind's slate.[10] He speaks often of the value of "contemplative philosophy," of "contemplating nature," and of contemplation and investigation as a pair, sometimes to the point of treating *contemplation* as a synonym of *philosophy* itself.[11] This is not speculation, then, nor is it yet what we call modern "objectivity." Embedded in Bacon's thought, however, was not so much an excision of speculation along the lines of Calvin, but rather, a model for a new "commerce between the Mind and Things"—a project that was consonant with both Plato's and Aristotle's systems, and with the natural philosophy in Augustine, Aquinas, and Roger Bacon.[12] Returning to the *vita contemplativa* and *vita activa*, Bacon wrote that he wished for humans to "dignifie and exalt knowledge" such that "contemplation and action...may be more neerely and straightly conjoyned and united together, than they have beene."[13] The inference, as Bacon updates a long line of philosophical and theological traditions, is that these two modes of philosophy and learning were already too far apart by his time.

In this focus on method and process, however, Bacon begins to sketch out two distinct roles for speculation, even if contemplation still seems to reign supreme for him. And as we trace the course of speculation in his work, we begin to see how he provides for it a crucial role in natural philosophy, in experimentation, and in knowledge production that carries on well beyond him. We start to see speculation's function when Bacon uses the Latin root *-spec* to name one of his Idols: he wants to banish "*Idola Specus*," the idols of the cave or den, the prejudices and biases that are learned from infancy. In his own Latin-English wordplay, he writes, "Let therefore your speculative prudence be so disposed in expelling and removing the *Idola Specus*." Thus, while the *Idola Theatri* are purely the result of "fabulous speculations," according to Bacon, he believed that "speculative prudence" was a mode of wisdom that could actually *govern* proper modes of naturalist thought.[14] He proposed that natural philosophy has two major branches: "operative" and "speculative."[15] These terms are the same ones in which Bacon has definitively sided with *opera* over *speculationes*; but here, he realizes that, in the end, they necessarily work in tandem, on the same model as contemplation and action. The former studies causes and axioms; the latter conducts experiments that have observable outcomes. The results of the experiments then lead to new axioms and more experiments, and thus knowledge advances.[16] (The current ideal of reciprocity between "design" and "implementation" has important origins here.) Like many characters and agents in the history of speculation, Bacon wants to discard the concept, but he ultimately needs it—here, for knowledge production.

That is to say, Bacon incorporates speculation in what becomes the processes of modern science when he comes to believe that knowledge can only advance "if men in their speculation will keepe one eye upon use & practise."[17] And therefore, natural philosophers must not "look down upon nature as from a high tower [*specula*] and from a great distance," but instead should "come down and draw near to particulars and take a closer and more accurate view of things themselves" so that they might "gain a more true and profitable knowledge of them."[18] Bacon elaborated in the *Novum organum* (1620) that unless observations and claims "terminate in matter and construction, according to true definitions, they are speculative, and of little use."[19] In other words, speculation now exists in a contingent, *temporal* relationship with activities and practices—here, experiments—and when those activities eventually help prove general, abstract principles, the "speculations" become useful and material. Experiments therefore must be reproducible endlessly into the future so that we can make final claims about universal conditions with certainty. Truth, for Bacon, was a matter of both philosophy and utility, but one could not pursue it without a "prudent" speculative disposition. In his Latin, Bacon performs an inversion: he aligns the upright, stalwart *sapientia* (judgment, reason, wisdom) with "speculative," and *prudentia* (discretion, foresight, applied good sense) with "operative"; *prudentia* is ultimately derived from *providens*, to see forward, to look toward the future.[20] Elsewhere, he and his translators even keep the Latin *speculatio* in his English texts as a potential end of human inquiry. Speculation/*speculatio* can have serious functions on either side of experimentation.

Bringing an element of futurity to his considerations, Bacon furthermore warned that when we "seek to adduce some science or theory from their experiments, [we] nevertheless almost always turn aside with overhasty and premature zeal to practice," overlooking the structures of thought necessary for knowledge and the need to "imitate divine foreknowledge and order" as natural philosophers.[21] That is, we *need* to look ahead, like God does, to understand divine plans, and therein lies the use of speculation's futurity. Speculation could be both guide for and product of experimentation. Bacon even came to refer to his own ideas in his *Great Instauration* (1620) as "my speculations," and invested himself in their future potential, that they "may in virtue of my continual conversancy with nature have a value beyond the pretensions of my wit."[22] A recent modern sphere of scientific postulation, inquiry, and verification that Bacon's heirs would institutionalize and spread was carving out a new space for speculation on the very grounds upon which it had been condemned and minimized. The relationship between speculation and practice was being retheorized and given new assumptions, instruments, and configurations as a means of understanding the interplay between the natural world and whatever lies beyond it. Speculation would help knowledge *advance*—move forward, into the future, where it would not be static or inert.

EXPERIENCE, PRACTICES, AND THE FATE OF SPECULATION

The interrelationships among speculation, experimentation, and knowledge that Bacon labored to cultivate would over the course of the seventeenth century redefine the terms through which scientific inquiry operates. In the process, speculation helped solidify its own conceptual and linguistic role. In part, this was because of the shifting vocabulary of the mid-1600s, when new generations of post-Baconian scientists refined and redirected Bacon's methods and terms. The language of experience and experiment became synonymous with what we now recognize as the new science, especially in the early years of the Royal Society (chartered in 1662).[23] As scientific inquiry was battling for the legitimacy of its methods and its vocabulary alike, the proponents of *practice* now sought to substitute this favored term and translate it into action, stripping it of historically negative associations. John Dunton, like many others, divided natural philosophy into two branches, speculative and experimental, while John Sergeant wrote in the opening of his *Method to Science* (1696) that "the METHODS which I pitch upon to examine, shall be of two sorts, viz. that of Speculative, and that of Experimental Philosophers; The Former of which pretend to proceed by Reason and Principles; the Later by Induction; and both of them aim at advancing Science."[24] Philosophy—both moral and natural—"ought to be [grounded] on Practice and Experiment, not on mere Speculation," as one figure later put it, and theologians like John Knox began using the terms together too.[25] Newton schematically contrasted "Experimental Philosophy," which "reduces Phænomena to general Rules" and only overturns those rules when "contrary" effect is actually produced, with "Hypothetical Philosophy," which "consists in imaginary explications of things & imaginary arguments for or against such explications."[26] In the renewed battle between advocates of ancient and modern wisdom, the former were often considered speculators, the latter practical experimenters—and the latter were claiming authority.

In important ways, the old battle between *speculation* and *practice* was now reframed as one between *speculation* and *experience/experiment*, and it could appear that *speculation* was destined to play a lesser role in modern science. Making new cognate terms, Newton elaborated further in his *Opticks* (1704) that "hypotheses are not to be regarded in experimental Philosophy," with "hypothesis" signaling anything speculative, or not deduced from human observation.[27] Only by dilating upon discovered and proven facts could one justifiably hypothesize, which for Newton left no room for speculation as an airy, inutile mode of thinking. ("I do not deal in conjectures," he remarked.[28]) As Mary Poovey notes, *conjecture* also underwent a transformation from the late 1400s to the mid-1600s, as it shifted—not unlike *speculation*—from "a mode of producing knowledge about the future from signs or omens believed to be portentous" to "offering an opinion on grounds insufficient to furnish proof, . . . guessing" that was "illegitimate" in the new science.[29] Descartes, for one, was dismissed by some in England as a purely speculative philosopher, because he purportedly did not adequately incorporate observation and material experience.

But *speculation*, despite all these divisions and potential for ostracism, was again impossible to chase away. It ultimately became a valuable term in two consequential contexts for its history over the next century and a half, far beyond Bacon's initial reach: the Royal Society and empiricist philosophy. In the first context, one of the Society's founding figures, Robert Boyle, in the same breath both attempted to dismiss the speculative philosophy and conceded that some of his own experiments could not be verified except by "Speculative and Metaphysical evidence."[30] That is, for Boyle, "evidence" can even exist immaterially, abstractly, as things known by cogitation alone. He also explained that

> Experiments considered in the Lump, or one with another, may very much assist the speculative Phylosopher, that is sollicitous about the causes and reasons of Naturall things; and that the speculative Phylosopher so assisted, may (on the other side) very much improve the Practical part of Physick. And consequently, that both of them may very happily conspire to the Establishing & Advancement of a Solid usefull Naturall Philosophy.[31]

Boyle would elaborate this logic that speculation and practice could "conspire" together in natural philosophy; or, as he called a lost tract of his, "Of the Usefulnes of Speculative & Experimental Philosophy to One Another." Thomas Browne agreed and argued that speculation clearly had a place in advancing science: "Let thy studies be as free as thy thoughts and contemplations; but fly not only upon the wings of imagination; joyn sense unto reason, and experiment unto speculation, and so give life unto embryon truths, and verities yet in their chaos."[32]

Right speculation, like imagination itself, could be trained to advance experimental knowledge. Eventually, a new formulation of the apparently paradoxical "practical speculation," or a useful and profitable abstract thought, became part of the discourse of speculative experiments, thought experiments, and inductive knowledge.[33]

Thomas Sprat, a founder of and strong public apologist for the Royal Society, framed the issues at stake clearly in his *History of the Royal-Society of London* (1667). He held that the new culture of experimental science meant that now, "a higher degree of Reputation is due to *Discoverers*, than to the *Teachers* of *Speculative Doctrines*."[34] Sprat argues that the "meer *Speculative Philosopher* . . . vainly reduces every thing to grave and solemn general *Rules*," while the "*Prudent* man is like him who proceeds on a constant and solid cours of *Experiments*."[35] But even with this apparent devaluing of speculation, Sprat gives an overview of the Society's experimenters, who themselves were being mocked as (ironically, he would see it) abstruse speculators who endlessly observe and never act. He defends them as not dealing only with ideas that "pass under the name of *Hypotheses*," and vows that "whatever *Principles*, and *Speculations* they now raise from things, they do not rely upon them as the absolute end, but only use them as a means of farther *Knowledge*. This way the most speculative *Notions*, and *Theorems* that can be drawn from matter, may conduce to much profit."[36] He adds that staring at the sun—a sort of secular form of "divine speculation"—will make one blind if it does not prompt action; "*Speculation* alone" is insufficient, but in a classic mode of abstraction, speculation can now be "drawn from matter."[37] Or, as Richard Allestree put it in *The Causes of the Decay of Christian Piety* (1667), speculation and experience are both necessary, but we cannot "so far let loose to Speculation, as to forget our Experience."[38]

If we step back and look at the Society's contexts, we see that Sprat tracks what he observes as the rise of "the *publick* Faith of *Experimental Philosophy*" and the progress it brings, as opposed to the "holy speculative Warrs" of Christian thinkers, which have "very much retarded . . . the knowledge of Nature."[39] But the "*Experimental Knowledge*" that he defends all the while relies on speculative thought and theoretical principles.⁴⁰ The Royal Society's *Philosophical Transactions*—the first journal of modern science in the West—would even publish in its early issues articles such as "Monsieur Auzout's Speculations of the Changes, Likely to be Discovered in the *Earth* and *Moon*, by Their Respective Inhabitants" (1667), which surmised what the postulated peoples of the moon would observe when looking at Earth. In the 1797 edition of the *Encyclopædia Britannica*, the "object of natural philosophy" was now given as "speculative truth," and the "natural philosopher was, at times, the 'speculative philosopher,'" meaning that experimentation had speculation not just as a means, but as an end, much as figures in the 1600s had theorized.⁴¹

Anticipation, in short, is built into the structure of the new science, through the duration of the experiment and the observation of outcomes, giving speculative thought another, as-yet-uncertain sense of potential prophecy in verifying universal truths *as* practical knowledge. A fast-forward glimpse to one of the foundational texts of modern natural philosophy elucidates how fully ingrained this language would become. Charles Darwin writes in the opening paragraph of *On the Origin of Species* (1859) that, only after "patiently accumulating and reflecting on all sorts of facts" and contemplating "that mystery of mysteries" (the origin of species) did he finally allow himself "to speculate on the subject, and [draw] up some short notes; these I enlarged in 1844 into a sketch of the conclusions, which then seemed to me probable: from that period to the present day I have steadily pursued the same object."⁴² This integration of speculation into science had ramifications for as many fields of thought as Darwin's own book reached.

In the mid-to-late 1600s, a more conscious effort then took place to remake speculation *as* practical, especially in the mental labor of thought. A signature move in early modern philosophy—the thought experiment, or the experiment on one's own mind—begins to clarify the promise of this conceptualization. (As Joseph Priestley put it in 1779: "Speculation without experiment has always been the bane of true philosophy."⁴³) Thomas Hobbes, who saw his own work as proceeding "by speculation, and deduction" (not induction), still asserted that real-world experiments and experiences could prove the value of their ideas.

He concludes book 2 of *Leviathan* (1651) with "some hope, that one time or other, this writing of mine, may fall into the hands of a Sovereign, who will consider it himselfe, . . . [and] convert this Truth of Speculation, into the Utility of Practice."[44] John Locke and David Hume wrestled with the categories of speculative and practical knowledge at length, too, and similarly concluded that while "facts" and "conclusions" were still distinct from "speculations," the advancement of knowledge over time could integrate the paths of speculation and practice and further the recuperation of speculation itself.[45] It seemed impossible now to treat speculation as purely "idle," and thus only as empty, vacant thought, for this was also to deny speculation's temporal dimension—its connotations of futurity and of projective cognition—and to see it as a term employed without time or space. To treat speculation as useless unless it became a path to righteous practices was to discipline and limit it to action-oriented cognition with a presupposed purpose and rigid moralism. From Bacon through empiricism, speculation now had all sorts of possibilities in conjunction with experimentation, practice, thought, time, nature, and more. What would happen, then, when speculation's potential object in future time became the anticipated or conjectural creation of wealth? Or, to ask a question that many asked in all sorts of ways: How might one experiment on money?

"AIR-MONEY": THE FINANCIAL REVOLUTION AND THE SPECULATIVE WORLD

Even if speculation's usages in finance are still several decades away, we now have its conceptual underpinnings in place, for it is hard to fathom the financial revolution without the premises of the scientific revolution. To understand how we got here, and why these shifts matters so much, we need to plot some economic transformations and *their* vocabulary. What P. G. M. Dickson called the "financial revolution" brought new senses and contexts to the notion of value itself—past, present, and future.[46] When William of Orange arrived and became king of England, Scotland, and Ireland, in 1689, he brought with him a set of relatively new financial practices (many of them later called "speculative") from the thriving markets of Amsterdam. Just five years later, he granted a royal charter to create the Bank of England, an entity that issued debt notes to public creditors, primarily to finance an expensive war with France. For the first time in British history, as J. G. A. Pocock characterizes it, the "institutions of new finance, of which the Bank of England and the National Debt came to be the most important, were essentially a series of devices for encouraging the large or small investor to lend capital to the state, investing in its future political stability and strengthening this by the act of investment itself, while deriving a guaranteed income from the return on the sum invested."[47] In other words, the state asked its subjects to lend money toward the future political stability of the state as if it were a stock whose success was necessary for those citizens' own collective security and well-being. Pocock explains the paradox: "Government stock is a promise to repay at a future date; from the inception and development of the National Debt, it is known that date will in reality never be reached, but the tokens of repayment are exchangeable at a market price in the present."[48] This mortgaging of the future in the present thereby fostered a "paradigm of a society now living to an increasing degree by speculation and by credit: that is to say, men's expectations of one another's capacity for future action and performance," as measured by market indicators.[49]

This process brought about new modes of "imaginary" wealth creation: over a hundred joint-stock companies, for example, suddenly existed by 1695.[50] To make broad generalizations: wealth and power needed less grounding in real estate, precious metals, coins and jewels, or tangible assets than before. Social standing became less discretely tied to immutable categories such as heredity and blood, and Catholic and Jewish subjects in England had more opportunities for gain. One could rise with astonishing rapidity in rank and in value—skip several rungs of the proverbial social ladder—by way of paper money, bank notes, and purely "fictional" credit. Profit, many observers on the ground felt, could be created without a material base, while ideas of money could breed more money, as if abstracting abstractions.[51] Property and assets were now more mobile and fluid than before, property prices were soon explicitly pegged in advertisements to the value of South Sea stock, and corruption in trading and pricing was presumed to be rampant.[52] So, while opinion, fancy, luck, credit, and a notion of futurity had always played a role in economic life, the state now rearranged them such that they supported the hypothetical promises of credit and abstractions of wealth that were reshaping the populace—and to which the state owed its financial life. Stock exchanges and currency markets themselves were largely understood as lotteries and their players as gamblers and diviners. The new state-sanctioned Million Adventure lottery (1694) and Malt Lottery (1697) arose from this same environment. Laws and regulations struggled to keep up with what instruments and practices could create, all while the state's need to borrow for perpetual wars presented more and more opportunities for profit for the most despised of investors.

As with speculations in experimental science, the relevant questions became: Were these forms of wealth substantiated and grounded in the material world and its practices, or were they mere creations of fancy, those benighted "idle speculations" now turned into dangerously consequential fictions? Was the new rising class of bankers, stock investors, debt holders, and currency speculators *actually* wealthy, or only dreaming themselves so? And could we know either way with verifiable certainty, within the paradigms of this changing "social epistemology," the same way gold could be assayed?[53] (Or was the value of gold itself extrinsic and dependent upon fancy?) Thus we find physiocrats, agrarians, and the equivalents of goldbugs asserting that the modern credit economy and the debt-financed state could be nothing more than sustained yet unsustainable fictions. With typical vitriol, Daniel Defoe, in his *Anatomy of Exchange-Alley* (1719), railed against the new "Stock Jobbers" who were "Abettors of Treason" in the ways they deceived the nation of its financial and trade resources and thrived on the state of continual war.[54] For Defoe, "Their Practise [is] more fatal to the Publick than an Invasion of Spaniards."[55] "Stock Jobbers" originated as an epithet in the 1690s, and it assumed hypocrisy and roguishness. Likewise, for many like-minded commentators, financial scheming was a devious *practice*, a false form of selling an imagined future through rigged gambling.

Defoe captured a growing ethos in which speculation was conceptually invoked when he inveighed specifically against the pervasive spread of "Air-Money," explaining that "I call it *Air*, . . . and the worst Sort of *Air* too, for it is ten times a more convectible Element than that we breath [*sic*] in. 'Tis an Element GOD never made, and 'tis a Trade he never bless'd, . . . 'tis a Fire has left more Ruins in this City, than that of Sixty six."[56] (The Dutch called the rapid exchanging of stocks *Windhandel*, or "wind-trading.") Defoe's figuration is, at first, scientific: Boyle had spent years investigating the "spring of air" and conducting experiments with his famed air pump. Air was both abstract thought and an object of experimentation, understood at once as inert nothingness and as fuel for fire. Science provided metaphors for economics, and vice versa; the new financial order offered a means to remake both society and the state. But the new finance, too, had a circular self-referentiality and artificiality in mental spheres that Defoe worried could never be disciplined and grounded in this world. He sees it, then, as *unnatural*, too: as if God had *not* made this air. It is an element somehow fabricated by hubristic humans, not of this universe, and thus it behaves according to laws we cannot understand. As he brings together categorically the colliding yet mutually thriving worlds of experimental science and experimental capitalism, Defoe illustrates the instability and controversy that accompanied the very speculative nature of their core functions of observation, valuation, and anticipation.

THE PROJECTOR AS PROTO-SPECULATOR

Defoe's commentaries gained notoriety, and remain touchstones now, because he saw natural philosophers, stockjobbers, writers, and others as interconnected figures in culture. That perspectival transition helps us reorient our view of how *speculation* as a term starts to shift when it migrates from Bacon's treatises, the Royal Society's journals, and philosophical texts to the fields of financial journalism and cultural criticism, and on to drama, poetry, and novels. But the dreams of wealth conjured in the financial revolution specifically were not yet called "speculations," and for that reason, we need to grapple with the history of a cognate term that clarifies the stakes of the intellectual history in operation. Defoe had a name for his era of scientific and financial revolutions: the "Projecting Age."[57] Prior to the mid-1700s, the keyword that most closely denoted what *speculation* in finance and political economy would become was *projecting*, from the Latin for "to throw or cast forward." In time, *speculation* would merge with, then eclipse, this term, and would do so with greater semantic range. But the history of *projecting* would influence speculation all the while. To *project*, meaning to "devise and scheme" (with both the positive and negative connotations of each of those terms), had by the early 1600s taken on increased significance, pointing to the act of conceiving futuristic plans that often aimed to deceive others and benefit the projector. *Projection* also meant "the transmutation of metal" in experiments, and thus it combined the headlong, forward-facing dangers that its Latin roots intimate with an alchemical connotation.

"Projectors" were staple figures in moralistic condemnations of those who would bilk the public. Ben Jonson posed and answered the question, through two characters in a play, of "What is a *Projector*? / I would conceive.... Why, one Sir, that projects / Wayes to enrich men, or to make 'hem great,"[58] while Shakespeare characterized Prospero as an arch-projector.[59] Hume soon warned that "when the nation becomes heartily sick of their debts, and is cruelly oppressed by them, some daring projector may arise with visionary schemes for their discharge."[60] Defoe himself had lost money in projects, yet in 1697 he published his *Essay Upon Projects*, in which he proposed a number of ideas on everything from highways to assistance funds for widows. In other words, Defoe had to reconcile the fact that he was a projector himself—an ambassador of the age that he decried. Projects and projectors were not new in human history, he notes: "The Building of the Ark by *Noah*, so far as you will allow it a human Work, was the first Project I read of."[61]

He is precise: he can "trace the Original of the Projecting Humour that now reigns" in his "Age" to "no farther back than the Year 1680, dating its Birth as a Monster then[,] . . . [when] the Art and Mystery of Projecting [began] to creep into the World," prompted by much of the rebuilding of London that had taken place after the fire of 1666.[62]

In a crucial shift that spanned literal and figurative senses, this meant that "projects" and "speculations" converged as "imagined plans" or "conceived ideas" for which the new finance was increasingly a crucible. They were often condemned in tandem, which in turn further pushed the ills of the financial sphere into the conceptual orbit of speculation.[63] This language is visible across a wide range of texts from the period: an account of church history condemns the past "Chimera's, or Idle Projects, by Men of Speculation"; another text discusses "those fine speculations and rare projects"; while another still speaks of "vain *Chimaera*'s, with weak and flat projects, . . . meerly in speculation and in thoughts."[64] Credit, typically personified as a fickle woman, was, in Defoe's words, "built on the Foundation of Project," and thus was "a *Deceptio Visus* upon the Imagination."[65] The language of deception and chimeras is telling here: projects and speculations were often understood as impossible conjunctions of disparate parts, monstrosities of human thought. Yet projects became rhetorical vehicles of cognitive projections of futurity of all types.

Just as speculation seemed to have been largely legitimized by figures in the new science, it once again risked being dismissed as nothing short of evil, and in that process, having its still-proliferating senses all channeled into one predominant (and negative) one. But the critical turn in Defoe's influential understanding of the Projecting Age is that *good* projects turn speculations into "practices" grounded in experiments: "Schemes, Projects, and infinite Arts and secret Practises" are therefore all lumped together.[66] Bad projectors were bad or untrained scientists, and thus poor predictors of the future. They read the evidence of the phenomenal world and extrapolated wild, impossible conclusions, even if we can't know the veracity or falsity of their conclusions until an unknown future time. They deceived others in the present—playing on opinion and fancy—into believing as *fact* the contingencies of the future. Samuel Johnson distinguished between the "folly and wickedness" of projectors and the necessity of projects for "the good of mankind, in searching out new powers of nature, and contriving new works of art," the latter of which "ought to be encouraged."[67] Good projectors combined the notions of fancy and fortune that reigned in the marketplace with the experientially validated methods of the new science. Sprat had another criterion for judging them: projectors were self-interested, while scientists and natural philosophers were interested only in truth, which was its own profit. This gave a burgeoning class of dreamers of all stripes the space to produce what we now call "inventions."

In the early 1700s, this also put projectors, as proto-speculators, on the border between those making legitimate, publicly beneficial proposals and those offering up harebrained schemes meant to enrich one person or small group—a dynamic that would soon fall under the conceptual rubric of speculation. Defoe proposed a contrast: "There is, it is true, a great difference between *New Inventions* and *Projects*, between Improvement of Manufactures or Lands (which tend to the immediate Benefit of the Public, and Imploying of the Poor); and Projects framed by subtle Heads with a sort of a *Deceptio Visus* and *Legerdemain*, to bring People to run needless and unusual hazards."[68] Again Defoe relies on visual imagery—our eyes are deceived, and sleight of hand follows—that reminds us of speculation's own roots in the visual observation and contemplation of physical evidence. Defoe ultimately believes that we can find a public consensus on "Honest Projector[s]" and "mere Project[ors]," and he counted himself among the former.[69] Defoe proposes a great deal in his *Essay Upon Projects* (which was a flop when published), including a betting pool concerning which towns will be taken in sieges in foreign wars, a public lottery, and educational resources for women. He refers to many of his plans as "experiments" and notes that they would need funding, but distinguishes his projects from the "Frauds and Tricks of *Stock-Jobbers, Engineers, Patentees, Committees*, with those *Exchange-Mountebanks* we very properly call *Brokers*," because they require that "Your Money to the Author must go before the Experiment."[70]

When pitched this way, as public goods, projects eventually became quite valuable—even if the public was wary of projectors' intentions, and even if the projects had high rates of failure. They stood at the intersection of experimental culture and economics.[71] Like joint-stock companies, projects soon had parliamentary backing, especially in the late 1600s and early 1700s, and the state welcomed plans for infrastructure and exploration projects that could benefit commerce and better meet the challenges of urbanization and early industrialization.[72] The innovations in means of financing them, and of creating wealth by way of projects, now tied speculation conceptually (though still not in direct linguistic usage) to a broad swath of endeavors: to hatch an investment was to experiment and speculate on others' visions of the future. And the consequences of that experiment's success or failure were pervasively connected to the future of the state itself, and to the future fortunes of a great number of individuals. The ends of science, the ends of monetary risk, and the ends of statecraft were circling around one another in the Projecting Age, and the *terms* for judging projects were greatly in flux. With them, so were the very epistemological grounds of evidence and value.

THE SPECTATOR SPECULATES

An emergent public sphere of print journalism and the developing English novel specifically then became the catalysts for a consolidation in the history of speculation as both concept and term. Speculation's crossings with projection, its ability to translate the methodologies of experimental science and finance into the broader domains of culture, and its growing expressive capacities challenged both lexicographers and language makers. But the term found even fresher, expanded discursive life in the early 1700s, in the journal that Jürgen Habermas highlighted for its role in the creation of the public sphere in England: Joseph Addison and Richard Steele's *The Spectator* (1711–1714). *The Spectator* focuses intensely on and thrives on "speculations," which signify both thought experiments and idle ideations.[73] We see all this in microcosm at the very outset: the epigraph to the first number doubles the titular play on the Latin *-spec* root with a quotation from Horace's *Ars poetica*: "Non fumum ex fulgore, sed ex fumo dare lucem cogitate, et speciosa dehinc miracula promat" (Not the smoke from the flame, but the light from the smoke does he contemplate, so that marvelous wonders may henceforth arise from it).[74] Here, *speciosa* means "wondrously beautiful," as the old form of "specious" did. (An unrelated journal founded later in the 1720s would attempt similar wordplay when naming itself *The Speculatist*.) The two editors construct a multitiered chart of *speculation*'s linguistic family as the premise for their forward-facing commentaries on society and culture.[75]

Addison and Steele straightforwardly note that they have "design[ed] this Paper as a Speculation."[76] It aims to implement detached observation and reasoned judgment in print—to look afar and into the future, not to the divine world of contemplation but to the contingent world of cultural change. *The Spectator* was especially keen to market the sense of "a speculation" as an active, public (published) meditation on future possibilities, an educated guess made using probable scenarios drawn from distilling past and present experience. A staple of many issues of *The Spectator*, then, is a column featuring the "Speculations" of "Mr. Spectator." This figure is the anonymous, impartial observer that modern science and modern empiricist thought had elevated, now turning his (male) eye to the sociocultural world. He claims from the start, in a nod to the continued Calvinist associations with *speculation*, that he is not "an idle but a very busie Spectator."[77] Mr. Spectator keeps track of his many speculations, referring to them by number (his "Hundred and sixty first Speculation," for example), and he prints letters from readers who engage with him on these speculations.[78] He proclaims, with even more wordplay on the *-spec* root, that "I live in the World, rather as a Spectator of Mankind, than as one of the Species; by which means I have made my self a Speculative Statesman, Soldier, Merchant and Artizan, without ever medling with any Practical Part in Life."[79] Incorporating "Spectator," "Species," and "Speculative," Addison's ironic rhetoric works on multiple levels here: soldiers, merchants, and arguably artisans are deeply invested in the "Practical Part of Life." The additional irony is that Mr. Spectator (called "Spec" for short) promises to employ "whatever Skill I may have in Speculation"—that is to say, speculation is a learned, applied "Skill" and not the airy, immaterial wandering of thought.[80]

The speculator figure in this journal is a perceiver par excellence: he consumes visual evidence of the changing world, contemplates and reflects upon it, and draws conclusions time and again. This is, in effect, a modified version of the figure that both Bacon and the Royal Society fellows had placed at the center of modern inquiry. Only here, speculation *itself* is both the practice and—beyond the phenomenal world—the object of inquiry as well. Thus Mr. Spectator spends much time in his "Speculations" detailing the "experiments" he conducts, whether in thought or in the observation of the worlds of society and culture.[81] In the paper's second year, it begins to tie together the language of speculation, spectatorship, and projecting: "I do not know," Addison writes, in his role as "the first Projector of the Paper," "whether I enough explained my self to the World, when I invited all Men to be assistant to me in this my Work of Speculation."[82]

Mr. Spectator's "Rambles, or rather Speculations" even take him to one of the first brushes between *speculation* and the new English financial system. Addison attempts to place a future (literal) value on his "Speculations": "When I think on the Figure my several Volumes of Speculations will make about a Hundred Years hence, I consider them as so many Pieces of old Plate [Spanish coins], where the Weight will be regarded, but the Fashion lost."[83] Addison imagines that his thoughts *themselves* will have future, projected value that will fluctuate just like metal coins, as a model of how speculative assets will be understood soon. The public speculations valued by *The Spectator* are those that have no defined path or results, no repeatable experiments to confirm their truths as static and fixed, in the present only. Rather, they need the whims of fortune, luck, or changing circumstances to bear out their application. Cultural criticism, in this case, was giving more conceptual variation to what natural philosophy and capitalism were innovating but not yet fleshing out as future-oriented valuation.

BUBBLES AND FLOATING ISLANDS

The signature "project" of the age Defoe named, of course, and the one that captured so many philosophical, economic, scientific, and cultural movements of the time, was the South Sea Bubble. Far from the isolated collapse of a single stock, the South Sea Company's rise and fall was so dramatic precisely because its primary charge became its assumption of England's national debt. The company, founded in 1711, had a government charter that, despite all the warning signs, gave it an air of security—all while it effectively behaved like a state lottery.[84] The stock grew nearly tenfold in 1720 before crashing, and it was recognized by plenty as a bubble even before it burst—yet that did not dissuade investors.[85] Newton's disciples had been important figures in the company, again sealing the connections between scientific and economic speculative imaginaries, and Newton himself was said to have lost money in the scheme; Alexander Pope, John Gay, and Jonathan Swift all lost substantial amounts.[86] Edward Harley, the government auditor and brother of the Earl of Oxford, claimed that investors had been duped by "a machine of paper credit supported by imagination."[87]

The South Sea Bubble became in cultural memory a symbol of the dangers and excesses of the new finance. It was also a minor literary event that drew projection and speculation even closer together. It prompted a spate of poems and ballads, not to mention a famous engraved scene by William Hogarth and a set of playing cards depicting the various characters in the scheme.

A typical such poem, Edward Ward's "South-Sea Ballad," speaks of the stock as a visual deception pulled off by disreputable knaves:

> Here, crafty Courtiers are too wise
> For those who trust to fortune;
> They see the cheat with clearer eyes,
> Who peep behind the curtain.[88]

Ward also describes the rise of the South Sea stock as the work of "alchemists" who are "cunning" in their ability to turn "nothing into all things,"

FIGURE 2.1 William Hogarth, *The South Sea Scheme* (1721). Hogarth's engraving—an early and important example of the political cartoon genre—employs imagery of fortune's wheel as a lottery, of rampant theft, and of prostitution tacitly sanctioned by both church and state.

Public domain.

and he rhymes "vapour" with "Paper." Another ballad, this one by "A Lady," called the stock—with several then-common anti-Semitic references and tropes—the "cleverest Project that ever was made: / For now the Contrivers are tipt with a Fee, / If they Souse the Subscribers into the South-Sea."[89] Swift also captured the alleged treachery of the "directors" of the venture in his poem "The South-Sea Project" (1721), which plumbs how finance operates and how wealth magically grows. Swift begs:

> Ye wise philosophers, explain
> What magic makes our money rise,

When dropt into the Southern main;
Or do these jugglers cheat our eyes?[90]

Swift and Defoe would disagree on many matters, but their understanding of the South Sea debacle was quite similar. Like Defoe's *deceptio visus*, Swift's metaphor fixes on the visual nature of money. "The pond'rous metal" of coin and gold "seems to swim" magically in the hands of projectors, but Swift's speaker is unsatisfied by the trick—no doubt because of Swift's regret at his loss. It's important to note here that while the South Sea project was indeed called a "bubble" in its time (thanks largely to Swift), it was *not* called a "speculation" or "speculative venture," and overall, it was *not* seen as a "fever" or "mania," as some have recast it in retrospect. Most blamed the directors and accused them of anything ranging from deception to foolishness. The "folly of projectors" became a common phrase in the early 1700s; thus, even as projects were recognized as potentially valuable, disastrous results recast them as some combination of fraud and quackery that bridged the present and the future.

In perhaps the most lasting and influential piece of literature to emerge from the South Sea Bubble, Swift's *Gulliver's Travels* (1726) would bind together fully and creatively the various intellectual, rhetorical, and conceptual threads that speculation now represented. Swift began composing the novel in 1720, and large sections of it are a satirical autopsy of the era that produced the Bubble. The novel begins in "projects." In the opening epistle to his cousin, Gulliver writes of his regret that he "attempted so absurd a project as that of reforming the Yahoo race in this kingdom: But I have now done with all such visionary schemes for ever."[91] Gulliver, we read, has long been a "great admirer of projects, and a person of much curiosity and easy belief;... for I myself had been a sort of projector in my younger days," and he still pursues promises of double pay on a ship as a surgeon, only to find himself attacked by pirates.[92] Swift, too, had proposed a number of projects, both earnest and satirical.

Projects and projectors fill the novel, none more memorably than on the flying island of Laputa, where the inhabitants spend all their time and energy on speculative questions of arts, music, and the stars, leaving them with little practical sense.[93] Gulliver notes, as we shift into speculations, that the "minds of these people are so taken up with intense speculations" that they must be roused constantly just to gain their attention.[94] The men in particular are "always so rapt in speculation," and elsewhere "so abstracted and involved in speculation," that they hardly speak to Gulliver.[95] The floating island has its status as an "airy region" doubled in its prized "academy of PROJECTORS" at the Grand Academy of Lagado in Balnibarbi.[96] In the satire of the Royal Society and the culture of uninformed wonder at scientific experiments, Gulliver encounters here a host of absurd inventions and mechanisms. Swift has Gulliver observe, for instance, that

> I had hitherto seen only one side of the academy, the other being appropriated to the advancers of speculative learning ... [There were] two large rooms full of wonderful curiosities, and fifty men at work. Some were condensing air into a dry tangible substance, by extracting the nitre, and letting the aqueous or fluid particles percolate; others softening marble, for pillows and pin-cushions; others petrifying the hoofs of a living horse, to preserve them from foundering.[97]

The projectors here claim to advance knowledge, as the new science claimed to, but they only advance "speculative learning," with no practical benefits. In fact, what Gulliver elsewhere calls "projectors in speculative learning" may believe that they "improv[e] speculative knowledge, by practical and mechanical operations," but they flatter themselves at the brilliance of their own ideas so that they never create useful inventions.[98] Quite the opposite, the projectors want to "destroy" a long-standing mill that functions naturally and replace it with an ill-conceived artificial one that operates by "pipes and engines"—Swift's recasting of the South Sea stock's effect.[99] But their "work miscarried, the projectors went off" and refused to accept blame, and still managed to "put ... others upon the same experiment."[100] These speculators float in air, they experiment in and on air, but they are condemned by Swift, because they come to earth with the same idle speculations that Calvin detested. Still, speculative thinking *is* experimental and is tied to empirically observable future outcomes; the question—and this is key to see—is less speculation's innate meaning than its method of application to and in the world.

Swift thereby gets at the circularity of speculation, and brings the period that we have covered here full circle: What makes a good speculation? A profitable result, which obviously can't be known in the moment of speculation, only in the contingent future. Swift's satire shows that by the 1720s, projectors were not to be understood simply as abstruse dreamers, nor purely as deceptive swindlers. The projectors in his novel *are* what we now simply call scientists. And they are hardly just fictional characters; in fact, they created the South Sea Bubble. "Speculators" are experimenting, whether impractically, or sometimes all too *practically*, if we return to the duplicitous sense captured in *practice*. They can produce knowledge, but that production depends on conditions and temporality that involve financial risks that will soon become the focal point of much thought about what speculation itself embodies. The future was hanging in the balance in the new science, and speculation was giving a new name and a new conceptualization to its operations—for good and bad, elevation and mockery. This widely applied and constantly modified idea could now enter a phase of its life in which morality seemed perhaps a trifling concern, and practicality and profit became lasting measures of speculation itself.

Even when it is called idle, speculation surely cannot be seen as inert philosophizing only: the ground beneath it has shifted permanently, and it too has done its share to renovate debates about value, evidence, and futurity in the early modern era. Defoe's language in *The Chimera* (1720), in which he discusses the Mississippi Bubble that John Law conjured in France that same year, draws even closer to the sense of *speculation* that will develop more fully in the coming decades:

the same Arbitrary Power [Louis XV] has rais'd an inconceivable Species of meer Air and Shadow, realizing Fancies and Imaginations, Visions and Apparitions, and making the meer speculations of Things, act all the Parts, and perform all the Offices of the Things themselves; and thus in a moment their Debts are all vanish'd, the Substance is answer'd by the Shadow; and the People of *France* are made the Instruments of putting the Cheat upon themselves, the Name of the thing is made an Equivalent to the Thing itself, transposing the Debts from the King to themselves, and being contented to Discharge the Publick, owe the Money to one another.[101]

Defoe plumbs the depths of the financial magic at work here by using multiple forms of the Latin *-spec* root ("species," "speculations") in order to indicate that—as Marx would famously phrase it—all that is solid is melting into air. But more specifically, "things" are dematerialized into "meer speculations," or ideas, into theories, not objects. A wand can transfer debts from the king to the people in a manner by which "the Substance is answer'd by the Shadow," or the outlined silhouette becomes the Thing itself. The speculator can be a modern-day sorcerer or alchemist, with power and knowledge relative to the degree of public, royal, scientific, or governmental sanction. But where else might one gain this power or foster the conditions of speculation? In a laboratory, in a public market, in the shadows, or in the pages of a magazine or a novel? Who can speculate, and how and where and why, will be the continued source of contention in the next phases of this concept's story.

3

GAMBLING ON A WORD

Of all th' ill-fated Words
Great JOHNSON's Dictionary affords, . . .
Not one was e'er so basely treated,
Of Spirit, Sense, and Meaning cheated,
Or e'er deserv'd Commiseration
Like this poor Word, call'd—SPECULATION.

—CHRISTOPHER ANSTEY, *SPECULATION; OR,*
A DEFENCE OF MANKIND (1780)

Dictionaries are not only fascinating windows onto meanings in their time. They are also telling for what they miss, which we can see in retrospect. In the late 1740s, Samuel Johnson began composing his monumental *Dictionary of the English Language*, which he would publish in 1755 and would revise multiple times through 1775. He wanted, in part, to stabilize an English language that had grown bewildering, far beyond any single speaker or reader's capacities. The *Dictionary* was to be a milestone—a marker, a snapshot of a heterogeneous, international tongue. And while Johnson captured in sharp focus the older mental and philosophical senses of *speculation*, and while he used the word itself in many other entries, he missed all the change and energy around speculation in his very moment. Speculation's rapidly expanding economic significance and its strong connotations of risk and gambling, which took hold in the mid-1700s, are absent from Johnson's *Dictionary*.[1]

There's more here than a simple oversight. What Johnson missed, and why he missed it, point up a stark set of divisions in how the British especially thought about, wrote about, and imagined the future through the frameworks that *speculation* now provided as a growing—and splintering—conceptual term. *Speculation* actually became a highly *unstable* term at precisely this moment. Its mid-eighteenth-century metamorphosis and variegated proliferation worked against what Johnson was trying to contain and pin down in his *Dictionary*. To reassemble its story from roughly the 1750s to the early 1800s, we'll have to look instead to commerce dictionaries, financial journalism, parliamentary reports, newspapers, and a host of other less singular texts than Johnson's. They will ultimately lead us to a different milestone: it was Adam Smith who sealed and advanced what would become *speculation*'s predominant meaning in the centuries that followed. Smith, in his articulation of conceptual vocabulary for the emergent field of political economy in *The Wealth of Nations* (1776), crafted *speculation* into a term crucial for his theory of capitalism, where he welded together an even wider semantic range of the same term that Swift had aimed to caricature. Smith granted speculation such a decisive function in modern capitalism by more closely linking experimental science and the largely disreputable domains of risk, gambling, chance, and insurance that the concept was increasingly encompassing in its orbit.

The world of capitalism that Smith described was reshaping the future with all sorts of speculative instruments of credit, contracts, stocks, certificates, and more, but also with the behaviors and terms of risk, renaming, valuing, pricing, and threatening. Where the previous chapter focused on the question of the force of thought (cognition, imagination, reasoning) in the production of knowledge about the future, this one shifts to the risk valuations of future wealth, what they motivate, and how people characterized their future effects. This attention to certain behaviors, from smuggling and gambling to investments and entrepreneurship, marks a stage in the history of speculation as a special *type of practice*. And while the concept of speculation had internal variety to this point, at this juncture we start to see it split into new strands that become at once difficult and necessary to reconcile in the minds of many thinkers in this period. A generation of Romantic poets and literary figures began asking, in the wake of the new dominance of *speculation*'s economic sense, how the term's philosophical sense had been indelibly altered by such a charged meaning. As we slow down and focus on the depth and intensity of meaning exchanged over a half century, we will start to see more clearly the debates over how speculators were manipulating the future by way of the present, and over how they were manipulating language in order to do so. Speculation largely fit into philosophical schemas thus far; now it starts to move around seemingly everywhere (a fear expressed in the epigraph to this chapter, from Christopher Anstey), almost out of control, beyond the reach of dictionaries to codify. But this lively period of speculation's life exhibits its new directions in political economy, journalism, and literature, where all sorts of figures priced their often-errant ideas of the future through an energetic, volatile concept.

SMUGGLERS, SCHEMERS, AND THE PRICE OF THE FUTURE

Speculation had previously been controversial because of its idleness, and then again because of its association with risky, unproven, and deceptive projects. But looking specifically at its linguistic function, around the mid-1740s, *speculation* was starting to become more clearly a legible term in then-cohering vocabularies of modern capitalism. As it was, it began to name an even more controversial and clearly immoral set of practices and associated instruments of capitalism. A House of Commons report on "running" (smuggling) in the international tea market, for instance, notes that "several Persons, who go under the

Denomination of speculative Buyers," purchase tea "merely on the Expectation of the Price rising afterwards"—that is, without a plan to consume or distribute the tea themselves, only to offload it as quickly as possible for a profit. The proximity of "merely" to "speculative" is no accident here; the connotation remained palpable from Calvin's time. One plan floated in the House of Commons to counteract this problem was to meet all demand for tea with an oversupply, so that "the Price [of tea] could not be raised by speculative Buyers and Smugglers Agents."[2] Across the 1750s and 1760s, there are increasing references, especially in media that cover trade and commerce, to such "speculative buyers," "speculative tradesmen," and generally "speculative men" in various economic fields.[3] As one writer explained in 1753, there was a widening pattern in which someone "of *Intelligence* and *Speculation* would then engage in the Speculative Part of Trade," by buying up foreign commodities at cheap prices and re-exporting them without their ever touching British soil.[4] These "speculative" figures are generally more interested in profit alone than in the intrinsic or consumable value of certain goods. They are versions of the scientific figures we saw in the early 1700s, now operating both in light and in shadows, and they are a new class of economic characters who are beginning to supersede what the term "projector" contained.

A "speculative merchant," that is to say, *could* be a reputable figure in (usually) local trade, and newspapers commonly reported on freight ships named *Speculator* and *Speculation*.[5] The influential writer Thomas Mortimer's *Every Man His Own Broker* (1761) discussed the impact of orders "sold on speculation at a low price, without being possessed of it," without a blanket condemnation of the practice.[6] But suspicion was widespread; the phrases "occasion'd much speculation" and "afforded great speculation" were often attached to these speculative buyers' habits, thereby adding an aura of suspicion to them. And time and again, smugglers were characterized as the "speculative men" of the commercial world, as in Stephen Theodore Janssen's widely circulated treatise on smuggling, from 1763.[7] These figures are ultimately mysterious— they peddle in winks and nods, and in airy dreams rather than hard currency or material commodities. They circumvent laws and create abstract markets of the mind for desirable goods, all by way of conjecture and leveraging risk.

Speculation's increasing cross-pollination within economic rhetoric became more salient, and over time it gained more traction in descriptions of reputable commercial activities, too, as we can see from a brief survey of sources, even as Johnson's *Dictionary* missed it. The translation of the French political economist and lexicographer Jacques Savary des Brûlons's 1757 *Universal Dictionary of Trade and Commerce* claims that "the speculation of money-negociations, in the way of commerce, between one foreign nation and another, . . . may prove occasionally not less profitable to the foreign trader than speculations in regard to commodities only."[8] By 1767, there are characterizations of stock and commodity buyers as "speculators" and "scheming speculators."[9] A 1768 history of the prices of grains and other provisions is declared a "good speculation for the landed gentleman," thereby indicating that the sense of "a speculation" that Addison and Steele had promoted now overlapped with this proper, even sanctioned mode of commercial behavior.[10] An economic dispatch from 1771 speaks specifically of a "Speculator" in potash.[11]

Speculation's power in commerce and finance, and in economic activity more generally, to evaluate whether a "speculation" was reputable or disreputable, legal or illegal, hinged largely on the user and the circumstance. This variability made it a fluid and adaptable term, and thus accentuated its malleability when its more pointed sense in finance and currency markets came into English, with input from several other foreign sources. Perhaps the most important source to single out is the famed Amsterdam merchant Isaac de Pinto's *Traité de la circulation et du crédit* (1761–1771), which prompted much debate when it appeared in English.[12] The treatise was a defense of financial speculation and public debt as boons to national economies. As was the case with Calvin's texts, the translation was pretty straightforward. Pinto's many uses of the French *spéculation* and *spéculateur*—with senses new to French at the time, too, as we will see momentarily—became *speculation* and *speculator* in English. Readers thereby confronted arguments about "speculative financiers" and claims that "the national debt of England,

and the funds that compose it, known under the name of Annuities, have for some time attracted the attention of princes, and the speculation of individuals."[13] We also see notes from the translator explaining the perils of "the gamester, or speculatist, who pledges his stock to the banker, or moneyed man, and of course on disadvantageous terms."[14] Pinto's essay discusses both ideas and material practices that it labels "speculative," with *speculation* toggling between its cognitive and financial semantic domains. This allowed for lines such as the claim in 1776 that paper money was flowing too freely, so that "Dutch, Scotch, and Jew" plundered banks with "speculation."[15]

We can pinpoint one important conceptual turn here that branched out from the world of new financial scheming. Putting together finance, contemplative thought, evidence assessment, valuation, and futurity, a landmark court case in 1766 channeled the energies gathering around *speculation* into an essential point regarding the new financial instruments—insurance contracts—that could monetize and make tradable the anticipated exchanges of the future, all without the need of their actually happening someday (much as Pocock's reading of state debt suggested). In *Carter v. Boehm* (1766), Lord Mansfield, who was then the Lord Chief Justice and a prominent reformist, established the principle of "utmost good faith" (*uberrimae fidei*) for commercial law in England. Insurance contracts, especially in marine and colonial settings, had been variously exploited and manipulated for decades, and in this case, an English governor (Carter) in Sumatra took out an insurance policy on a fort built for the British East India Company, fearing it would be raided. His indemnifier (Boehm) argued that Carter knew the fort could withstand *only* an attack by natives, and thus was susceptible to attack by the French, who eventually took the fort, at which point Boehm refused to pay. One of the questions at stake was whether "the insured" was "obliged to discover facts" only, or whether he should also necessarily consider "the ideas or speculations which he may entertain, upon such facts," when working through future possibilities in his mind. Seeing that both parties were staking real and hypothetical money on future events that may or may not ever happen, yet that both were projecting ideas within an information asymmetry, Mansfield turned to *speculation* in order to craft a new sense of the term that would endure for centuries:

> Insurance is a contract based upon speculation. The special facts, upon which the contingent chance is to be computed, lie most commonly in the knowledge of the insured only; the under-writer trusts to his representation and proceeds upon the confidence that he does not keep back any circumstance in his knowledge, to mislead the underwriter into a belief that the circumstance does not exist, and to induce him to estimate the risque as if it did not exist. . . .
>
> Good faith forbids either party by concealing what he privately knows, to draw the other into a bargain, from his ignorance of that fact, and his believing the contrary.[16]

For Mansfield, insurance contracts cannot exist in a world where everything is certain and provable by experimentation; rather, they are "based upon speculation" that differs between individuals, and thus can only be brought to the same plane by trust and good faith. He distinguishes between what is a "fact of the case" and what is a "mere speculation . . . [or] conjecture" that was "dictated" to the governor "from his fears"; and the fact that insurance was broadly considered a lottery helped solidify speculation's imbrication within the world of gambling.[17]

The theoretical consequences of these interconnections were far-reaching for the long-term conceptual evolution of speculation. In a searching interpretation of the origins of modern finance capitalism, Ian Baucom writes that insurance took the speculative nature of capitalism in this moment one step further: not only is insurance predicated on future contingencies, but in fact, it asserts that "the real test of something's value comes not at the moment it is made or exchanged but at the moment it is lost or destroyed."[18] Thus, paradoxically, value "neither depends on its being put to use or entered into exchange as a commodity but results purely from the ability of two contracting parties to imagine what it would have been worth at that imaginary future moment in which it will have ceased to exist," whereas the insurance contract itself, by contrast, gains value immediately, when it is signed.[19]

In that way, hypothetical prediction—going back to Bacon—becomes critical to provisional judgment, all while insurers added mathematical bases for their calculations and developed their own sets of data and interpretive standards that sought to provide more evidence for such judgment. A deep irony forms around imaginative projections in the dynamic of insurance as a type of "technology of risk" that François Ewald has identified: scientific and mathematical formulations of probability promised to stabilize future states of affairs (by way of insurance payouts based on actuarial calculations, for instance), but the gambles that one had to take in order to employ those instruments seemed even riskier than the threats they sought to guard against, all because they issued from the unstable world of new finance.[20] Accidents and chance seemed at once highly unlikely and statistically inevitable at unknown future points.

Such a reading of speculation underscores the long-standing skepticism toward insurance contracts among various religious groups who felt that insurance attempted to circumvent God's plans and providence—adding another layer to their hostility to speculation. Insurance policies could show a lack of faith in God's plans: if you lost your house in a flood, it was for a reason, and you should not collect money on what the insurance industry still terms "acts of God."[21] And well before Smith's secular "invisible hand," figures from Aquinas to Calvin argued that there was a divinely sanctioned natural order to economies and markets, and that avarice and usury violated that order, whereas insurance bypassed it. The new modes of wealth creation during the financial revolution could—to borrow a phrase from Montesquieu—"swell people's fortunes beyond the bounds prescribed by nature."[22] One could reasonably raise the price of a good by, say, 5 percent, but to raise it by 50,000 percent overnight would seem sinful; the same held for accruing wealth, especially when earned *without* having worked. (Proverbs 13:11 put it plainly: "Dishonest money dwindles away, but he who gathers money little by little makes it grow."[23]) It's not just smugglers who speculate, then; it's also insurers and policy holders, financiers and debtors. The domain of what *speculation* named by the 1760s and 1770s was growing to include far more than the experimental works of early modern science and risk that *projecting* denoted, and as England grappled with what was illicit in its political economy and how the future was to be priced, *speculation* became an even more crucial piece of conceptual vocabulary.

SPECULATION'S BIG GAMBLE

In the booming new field of financial journalism, the consensus was that those figures engaged in economic "speculation" were taking gambles of various types on an unknown and unknowable future, and here we can connect some dots that lead us to Adam Smith's intervention. We have seen hints and elements of gambling drawing in proximity to *speculation* already, whether in the sense of risk that *projecting* encompassed or in the association of *idleness* with a proclivity for gaming. The worlds of international trade, finance, smuggling, and now insurance policies became the subjects of anti-gambling tracts from all corners. The term *gambling*, which slowly began to overtake *gaming* in the mid-1700s, still signaled more clearly "to cheat or swindle," not the common sense of *gambling* we have now—as a calculated risk, often in a regulated space. Gambling was unquestionably rampant, and there was a particular fervor for it in England in the late 1700s.[24] But lotteries had been used to raise government funds and to invest in colonial ventures at least since Elizabethan England, despite brief bans on them, and most early insurance schemes were structured like lotteries, too. In the mid-1700s, there are references to lottery tickets sold "on Speculation," once again drawing the term further into this linguistic orbit, and when an expanded version of the translation of mathematician Abraham de Moivre's influential *Doctrine of Chances* appeared in 1756, it repeatedly referred to "speculations" and "speculations of chance."[25]

The line on gambling in Reformation thought, and specifically in Calvinism, was that one did not wager on God's providence, and that one should work hard to accrue money rather than seeking immediate fortunes on speculation. Gambling, like speculation, was empty, inert.

Proverbs 16:33, for instance, gave a lesson of anti-chance thinking that Calvin would promote: "The lot is cast in the lap, but its every decision is from the Lord." If God sought to endow you with a monetary fortune, he would find a way to do so; it wouldn't come from your own devising. In his *Compleat Gamester* (1674), Charles Cotton refers to "gaming" as "an enchanting *witchery*, gotten betwixt *Idleness* and *Avarice*," and as an "itching Disease." The paralyzing effect of gambling "renders a Man incapable of prosecuting any serious action," and eventually, the gambler is "plung'd to the bottom of Despair by Misfortune" and utterly destroyed.[26] The nascent literature exploring the psychology of the gambler, which again relied on notions of idleness and deceptive projections, would feed the medical diagnoses of speculation that we'll encounter in chapter 4.

But gambling was acceptable especially among the upper classes, precisely because they did not need new fortunes, and card games, backgammon, and billiards in particular could keep all winnings in-house among socially legible and trusted individuals.[27] To some, this mode of gambling itself signified the degeneracy and decline of the aristocracy. A specific form of gambling called "political speculation" even arose in this moment as a means of tying speculation to the political fortunes of states that we will soon encounter; here, bettors wagered on the outcome of wars and elections.[28] And of course, there were more figurative gambles, such as immigrating to new worlds, which were commonly understood as calculated risks against the vicissitudes of chance.[29] The effort to separate speculation from gambling, which scholars such as Ann Fabian have documented, was not yet successful: speculation increasingly *was* understood as gambling, pure and simple, in many cases.[30] As Henry Ward Beecher would concede in 1846, in a line of thought that still persists: "indeed, a Speculator on the exchange, and a gambler at his table, follow one vocation, only with different instruments."[31]

In the late 1700s, many of the trends we have now identified were converging. Stock markets were widely understood as glorified houses of gambling and cheating, just as the South Sea Bubble had been understood by most simply as a new form of lottery. To buy on credit was to gamble on promises and faith, which was far from investing in the growth of real properties. Gamblers were also bad scientists and experimenters: they did not use empirically verified evidence to make decisions about future outcomes. On the contrary, gamblers rejected meaning discovered from natural philosophy and scientific inquiry and instead placed too much faith in the whims of fortune and luck. Gambling created instant profits and losses that could be exorbitant or catastrophic; it compressed the time-spaces of economic life in fundamentally anti-natural ways, putting falsified promises and prices on the future. It cut against the Protestant narratives of self-mastery and self-determination that T. J. Jackson Lears has laid out, and it left waste, degeneracy, and destruction in its wake.[32] And gambling was not and never could be rational, even when probabilities and mathematical studies might make it seem so.

Just as gambling amplified these dangerous conceptual elements within *speculation* in the 1760s, we find in 1772 two explicit and consequential new articulations and applications of *speculation* that set the term most clearly on its course for its now-familiar life in the sphere of financial markets. They occurred in print almost simultaneously, first in America (a point we'll explore fully in the following chapter) and then in Scotland. In the *Pennsylvania Gazette,* a columnist writes briefly that in English and Scottish markets and exchanges, there is an "avaricious spirit" linked to "gambling," creating an "illegal traffic, usually called Speculation."[33] ("Usually" suggests a custom by this point, though it's hard to tell how long the custom of calling it "Speculation" had existed.) Meanwhile, in Scotland, a crisis roiled the banking world—a crisis that would factor into *Wealth of Nations.* The most spectacular event of the crisis was the collapse of the once stalwart Douglas, Heron & Co. bank (also known as the "Ayr Bank," after the location of its head office, with puns on "air" never far away).[34] The bank had seen a dramatic rise built on dubious practices such as fictitious "bills of exchange," in which sales and trades that never took place were recorded in order to bolster credit.[35] The well-known *Scots Magazine* decried such "adventures of speculation" in economic commerce, linking them specifically to "gambling-practices." "Such practices," the magazine notes, "are certainly incompatible with the principles of a banking company; indeed, where-ever they are introduced, the ruin of that company must be at hand."

"Speculation," that is, has now fully become a *practice*—the low, deceptive practice of gambling. Not in darkness with dice, but in daylight in banks. The magazine continues to explain, as if it were a dictionary itself, that "the words *speculation* and *speculator*, as now understood, are very modern, and very significant": "The stock of a speculator is his own brain. He is a gamester, one of the very worst species. The worst faculties of a speculator are bent upon contriving schemes to get money into his hands from every quarter; from rich and poor, friends and strangers.... The speculator is a collector who raises contributions on all the world to go a-gaming on the cash of others.... Such is the man of speculation."[36] In its call to "expel speculators, gamblers, and adventurers," the magazine invokes one of the first clear statements of something we'll see continuing into the present: speculation is gambling detached from the presumed *natural* materiality of economics, and it should be condemned morally. If the "stock of a speculator is his own brain," then speculation now highlights the ways in which an otherwise apparently sanctioned investor can gamble with great risk on the figments of his own imagination.[37]

The sense of *speculation* is "very modern" and "very significant" precisely because it keeps accruing so much new meaning by the day.[38] Combining connotations of prognostication and fraud, evidentiary readings and swindles, *speculation* signaled a threatening approach to the collective financial future. In the following years, the spread of *speculation as* gambling, and as an addictive personal vice with profound public implications, was rapid, and it's worth noting right away several of the important figures who helped put it into further circulation. Horace Walpole, for example, condemned bidding up "pictures at auction" as a type of "speculation" akin to "gaming."[39] (The speculative art markets were thriving in this moment, not the least because of the plundered antiquities and foreign art objects that were flooding Britain.[40]) And, more substantively, the renowned diarist Hester Thrale captured this new sense of a "*Gaming* method of Commerce called

Speculation" in the 1770s. Thrale writes that "Mr. Thrale over brewed himself last Winter" and thereby "made an artificial Scarcity of Money in the Family," and "so the Wings of *Speculation* are clipped a little." She continues: "Oh what a Curse upon Commerce is this modern Spirit of *Speculation* as 'tis called.... By Speculation is meant Trading upon Conjecture" in hopes for "a sudden & expected Rise to sell out with immense Profit & Advantage."[41] It is a "rapacious and monopolizing Spirit" that leaves the "*Speculator*... to contemplate his unsold Commodity" while he wastes away in ruin, she concludes. We must "punish the Spirit of Speculation at *our House too!*" she declares, "if God Almighty finds it fit to make *one* other Example of those who fall into this fashionable Frenzy."[42] Channeling the senses of speculation's threat to Christianity, its artificiality, and its position in a shifting capitalist order, Thrale highlights just how many realms of thought and practice *speculation* was tying together by the time Smith picked it up in the 1770s.

ADAM SMITH'S COMPROMISE

Adam Smith's two most famous works—*The Theory of Moral Sentiments* (1759) and *The Wealth of Nations* (1776)—were composed and published in a period whose study allows us to understand quite precisely how a concept that was being transfigured around him ended up pressing terminologically upon the major questions he tackled in his studies. In the former work, Smith speaks of "men of reflection and speculation" and "men of retirement and speculation."[43] These figures are philosophers and ponderers; a "man of speculation" would think about the moral implications of the earthquake in China that Smith posits in a famous thought experiment. Having returned from a stimulating trip to France and Switzerland, where he conversed at length with the French physiocrats, Smith resettled in Scotland and went to work on *The Wealth of Nations*. He returned in an early draft, which would become part of the first chapter of the book, to those same "men of speculation"; they are now something different: "Many improvements have been made by the ingenuity of the makers of machines, when to make them became the business of a peculiar trade; and some by that of those who are called philosophers, or men of speculation, whose trade it is not to do any thing, but to observe every thing, and who, upon that account, are often capable of combining together the powers of the most distant and dissimilar objects in the progress of society."[44] Like Mr. Spectator, Smith's "men of speculation" are impartial observers and contemplators with omnivorous powers of apprehension. (He had written extensively on the idea of the "impartial spectator" all across the *Moral Sentiments*.[45]) They think synthetically, often chimerically, as by combining "distant and dissimilar objects," and the result is that they become important experimenters and inventors, as we saw at the end of the last chapter.[46] Smith had written elsewhere in an early draft—indeed, one of the very first sections he drafted, on "opulence" and the division of labor—that the person who "first thought of employing a stream of wind" in a corn-grinding mill "was probably no workman of any kind, but a philosopher or meer man of speculation; one of those people whose trade it is not to do any thing but to observe every thing," and thus someone able to combine dissimilar objects. Smith adds in his draft that "even the speculations of those who neither invent nor improve any thing are not altogether useless. They serve at least to keep alive and deliver down to posterity the inventions and improvements which had been made before them."[47] Speculation, it turns out, has practical value even in failure.[48] "It was a real philosopher only who could invent the fire engine," Smith continues, because "in philosophy as in every other business this subdivision of employment improves dexterity and saves time."[49] Speculators, in short, can often be beneficial scientists and inventors, but they are necessarily much more.

The Wealth of Nations continues by elaborating not simply a theory of political economy but also a discourse that characterizes modern capitalism, as we can see by Smith's renovations of the common senses of terms like *labor* and *production*. Smith also characterizes a number of "types" that make the economic world function as a semiautonomous machine. These include the rational economic man and the "sober" investor, and also what Smith calls the "prodigals and projectors."[50] As opposed to "men of speculation," projectors inspire mostly negative assessments from Smith—and he surveys the world to find and castigate them. He notes ambivalently that Christopher Columbus himself was a projector. He argues that "over-trading" by "some bold projectors in both parts of the United Kingdom, was the original cause of this excessive circulation of paper money."[51] And he contends that the idea of "a new mine in Peru... is considered there in the same light... as a lottery," both of which "tempt... many adventurers to throw away their fortunes in such unprosperous projects."[52] Moreover, for Smith, John Law's Mississippi scheme was "the most extravagant project, both of banking and stock-jobbing, that perhaps the world ever saw," premised on a wild dream of "multiplying paper money."[53] Regarding the Scottish banking crisis, he calls the primary culprits "chimerical projectors," too.[54] Smith therefore favored government initiatives to keep borrowing rates low, so as to discourage the "imprudent" risk takers who would not be dissuaded by higher rates.

In Smith's view, projectors, with their "golden dreams," are most often the foolhardy experimenters of scientific culture, and thus become gamblers in economic domains. Like the "invisible hand," Smith's "golden dreams" yokes together the durable precious metal and the immaterial, substanceless fancy. But projectors are unworthy characters for Smith because they seek returns on their investments far beyond what the "greater part" of regular "projects" allow. Feeding his understanding, too, was his theory that some labor was productive, while other labor was not. Productive labor, in keeping with Smith's broader theory of value, also adds to the value of an object, whereas nonproductive labor neither imputes nor generates new value. Projectors, guided by unruly passions, seek to profit by the rapid, alchemical accrual of value in some object or idea. They most often fail, and yet the anomalous victors are taken by others to be a norm and standard—a basic misreading of empirical evidence. In laying this out, Smith still uses the terms *projects* and *projectors* extensively, and by way of Smith's reworking and expanding "speculation," projectors gradually become emblems of the economic and terminological past.

Cognizant that the language of *speculation* was shifting under his feet as he composed, Smith then pivots and further advances his own terms and their implications. He writes that "sudden fortunes, indeed, are sometimes made... by what is called the trade of speculation."[55] (Note again the phrase "what is called": like Chaucer, Smith is hedging and explaining.[56]) *Speculation* is its own field of *trade*, not just a habit of thought, in this expansive formulation; and by "trade" he means to invoke both an occupation and international exchange. The "speculative merchant" (a merchant who bought and sold goods purely as a trader), he notes, "exercises no one regular, established, or well-known branch of business. He is a corn merchant this year, and a wine merchant the next, and a sugar, tobacco, or tea merchant the year after."[57] The speculative merchant does what Smith described earlier: he combines elements of dissimilar practices and synthesizes them into a single, common enterprise that coheres only in his mind. Smith's figures who appear to do "nothing" are actually driving *everything*, despite existing in what one American critic would soon call the "Common Sewer of Speculation."[58] Smith then understands the difference between typical practices of capitalism and of speculation as a difference of proportion—proportion grounded in the predictability of returns over time. He explains that, normally, a merchant's "sum or amount of his profits is in proportion to the extent of his trade, and his annual accumulation in proportion to the amount of his profits." Smith proposes a natural order, regularity, predictability, and steady accrual of wealth in the postmercantilist order. It takes a "long life of industry, frugality, and attention" to build wealth "naturally"; gambling, like a lottery, does so too quickly, unnaturally, through "adventures."

But Smith does not leave speculation here, and as he sketches out his broader theory of capitalism, he carves out a surprising and heretofore unrecognized role for *speculation*. Smith asserts that "the establishment of any new manufacture, of any new branch of commerce, or of any new practice in agriculture, is *always a speculation* from which the projector promises himself extraordinary profits."[59] That is, speculation and projection are absolutely fundamental to capitalism, if not to human behavior as a whole: without airy, fanciful ideas as stimuli, no "new branch of commerce" ever takes root. Smith does a great deal to recuperate speculation, then: speculators seem to do nothing and yet they create vital innovations; they have no knowable business interest yet are the driving force of commerce itself. For Smith, several things are true at once: "men of speculation" (he does not yet call them "speculators") *do* or *practice* nothing but ceaselessly observe and *project*; they are out of synch with the major shifts in markets, because they are constantly shifting; they play a high-risk game, and yet, their future-oriented thinking is endemic to capitalism. They are both the aberration and the center, the dismissed and ineffectual outlier, yet the generative creator. They are the bridge between dreams and actions that previously seemed separated by an impossibly large chasm. Smith notes that a "bold adventurer may sometimes acquire a considerable fortune by two or three successful speculations, but is just as likely to lose one by two or three unsuccessful ones." Likewise, the "regular, established, and well-known branch[es] of business" will survive despite the "occasional competition of speculative adventurers."[60] That is, speculation can still be done poorly, but the natural order of capitalism will bring about a corrective when humans err in reading evidence.

Smith has *incorporated* the gambling spirit of speculation into legitimate, even enlightened practices. Speculators are as rational as farmers and as sound as any entrepreneur: they are not by definition the swindlers that projectors often were, nor are they smugglers and fleecers. Where speculation had previously been redeemed as an intellectual category, Smith now redeemed it as a practice—so long as it was practiced judiciously, not as pure gambling. Thus, this is not a full-throated defense of speculation, or even a specific type of speculation (as Pinto had offered). For Smith, an economy had to remain material at its core: "The commerce and industry of the country, . . . though they may be somewhat augmented, cannot be altogether so secure, when they are thus, as it were, suspended upon the Daedalian wings of paper money, as when they travel about upon the solid ground of gold and silver."[61] Finally, using the older language of *speculation*, Smith contends that the "popular fear of engrossing and forestalling may be compared to the popular terrors and suspicions of witchcraft" (as Charles Mackay will argue at length; see chapter 4).[62] The best "antidote" to the "poison of enthusiasm and superstition," Smith argues, is "science," and the ideal capitalist is a type of scientist, in the end.[63] Moreover, unlike enthusiasts, projectors can be regulated; the apparently "abstruse... principles of the banking trade," for instance, can be "reduced to strict rules" that will make "some flattering speculation of extraordinary gain" appear "extremely dangerous" and likely "fatal" to any "banking company."[64] This is necessary, Smith holds, because failed projects diminish the available financial resources for good projects and for public works.

And so, even while Smith dismisses "speculative systems" of philosophy as "frivolous" and irrelevant to political economy, he concedes that *The Wealth of Nations* itself is a "speculative work," describing a system that is not yet fully in place.[65] But whereas the physiocrats posited a system that has "never been adopted by any nation, and it at present exists only in the speculations of a few men of great learning and ingenuity in France," his speculative work would have immense practical value—or so he imagined, like Hobbes did before him.[66] The vast domestic and international success of *The Wealth of Nations* disseminated this turn in speculation farther. The book sold out in six months, reached ten editions in a few short years, and appeared in at least four other languages within four years.[67] And it was praised in reviews as belonging to "the highest rank among the speculative books."[68] Without Smith's extended meditations on what speculation and speculators meant for this emergent economic order, it's quite possible that *speculation* never becomes more than market jargon, rather than a term that will label everything from high-risk gambles to basic ingenuity—with more to come.

And it's quite possible that *projects* would continue to signify more than *speculations* did in the decades to come, too. If that had been the case, this book would look very different: much of what follows in the chapters to come relies on wordplay grounded in the visual and perceptive roots of *speculation*, and the linguistic innovations that we'll encounter rely on the term's singular features. Suffice it to say, an alternative history of what *projects* could have yielded would be fascinating, "new branch of commerce" ever takes root. Smith does a great deal to recuperate speculation, then: speculators seem to do nothing and yet they create vital innovations; they have no knowable business interest yet are the driving force of commerce itself. For Smith, several things are true at once: "men of speculation" (he does not yet call them "speculators") *do* or *practice* nothing but ceaselessly observe and *project*; they are out of synch with the major shifts in markets, because they are constantly shifting; they play a high-risk game, and yet, their future-oriented thinking is endemic to capitalism. They are both the aberration and the center, the dismissed and ineffectual outlier, yet the generative creator. They are the bridge between dreams and actions that previously seemed separated by an impossibly large chasm. Smith notes that a "bold adventurer may sometimes acquire a considerable fortune by two or three successful speculations, but is just as likely to lose one by two or three unsuccessful ones." Likewise, the "regular, established, and well-known branch[es] of business" will survive despite the "occasional competition of speculative adventurers."[60] That is, speculation can still be done poorly, but the natural order of capitalism will bring about a corrective when humans err in reading evidence.

Smith has *incorporated* the gambling spirit of speculation into legitimate, even enlightened practices. Speculators are as rational as farmers and as sound as any entrepreneur: they are not by definition the swindlers that projectors often were, nor are they smugglers and fleecers. Where speculation had previously been redeemed as an intellectual category, Smith now redeemed it as a practice—so long as it was practiced judiciously, not as pure gambling. Thus, this is not a full-throated defense of speculation, or even a specific type of speculation (as Pinto had offered). For Smith, an economy had to remain material at its core: "The commerce and industry of the country, ... though they may be somewhat augmented, cannot be altogether so secure, when they are thus, as it were, suspended upon the Daedalian wings of paper money, as when they travel about upon the solid ground of gold and silver."[61] Finally, using the older language of *speculation*, Smith contends that the "popular fear of engrossing and forestalling may be compared to the popular terrors and suspicions of witchcraft" (as Charles Mackay will argue at length; see chapter 4).⁶² The best "antidote" to the "poison of enthusiasm and superstition," Smith argues, is "science," and the ideal capitalist is a type of scientist, in the end.⁶³ Moreover, unlike enthusiasts, projectors can be regulated; the apparently "abstruse... principles of the banking trade," for instance, can be "reduced to strict rules" that will make "some flattering speculation of extraordinary gain" appear "extremely dangerous" and likely "fatal" to any "banking company."⁶⁴ This is necessary, Smith holds, because failed projects diminish the available financial resources for good projects and for public works.

And so, even while Smith dismisses "speculative systems" of philosophy as "frivolous" and irrelevant to political economy, he concedes that *The Wealth of Nations* itself is a "speculative work," describing a system that is not yet fully in place.⁶⁵ But whereas the physiocrats posited a system that has "never been adopted by any nation, and it at present exists only in the speculations of a few men of great learning and ingenuity in France," his speculative work would have immense practical value—or so he imagined, like Hobbes did before him.⁶⁶ The vast domestic and international success of *The Wealth of Nations* disseminated this turn in speculation farther. The book sold out in six months, reached ten editions in a few short years, and appeared in at least four other languages within four years.⁶⁷ And it was praised in reviews as belonging to "the highest rank among the speculative books."⁶⁸ Without Smith's extended meditations on what speculation and speculators meant for this emergent economic order, it's quite possible that *speculation* never becomes more than market jargon, rather than a term that will label everything from high-risk gambles to basic ingenuity—with more to come.

And it's quite possible that *projects* would continue to signify more than *speculations* did in the decades to come, too. If that had been the case, this book would look very different: much of what follows in the chapters to come relies on wordplay grounded in the visual and perceptive roots of *speculation*, and the linguistic innovations that we'll encounter rely on the term's singular features. Suffice it to say, an alternative history of what *projects* could have yielded would be fascinating, but strikingly different. Instead, by 1778, "speculative commerce" was becoming its own minor field of inquiry in political economy, and several years after that, so was "speculation in trade," with both phrases now incorporating allusions to gambling.[69] Thus it seemed logical for *The Times* of London to claim in 1793 that "speculation and enterprize are the very soul of commerce."[70] And at the same time, Edmund Burke could characterize the "science of speculative and practical finance" as a domain to itself.[71] The popular British book *The Art of Stock-Jobbing Explained* (1816) soon characterized speculation as gambling, but—however devious or morally offensive—a highly rational and ubiquitous form of it.[72] Smith gave theoretical and material circulation to a term that now moved almost effortlessly from gambling to insurance to the heart of the new capitalism, all while maintaining its connotative and denotative roots that we have seen thus far.

ROMANTIC SPECULATION

Smith successfully launched *speculation* like a linguistic product of the capitalist system he described, and the uptake of this new commercial sense of *speculation* was so swift and so pervasive that it immediately threatened to overwhelm all other meanings and senses. Literary authors of a variety of backgrounds therefore found *speculation* to be a word worth focusing on and yet, at the same time, worth criticizing and perhaps lamenting for its overuse. Just four years after *The Wealth of Nations*, Christopher Anstey's poem *Speculation* mourned that *speculation* was so hopelessly lost to a debased world of commercial slang. The same word that Boethius had used to reach the heavens and that philosophers had used to signify pure cogitation was now nothing but the schlock and dross of mass modernity. Anstey writes that, as a word, *speculation* has been treated "basely," indeed worse than any other word before it. Anstey is already playing with the crossover economic sense of the term—it was "cheated" out of having greater meaning, just as speculators themselves cheat, and it is left a "Poor Word."

How did such a fate befall *speculation*? What happened, Anstey contends, is that when the new economies of credit states, lotteries, and swelling national debts mingled with omens and alchemy, language came to operate like a fictional monetary "system":

> Since Language every Day submits
> To some new Phrase from modern Wits,
> And like its Speaker, or its Writer,
> Grows richer, chaster, and politer,
> Whatever wild, fantastic dreams
> Give Birth to Man's outrageous Schemes,
> Pursu'd without the least Pretense,
> To Virtue, Honesty, or Sense,
> Whate'er the wretched basely dare
> From Pride, Ambition, or Despair,
> Fraud, Luxury, or Dissipation,
> Assumes the Name of—Speculation.[73]

In other words, language itself is a constant game of speculation, and the word *speculation* is an asset that sharply rises and falls in value. Anstey returns several times to the word *basely*, playing on the sense of "base" from the world of coinage—using a "base metal" as an alloy—where *debase* meant to "counterfeit." A similar pattern holds with his uses of *accrue* and *richer*.[74] *Speculation* has been drained of its "spirit" and "cheated" of its immaterial signification by the vulgar world of scheming for gain. It had been cheated of the opportunity to accrue semantic value gradually and naturally over time, and instead had multiple divergent new meanings foisted upon it by linguistic frauds.

Within this increasingly inward, linguistic turn on *speculation*, Anstey feared he could not save the word. This "harmless Term" that once expressed "no more / Than ocular, or mental View," is now "Abus'd by Wights of all Professions, / Hack'ed at the Bar, in Pulpit tortur'd."[75] Lady Fortune eludes the frauds and quacks who now speculate everywhere, but *speculation* suffers merely by their practices. Beyond this poem, economic treatises and especially columns played on the polysemy of *speculation*, as evinced by columns in the *London Magazine* such as "A Speculation on Paper Wealth" (1776), which marks the groundless "frivolity" of the present as "the *paper age*."[76] The writer argues that speculation was doing the same thing that paper money itself was doing: asking for faith and for future credit on an idea that may rise or fall in material value due to a thousand "frivol[ous]" causes, distinct from intrinsic value.

In fact, Anstey was even beaten to the punch with the use of this growing term as his title: "Speculation, a Poem" appeared anonymously in London in 1776, while the poet William Tasker offered a brief "Ode to Speculation" in 1779.[77] The journal *The Speculator* arrived soon after, in 1790. It accepted that "the Speculator is one who has contributed little, perhaps, to the practical utility of the arts of life," and was careful to delineate how a good "speculator" thinks, and thus to vindicate its own title: "The air-built systems of abstract philosophy, and the sordid calculations by which the vice and weakness of mankind is made subservient to interested design, have been equally remote from his bosom."[78] *Speculation* was the title of a rather clunky but illustrative and widely produced five-act comedy by Frederick Reynolds, first performed in London in 1795, featuring a speculator named Mr. Project. Everyone seemed to want to wrest *speculation* to their corner just as it seemed to be bursting with new meaning. "Speculative fiction" and "speculative literature" emerge in this moment, even though "fiction" and "literature" themselves were then less generically stable categories than they would become (see chapter 5).[79] Anstey was right about the proliferation of usages of *speculation*, but wrong to claim that it was devalued—if anything, the term's stock was soaring.

And yet, all the while, for these very same reasons, the sense of contemplation, of anticipation, and of a type of thought contrasted with practical, moral, or applied philosophy that *speculation* still retained became even more valuable and rare to some.[80] Key literary and philosophical figures turned back to it, then, just as its newer economic senses were becoming more predominant in the concept's overall currency. This serene, reflective counterpart to commercial speculation was developed in particular by Romantic writers, who were coming of age just as *speculation* was being dramatically transformed, rethought in its role in knowledge production and reflective creativity. One could easily envision the Romantics being drawn to *speculation* for its combined sense of divine contemplation and an all-powerful faculty of visual apprehension. But what we find first is a careful, often painstaking effort, beginning in the late 1700s, to cordon off financial speculation as dirty and tainted, a mode of speculation to be quarantined. Note the language in Mary Shelley's *Frankenstein* (1818), when the creature recounts his first feelings upon discovering German Romanticism: "The *Sorrows of Werter*, besides the interest of its simple and affecting story, so many opinions are canvassed and so many lights thrown upon what had hitherto been to me obscure subjects that I found in it a never-ending source of speculation and astonishment."[81] *Speculation* here is a powerful, sublime wonder, the kind of awe we are accustomed to seeing the Romantics elevate. German philosophy (including mysticism) from the late 1700s and early 1800s had become the acknowledged torchbearer of "speculative philosophy," especially as it responded to empiricism, and German idealism in particular was often called "speculative" by British thinkers and writers. Beyond Goethe's uses of the term, Hegel, who favored the word *spekulative* in his works, was closely associated with speculative philosophy and wrote at length on speculative science, speculative logic, and the nature of speculative thought, to which he assigned a high place in philosophical endeavors.[82] The American *Journal of Speculative Philosophy*, which ran from 1867 to 1893, would trace its own roots to Hegel.

Frankenstein continues and rounds out this logic near its end. Victor Frankenstein first explains to Robert Walton that his creation of a human lifted him above the ranks of "common projectors," before he ultimately concedes that he is little more than a failed speculator: "All my speculations and hopes are as nothing, and like the archangel who aspired to omnipotence, I am chained in an eternal hell. . . . but how am I sunk!"[83] Frankenstein, who separates himself from the animalistic "herd" rhetorically by way of his "reflect[ion]" on his work, could have been the greatest speculator in human history with his imaginative, future-making projection of human life reassembled. Instead, he is little more than the commercial swindlers he denigrates, and his common (not sublime) speculations do nothing but condemn him and his future potential. Frankenstein is not frenzied, and he is acting in solitude rather than in the crowd, yet *speculation* is still not good enough for him, and it does not hold the promise that it did for a generation prior.

More broadly, this sense that the new life of *speculation* in a murky, corrupt world of financial scheming had ruined the term was common among many Romantics.[84] Keats's letters, we can see, are full of "Speculations" as thought experiments and as prompts for contemplation: he speaks of his "favourite Speculation" as an idea about Adam, or a dream of sensations that cannot be empirically verified.[85] A century later, the poet-critic John Middleton Murry picked up on the idea that, for Keats, *speculation* retained its sense of "contemplation," unsullied by its then-recent changes: "physical vision" combined with "disinterested beholding," which then leads to "intensity."[86] By making speculation "a sensation rather than a thought," Keats is able to position himself as a "magnificent materialist" rather than a Platonic idealist, on Murry's reading.[87] Therefore, in his "Gripus" fragment, Keats criticizes avarice and the desire for material wealth ("gold and silver are but filthy dross"), and thus dismisses a marriage between an aristocrat and a servant as "no light affair; / 'Tis downright venture and mere speculation. / Less risk there is in what the merchant trusts / To winds and waves and the uncertain elements."[88]

Despite the Romantics' best efforts, then, *speculation* was *too* polyvalent and too associated with economics now to signal the kind of clear, pure thought that they wished to elevate. Instead, imagination famously became their preferred concept, and in becoming so, took with it parts of speculation's history. Where "flights of lawless speculation" were misleading and distorting, for Coleridge, *imagination* performed the cognitive, metaphysical, and semiotic work that *speculation* no longer could—and more.[89] *Speculation* seemed aligned with and condemned to the second-order status of *fancy*.[90] The power that Romantics—despite the internal differences among them—consistently invested in imagination as a cognitive faculty that apprehends, synthesizes, and re-creates the phenomenal world sounds very much like the senses of *speculation* we have seen articulated in previous decades and centuries. Imagination's power extended into the past (remembering and recalling), the present (perception), and the future (projection). M. H. Abrams's classic formulation of the Romantics' shift in metaphors for how the mind operates—from a reflective (mirror) to a projective (lamp) model—also points us back to where we began this book, with the entwined mirror and watchtower of the Latin *specula*.[91]

Then, in Coleridge's treatment, the active and vital imagination brings speculation into line, giving it a subordinate and orderly place.[92] It is a mental power indeed, but it is not elevated as it had been for Boethius. Instead, imagination now both discovers and creates cosmic, eternal truths; speculation merely copies them, or provides distorted impressions that are meant to be refined and perfected. Imagination has the power to unify dissimilar objects and perceptions, much like Smith proposed, and it stands over and above reason. It also has its classic Wordsworthian function of contemplation in solitude as a mode of quasi-divine insight. Thus, where Samuel Johnson charged in *Rasselas* (1759) that "to indulge the power of fiction, and send imagination out upon the wing, is often the sport of those who delight too much in silent speculation," the Romantics largely embraced the idea that imagination could subjugate the errant ways and contamination now tied to speculation.[93] Commercial speculation is safely separated out, and *poets*—rather than speculators—now assume the future-creating and projective power as "hierophants of an unapprehended inspiration, the mirrors of the gigantic shadows which futurity casts upon the present," in a world that they help utter into being.[94] That is, multiple senses of *speculation* have been bound together and critiqued here (capitalist, philosophical, and cognitive) in an effort to clear a path for a new mode of imagination that would operate differently and more clearly.

Projective thought, experimentation, gambling, capitalist enterprise, quiet contemplation: *speculation* was now doing a great deal of work in all corners, perhaps not at all feeling the strain that Anstey feared. Rather, *speculation* seems liberated by all the new significance it holds, and it was instead the job of lexicographers and language makers—whether Adam Smith or Samuel Johnson or anonymous newspaper columnists—to catch up and interpret it as it was circulating in mouths and texts everywhere. *Speculation* means far from one thing, far from a narrow set of things, even. It is a powerful, highly connotative, and now almost too-literary way of naming how we take risks, how we fix prices on the contingencies of what might happen one second, one minute, or one month from now—whether through the legitimized circuits of capitalism, the underground circuits of smugglers, or the wild experiments of projection. And by missing these chapters of *speculation*'s emergent new lives in English, Johnson also missed an important exchange across languages, cultures, and countries. Just as other tongues shaped the entry of *speculation* into English in the 1300s, so too did they influence the course of *speculation* in this moment (and vice versa), as we saw above. The cognates of *speculation* in Romance languages meant essentially the same thing as the English term until the late 1700s. The dictionary of the French Academy from 1762, for example, records no economic connotations, only contemplative mental projection; by 1798, though, *spéculation* has an economic meaning in the latest edition.[95] In the Royal Spanish Academy's dictionaries, the financial sense does not appear until 1822, having been absent in editions from 1780, 1803, and 1817.[96] Most Romance languages also retain a term for "mirror" (such as *espejo*, *espelho*, *specchio*) that preserves the Latin root's developed sense of inward contemplation. German dictionaries have the "contemplation" sense of *Spekulation* arriving only in the late 1700s, with the economic sense cited in Goethe's letters joining it around the turn of the 1800s.[97] It appears, then, that the financial sense possibly arrived in English via French, then was exported back to Romance tongues and German—but it's difficult to plot the timing precisely, especially because we can only fix the term's exact financial meanings in retrospect. Regardless, the financial sense of the term seems to have flourished rapidly and translingually.

It's worth looking ahead for a moment, though. Major English-language dictionaries took some time to record its new uses, but Noah Webster's 1828 *Dictionary* has the following for *speculate*, beginning with the sense that the Romantics had influenced:

1. To meditate; to contemplate; to consider a subject by turning it in the mind and viewing it in its different aspects and relations . . .
2. In commerce, to purchase land, goods, stock or other things, with the expectation of an advance in price, and of selling the articles with a profit by means of such advance; as, to *speculate* in coffee, or in sugar, or in six percent stock, or in bank stock.[98]

Similarly, *speculation*, which has six meanings, is at once a "mental view of any thing in its various aspects and relations," a "mental scheme; theory; views of a subject not verified by fact or practice," and "in commerce, the act or practice of buying land or goods, &c. in expectation of a rise in price and selling them at an advance." Webster concludes the final of these with a moralizing note: "In the United States, a few men have been enriched, but many have been ruined by speculation."[99] Above all, Webster was alert to the particular moral and political valence that *speculation* was developing in the United States, where we'll next turn our eyes.

4

AMERICA THE SPECULATIVE

> *It is true the Americans have proved that they, in more than one sense, can* speculate *without bounds.*
> —HENRY DAVID THOREAU, *A YANKEE IN CANADA* (1850/1866)

The American experiment: this familiar phrase captures the long-standing sense that the country's founders were testing, examining, and refining through political practices an idea whose results would be uncertain. And thus, at this point in the history of speculation, it should not surprise us that, just after 1776, the prominent general Nathanael Greene called the signing of the Declaration of Independence a "bold speculation."[1] Greene invoked the rapidly multiplying senses of *speculation* as a projective thought, a conjectural gamble, a commercial enterprise, and a considered reflection on knowledge creation. In the same moment, the Philadelphia statesman and future senator William Bingham similarly linked a "Spirit of American Speculation" to the country's new diplomatic prospects, while the Frenchman Étienne Clavière added that "we know of no period when the speculative spirit has been so widespread as it is now, or of any revolution in history similar to that achieved by Free America."[2] With all the fresh energy around the term *speculation* itself, to call the new country a "speculation" seemed appropriately forward-looking, even if something of a hedge. When the British travel writer William Priest visited the country in the 1790s, he confirmed, "Were I to characterise the *United States*, it should be by the appellation of the *land of speculation*."[3]

Speculation was spreading ever farther and wider—discursively, practically, and behaviorally—in the late 1700s, but the early United States had a particularly focused and salient role in renovating the concept in this moment. Yet America could not be just one type of speculation—a pure, simple, or easily validated kind, and not the crude cheat that we have also seen. Once we start to explore what it meant to call America a "speculation," and why so many figures suddenly labeled the new country this way, we start to pinpoint a crucial new turn in the history of speculation itself, leading to what became the common trope of "speculative mania" that endures into the present. This turn occurred around the same time as the events recounted in the previous chapter, where we identified what was understood as uniquely "speculative" about the American idea, its people, its financial system, and its future risks. There was a precise moment when speculation was transformed from a set of individual ideas and behaviors into a collective "mania" and frenzy. Here, the important early American physician Benjamin Rush was instrumental in casting speculation as a contagious and addictive fever that produces widespread conditions that overtake bodies and minds alike. If we consider that this purported physiology of speculation generated a new relationship between contemplative reflection and unthinking, frenzied behaviors, we see one way that the American experiment tied together many threads of speculation throughout history.

Where Adam Smith conceded that speculation was integral to capitalism, Rush, who gained fame for his new diagnoses and categorizations of mental illnesses, believed that this same mode of financial gambling now called "speculation" was not just a personal vice, but a rampant mental illness and "spirit." He went so far as to attribute a rise in suicides in America to "unsuccessful . . . speculation."[4] The "spirit of speculation," he foresaw, was not a good-hearted "spirit" of nation-building, but in fact could "destroy patriotism and friendship in many people"; thus, he longed for a return to the imagined moment (still very recent) when "our country was... untainted by speculation."[5] This paradox—that speculation was the foundation of the United States, and would also be its imminent downfall—frames how early Americans used *speculation* to conceive of their new country, how they used practices that were now called "speculations" to fashion it, and how they attempted to entwine and separate these types of speculations such that America became a privileged site in speculation's history.

The American experiment, with its promise and its wildness, seems to take us far from Boethius's vision of speculation leaving earthly matter behind. In the sprawling laboratory of America, many new kinds of speculation were tested and reformulated, in ways that most in the moment felt were out of control: if speculation was a commodity to Christopher Anstey, it was a mania all across America.[6] But eventually one of speculation's first conceptual historians, the Scotsman Charles Mackay, attempts a taxonomy of speculation as a type of possessed madness. Ralph Waldo Emerson then caps this line of rhetoric, in 1844, when he validates the mad speculations in his country and calls America "the country of the Future," a "country of beginnings, of projects, of vast designs, and expectations."[7] The reserved, pondering speculator and the crazed, profit-seeking speculator that coexist today are in prototype by the mid-1800s, and the new permutations of *speculation* allowed them to be critiqued in one term. As writers find speculation diagnostically useful, politically expedient, financially instructive, and poetically savvy, the concept's scope again widens and its uncanny ability to frame diverse phenomena together is again on display. Rather than being overwhelmed by the term's sprawl, several figures neatly and historically categorized it into frameworks for future usage—now tied to the fortunes of nations and bodies.

THE NATURE OF AMERICAN SPECULATION

Starting from Smith's *Wealth of Nations*, the special attachment of *speculation* to the early United States led to a fast-moving series of new characterizations and provocations. This process began when Smith not only laid out a general theory of capitalism in which speculation is a central concept but also helped push *project* into the linguistic background. Thus, in the final paragraph of his book, written at the moment of American independence, he offers a stinging rebuke: "The rulers of Great Britain have, for more than a century past, amused the people with the imagination that they possessed a great empire on the west side of the Atlantic. This empire, however, has hitherto existed in imagination only. It has hitherto been, not an empire, but the project of an empire. . . . If the project cannot be completed, it ought to be given up."[8] The American colonies, for Smith, were like the many failed "projects" that littered economic and scientific history—ill-conceived experiments that were doomed to fail. (In fact, digging even further beyond *projecting*, Smith also revives an older predecessor term for *speculation* to describe colonialism: "engross[ing].")[9] America might be the future of capitalism, but the history of America as a colonial "project" is little more than an airy dream of Swift's projectors at Lagado. To call America a "project," that is, was to assert certain claims about the nature of the United States, and beyond Smith, it also became a common term among Loyalists who sought to delegitimize it. Charles Inglis's response to *Common Sense* in 1776, for instance, was written to "oppose the destructive project of Independency," while Peter Oliver condemned "those who were the principal Agitators in projecting & pursuing . . . this unparalleled Rebellion . . . to its present Form."[10]

Of course, to call the new country a "speculation," by contrast, cut multiple ways, in yet another example of how articulations of this term were attempts to intervene in debates on the state of claims about the future, and about knowledge of the future. This was especially true in light of the extremes of higher thought and debasement and fraud that speculation represented, among many other things, by the mid-to-late 1770s. Even before the Declaration of Independence was signed, John Adams feared that "curious Projectors and Speculators in Politicks, will ruin this Country—cool, thinking, deliberate Villain[s], malicious, and vindictive, as well as ambitious and avaricious."[11] The new stereotype of the "political speculator" embodied the worst of two worlds (corrupt politics and avaricious gambling), one who sought to profit from office, and he was warned against from all corners.[12] But nowhere were speculation's conceptual and semantic stakes in the new country clearer early on than in the fierce debates surrounding the financial structure of the republic—especially regarding the prospect of the Bank of the United States. The kinds of financial gambles that now marked this increasingly dominant sense of *speculation*, of course, had been present since the earliest colonial days, including Puritan land speculation, colonial lotteries, and rampant debt schemes.[13] As historians have amply demonstrated, the United States was founded not simply on its self-mythologized plans of enlightened democracy and the social contract but also on public credit and unstable debts, on compromises in a crudely materialistic world of economic gain.[14] And it was also convenient to blame speculation (in general) and speculators (as individuals) for most any crime one sought to condemn, and here, *speculation*'s keyword function in claims about the American experiment was amplified in particular ways. We see it in the words of most of the country's founding figures. George Washington—who had been "one of the greatest land speculators of the [1750s]," in Robert Sobel's words—complained that "virtue and patriotism are almost extinct. . . . Stockjobbing, speculating, engrossing, seem to be the great business of the day."[15] He wrote to his cousin Lund Washington that "I cannot, with any degree of patience, behold the infamous practices of speculators, monopolizers, and all that class of gentry which are preying upon our very vitals, and, for the sake of a little dirty pelf, are putting the rights and the liberties of the country into the most imminent danger, and continuing a war destructive to the lives and property of the valuable part of this community."[16] Thomas Jefferson, for his part, consistently railed against speculation, and he lamented, when writing of England, "I wish any events could induce us to cease to copy such a model, and to assume the dignity of being original. They had their paper system, stockjobbing, speculations, public debt, moneyed interest, &c, and all this was contrived for us."[17]

But the substantive issue was a fundamental disagreement on whether speculation had a place in the natural course of American commerce, or whether it was a perversion and aberration. It was a disagreement, too, on whether speculation per se was the problem, or whether it was certain *types* of speculation (land versus finance) by certain people (Christian versus Jewish), or whether waste, corruption, and idleness, as *effects* associated with speculation, were the target of opprobrium.[18] Either way, speculation in the present was a threat to, not a condition of, future wealth—and yet it was precisely the path to future wealth that Americans were pursuing. James Madison and his allies believed, for instance, that commerce should thrive and the economy—especially manufactures—should expand, but only within a vaguely defined realm that unseen laws and forces of both nature and humanity dictated. Madison supported federal banking but believed "nothing but evil" would spring from the "imaginary money" of state paper, which would lead, he claimed, to speculative swindles.[19] John Adams declared that every dollar issued beyond the exact quantity of gold and silver in the vaults represented nothing and was, therefore, "a cheat upon somebody," while Alexander Hamilton himself discussed speculation extensively, especially in his reports of the early 1790s.[20]

A set of exchanges between John and Abigail Adams, in light of their own financial practices, illustrates both the stakes of and the transitions in conceptual terminology here. John Adams worried about "commercial Projects and private Speculations," and in a letter to his wife just a month after the Declaration of Independence was signed, he reiterated that "thousands of schemes for Privateering are afloat in American Imaginations. . . . Out of these Speculations many fruitless and some profitable Projects will grow."[21] The high rate of failure of these airy schemes worries Adams: How many of them would it take to sink the new United States as a whole? Or speculation could threaten American democracy by creating a new wealthy ruling class overnight. In his diary a year later, Adams again drew on the polysemy of both *speculation* and *constitution*, noting that "my Constitution is too much debilitated by Speculation."[22] Abigail Adams herself played on the multiple senses of *speculator* in her letters to her husband. She wrote in 1783, "We certainly see a country sufficiently disorderd, and embarrassed to satisfy any speculator in the utmost wantonness of his imagination. But where and to whom shall we look, for a restoration of internal peace and good order, so necessary for the preservation of that very freedom for which we have so long and so successfully contended[?]"[23] John believed that "nothing will damp the Rage for Speculation but a Peace which may break a few hundreds or thousands of speculators."[24] And in fact, while John argued in the 1790s that Hamilton was to blame for having "made of a whole Nation Stockjobbing, Speculating, selfish People," Abigail disagreed: "Nor do I think the System of Finance conceived by Mr. Hamilton the origin of the Speculating, Stockjobbing ... Rage."[25] This debate was even personal for the Adamses, for while John was in Paris in 1783 negotiating an end to the war, Abigail began to speculate in depressed war bonds, then sought to acquire a risky piece of disputed real estate in Vermont near the Canadian border (and used straw men to get around purchasing regulations). She also came up with a plan for John to ship goods from Europe to her, where she would then mark them up and sell them to local stores whose shelves were depleted due to the Revolutionary War.[26]

The underlying question, to return to the discourse around gambling examined in the last chapter, was the *natural* and thus sanctioned mode of commerce for the future of the new republic. What should legalized monetary gambling look like, and what kind of future and valuation would it produce? And how might we know that *now*? *Speculation*'s connotations of abstraction and immateriality bore on the proposed answers to this question, too. Looking back, Henry Adams asserted that in the early republic, there was a commensurability in which "the traits of the American character were fixed; the rate of physical and economical growth was established; and history, certain that at a given distance of time the Union would contain so many millions of people, with wealth valued at so many millions of dollars, became thenceforward chiefly concerned to know what kind of people these millions were to be."[27] By contrast, as Bruce Mann writes, "speculative debt" was not commensurate, but was "utterly independent of the natural calendar" and unrelated to "natural" growth; it was "detached from the land and had no connection with the production or exchange of goods, whether agricultural or manufactured."[28] International trade—that major vehicle of speculation—did not *produce* anything, in the physiocratic and agrarian line of thought; it was, once again, idle, and it diverted people from their pursuits of honest labor and steady growth.[29]

Worse, the debts that issued from trade and from new banking practices were being paid off via a variety of inventive monetary instruments whose character pressed further upon the volatile sense of speculation. One newspaper writer contended that "the Continental currency was not the sole cause of the idleness and speculation, which prevailed in this country about the years 1780, 1781, and 1782," but that "vast quantities of specie" and "clandestine intercourse with British garrisons" had contributed to it.[30] The Massachusetts attorney general and future governor James Sullivan, in his *Path to Riches* (1792), outlined a vision of commerce in which banks could "*prevent a flood of paper money*" circulating "without any *specie to be represented by it*," which would thereby reduce "speculation" and render "the measure of trade . . . permanent, certain, and steady."[31] Fusing the Puritan language of "grace" to the new republic's economic foundations, Noah Webster recalled in 1794:

> I met a fat plump faced Speculator, the other day, staggering under a heavy canvas bag. With true yankee freedom I asked him what he had in his bag. "*The Grace of God,*" replied the wag. Ah, said I, I have often heard of that article, but never saw it in a bag. . . . I was surprised to hear a Speculator say, he had the *grace of God*, especially such a load as to stagger under it; but upon explaining himself, my surprise ceased, and I smiled. He had cleared three hundred dollars, that morning, by the sale of public paper—He was too much pleased with the abundance of his *grace* to stand discussing nice points—and we parted.[32]

The Puritan backgrounds cited here—too lengthy to explore fully—further indicate the ways that speculation altered the core of a powerful version of American identity that prevailed at the time.[33] In 1795, the *London Magazine* reported danger across the Atlantic and warned against "American speculation" as a source of bad trade.[34] Speculation promoted idleness and gambling, which in turn led to degeneracy and lost productivity, which in turn led to more idle gambling in hopes of winning back losses. The result is the kind of waste that cut against Benjamin Franklin's mythologized advice—which would figure so prominently in Max Weber's work—that "Time is Money," which meant that one who "sits idle one half of that day" was "throw[ing] away" money itself. Franklin insisted, too, that "money is of a prolific, generating nature. Money can beget money, and its offspring can beget more," countering the long-standing claims against the unnaturalness of usury and instead opening American economics up to legitimized speculation, so long as it followed a natural (begetting) and measurable model of reproduction.[35] And regardless, the founding figures themselves simply could not stop speculating. Stuart Banner quotes an English traveler who claimed in 1802 that Americans "speculate on the future, but the future with them is not as distant as it is with us."[36] America was bound to be a speculation, a country full of speculations and speculators, but what *kind*? What future values would American speculations risk and generate, and how, and when? The conceptual terrain of the speculations that seemed so pervasive in America in particular, whether in land, politics, specie, or paper, only shifted by way of a set of interlocking theories of how speculation inhabited both individual bodies in the new republic and the body politic itself.

SPECULATION MANIA

For all its threats, and for all these debates and claims, speculation largely did not yet seem to many Americans as something frenzied, diseased, and collectively manic. However, right on the heels of *speculation*'s newly minted significance for gambling and for capitalist enterprise, *speculation* was radically transformed yet again between 1787 and 1792.[37] In this moment, Benjamin Rush was a dominant influence in shifting understandings of madness and mania away from religion, superstition, and lunar patterns, and toward material, embodied, scientifically observable phenomena.[38] As Sari Altschuler has argued, Rush equated the political health of the new republic with the physiological health of its citizenry—particularly in the terms that he himself had reconceived.[39] As surgeon general of the Continental army and a prolific publisher of studies of mental illness, Rush published a widely circulated, semi-satirical article in 1787, "On the Different Species of Mania." In it, he lists twenty-six types of "manias" that had become pronounced in America, from "land mania" to "horse mania," "machine mania," and even "monarchical mania."[40] These manias begin in individuals and then spread to masses, Rush believes, thereby infecting the health of a democracy that relied on rational decision-making. The grip of this manic pursuit of future money had forever reshaped the America around him.

While we have seen hints of speculation as a frenzy or malady, consistent references to speculation as a "mania," which was a key part of the emergent vocabulary of medicine in this moment, are nearly nonexistent prior to 1787.[41] With this characterization, Rush crucially reads speculation as both an individual mental disorder and as a contagious epidemic—readings that persist all the way to the present.[42] We should not skip over the connection that Rush makes: mania itself may not be a contagious disease, but speculation can be regarded as a mental epidemic that goes beyond even the characterizations of gambling addiction at the time. The very next year, for instance, the English clergyman and American immigrant William Gordon discussed currency decisions in the earliest days of the new republic:

> All classes were infected. It produced a rage for speculating. The mechanic, the farmer, the lawyer, the physician, the member of congress, and even a few of the clergy, in some places, were contaminated, and commenced merchants and speculators. The morals of the people were corrupted beyond any thing that could have been believed prior to the event. All ties of honor, blood, gratitude, humanity and justice were dissolved.... Brothers defrauded brothers, children parents and parents children.[43]

Speculation now has both its familiar connotations from the world of gambling—corruption, immorality, fraud—and a new quality of infectious rage that cuts across "all classes." Rush was very particular, too: he argued that "madness has increased since the year 1790" in the United States because of "the funding system, and speculations in bank scrip, and new lands," all of which have remained "fruitful sources of madness" for the populace.[44]

A particular event in the summer of 1791 epitomized and named the ways in which economic speculation, political speculation, and speculative madness were now understood to be merging in the new country, all with purportedly disastrous results: "scripomania," as it was called, after Bank of the United States certificates of subscription.[45] As scrip in the new Bank saw a dramatic rise in value in 1791, the Philadelphia *General Advertiser* cried out that "an inveterate madness for speculation seems to possess this country!"[46] "Where this infatuation will end it is hard to say," opined another piece, "but some will doubtless ere long *speculate* in the mad-house."[47] A much-reprinted dispatch amid the frenzy in Philadelphia that year declared that *"Speculation Mania* which now rages, in the *United States,* for *Bank Stock*, is unequalled by any thing, ancient or modern, except the *South Sea* or *Mississippi* schemes."[48] And like the South Sea Bubble, scripomania was a minor literary event that captured this new idea of speculation and helped disseminate it widely. The *New York Daily Gazette* offered a poem in August 1791 called "Speculation," which asked,

> What magic this among the people,
> That swells a may-pole to a steeple?
> Touch'd by the wand of speculation,
> A frenzy runs through all the nation;
> For soon or late, so truth advises,
> Things must assume their proper sizes—
> And sure as death all mortals trips,
> Thousands will rue the name of SCRIPS.[49]

Karen Weyler adds that the poet Philip Freneau named 1791 the year of "The Reign of Speculators," because of what he called the "Banks, bubbles, tontines, lotteries, monopolies, usury, forgery, lying, gambling, swindling, &c. &c" that seemed hopelessly pervasive. His satirical order of American nobility then ranked "The Order of Scrip" at the top.⁵⁰

Just as with Anstey and English writers treating *speculation*, some colorful and emblematic literary characterizations quickly arose and modified *speculation* further, pushing on its newly emergent metaphorical senses. Freneau's "On a Travelling Speculator" (1791), for instance, recounts a character who "bought where he must, and cheated where he could," including "Vast loads amassed of scrip, and who knows what." Eventually,

> Three weeks, and more, thus passed in airs of state,
> The fourth beheld the mighty bubble fail,—
> And he, who countless millions *owned* so late,
> Stopped short—and closed his triumphs in a JAIL.⁵¹

That is, for Freneau, jailing the individual speculator is the only possible hope to counteract the mass hysteria that he provoked. The proliferating poems of speculative mania seemed themselves a contagion. Another anonymous poem, called "The Glass; or Speculation," offered an "account of the ancient, and genius of the modern, speculators," which reached back to *speculum* to offer the following epigraph:

> Here speculating lads may plainly see
> How with true reason their sage acts agree;
> Here they may view, as in a proper glass,
> Their sad deformity of mental face.⁵²

The author asserts, furthermore, that "SPECULATION now employs the heads and hearts of all the monied characters in the State—so immense are their profits, that they bid fair to be the richest citizens in the world," but that this rage for economic speculation threatens to overshadow the public benefits that good projectors could offer. The author rails against the "speculating tribe," and the characterization continues to develop the idea that speculation is much more than individual or even small-group conjecture or deceit:

> *Speculation*, like a baleful pest,
> Has pour'd his dire contagion in the breast;
> That monster that would ev'ry thing devour,
> But finds his proper food among the poor.[53]

This sense of *speculation* as a "dire contagion," something that is uncontrollable and "trib[al]," even means that the formerly condemned projectors are now held up as ingenious proponents of "improvement." It might be too late already, the author fears, for the "Artifice" of speculation, which is linked to *"Gambling"* and *"stock-jobbing,"* drags all its agents to hell. And it reaches beyond money: "But not alone in *notes* they *speculate*, / They grasp all property within the state."[54] America races toward having its own *"speculating king"* and creating still more despots, like Nero and Caligula, and the "num'rous SCRIPTS" that have "puff'd *speculation* by thy magic pow'r" will leave the country full of nothing but "fools of nature."[55] In 1792, America's first infamous speculator, William Duer, was called by Madison the "Prince of the tribe of speculators."[56] Here, too, we notice the primitivist characterization of speculators as "tribal" figures. Phrases like "the pestilent spirit of speculation," "rage for speculation," and "speculating mania" became increasingly common in American media.[57]

Across diverse sources and in a wide range of fields, "speculation mania" became a common, often sensationalistic phrase in the United States across the 1790s. Many commentators suddenly saw such maniacal periods as regular occurrences endemic to the American character; one newspaper discussed "the bubbles brought forward in the present *mania* for speculation in order to deceive the public."[58] The *Philadelphia Gazette* claimed in 1795 that we now lived in an "Age of Commerce" defined by a "universal Mania" that was visible in the South Sea and Mississippi Bubbles, and again now.[59] In 1797, the *American Mercury* looked back and drew a comparison across the earlier part of the decade to demonstrate that "when the revolution broke out in France the speculation mania was raging in this country—the French had their heads turned with fanatical theories of perfection of man, democracy and atheism—The Americans became mad with fortune-making—a rage that has sent many a poor bankrupt to his cell."[60] What had previously seemed like a political and financial threat to the United States was now a full-blown and uncontainable madness. It's not that Americans alone were especially *maniacal speculators*, genetically or otherwise, but rather that the two terms and their link to embodied behaviors had become bound here, and the rhetoric tying them together would spread rapidly beyond America's shores.

This shift in understandings of speculation, for example, even prompted rereadings of the South Sea Bubble, which became the reference point for recasting *all* financial crises, whether in Amsterdam in 1637 or in the United States in 1791. We recall that the South Sea debacle was not called a "speculation" in its day, but rather, was understood as the product primarily of individual folly, or connivance among a cabal of "directors" and "projectors." Rarely was it characterized as the kind of contagious unreason that *frenzy* implies—and in fact, many economists now doubt that it was much of a "mania" at all. In *Some Considerations on the Late Mismanagement of the South-Sea Stock* (ca. 1720), for instance, the anonymous author points to "Follies" and "imaginary Schemes" that harmed the "poor deluded unfortunate People," but there is no language of "mania" or "frenzy" surrounding it.[61] Adam Smith, too, pointed to the "folly" and the "knavery and extravagance" of that "stock-jobbing project," but not to any sort of mania.[62] Earlier fears about speculation were largely about secrecy, insider knowledge, clandestine managers, lack of good faith, and individual folly—the kinds of things Lord Mansfield addressed. Nor do we yet have the common language of economic "cycles," which rationalized bubbles. But by the end of the century, the South Sea project was fully rewritten as a "speculation," and in 1798, when William Coxe looked back on it, he concluded that "the general frenzy in favour of the South Sea speculation had risen to an enormous height."[63] We'll return to this touchstone momentarily through Charles Mackay.

THE MANIACAL SPIRIT

America was not just a speculation, but a country ravaged by a speculative fever. But speculative fever was not passed by contact with skin or blood: So what kind of contagion was it, and what does its spread say about its meaning in America and beyond? The answer to this question underscores the immense shift in theorizations of speculation that *mania* implies: speculation was now a *spirit*. One magazine columnist warned that Americans must not be seduced into "giving substance and existence to the frothy essences and fantastick forms of speculation; nor is it by paper money, or an abolition of debts" that America's economic turmoil can be resolved.[64] A spirit was something ethereally embodied and not just a visceral, materialistic thrill—something that inhabited bodies without being treatable by medicine, for instance. A spirit, like a "pest," was permanent and contagious; the individual desire to gamble, for instance, could be regulated and tempered more visibly, but controlling an infectious spirit was more difficult, if not impossible. The same idea—a spirit—that was said to lift the American experiment was once again its potential downfall.

This rhetoric, which draws on much from speculation's preceding history as an abstract idea, pervades the annals of the early U.S. congresses. In 1790, Theodore Sedgwick of Massachusetts refused to believe that "speculation, to a certain degree, is baneful in its effects upon society," and held that a "pernicious temper, or spirit of speculation," could be safely "counteracted" if blunted "early."[65] But if a spirit becomes a "mania," control seems prima facie impossible, others asserted. James Jackson, then a congressman from Georgia, spoke against Hamilton's treasury plans in 1790 in part because he feared that they had encouraged a "demon of speculation" that had "extended its baleful influence over the remote parts of the Union." He notes that "a spirit of havoc, speculation, and ruin, has arisen" especially among those who had privileged access to financial information.[66] As the New Hampshire congressman William Gordon argued in 1799, "the natural operation of commerce" had now given way to a "spirit of speculation which ha[s] raged to a great extent in this country; which has driven the merchant from his counting-house to speculate in land, and produced a sort of mania among the people of the United States."[67]

Here we have a new reading of *speculation*'s mediation between what we might sketch roughly as abstract idealism (spirit) and practical manifestation (material gambles), grounded in new risky capitalist and political experiments unique to the American moment. And once again, such a new reading became a convenient rhetorical device in American political and economic commentary. A survey of the rhetoric in this moment finds many new manias attested, like the "rage" and "mania" for the "speculation" of "*hydromania*" to supply Baltimore with "good and wholesome water" in the early 1800s, or a scene where "the harpies of speculation laid hold of [Washington, DC] as their prey—what was imaginary, or could only be brought about in a long series of time, their cupidity represented as already existing . . . during the speculating mania, when the federal city was supposed to be an Elysium."[68] By the 1810s, countless writers assert that the "mania" for "speculation" will spell the end of America. One paper noted that speculation had "pervaded almost every class of community," which thereby created "hordes of speculation" that behaved like "noisome vipers, that breed and fatten on the corruption of national morals."[69] Another exclaimed: "*Speculation!*—One of the most remarkable events of the present eventful times, is the extensive and increasing mania for *commercial speculation* and *monopolies*. The late famous *butter monopoly* has dwindled almost into insignificance before the multiplied and enormous speculations in *groceries* . . . the *mania* of speculation."[70] Another round of "bank mania" ensued in 1814, and one letter to the editor conceded in 1817 that "it is our lot to live i[n] an age, ruinously affected with the *mania* of Speculation, and possibly this disease may have got hold on the crops."[71] Soon, most every economic trend is labeled a "mania" of some type, often with a "fever" or a "reckless" and "wild" spirit attached.[72] "Canal Mania" and "Railway Mania" were common phrases, with the latter signaling both an object of investment and a metaphor for high-powered ambition in speculative gambles.[73] Americans, allegedly more than any other peoples, were relentlessly running headlong into wild schemes that promised no future but ruin.

Several presidential pronouncements in the 1830s and 1840s capture this state of affairs perfectly and frame the next chapter of speculation's history. Andrew Jackson's associate William Leggett in 1836 castigated "that fool-hardy spirit of speculation, which, but a little while ago, kept hurrying on from one mad scheme to another, as if it possessed the fabled art of turning all it touched into gold. A commercial revulsion has commenced, and we fear will not terminate, till it has swept like a tornado over the land, and marked its progress by the wrecks scattered in its path."[74] Jackson wrote to Chief Justice Roger Taney in 1836, in a variation on a theme we've seen since the 1770s, that "it seems to me that one of the greatest threatners of our admirable form of Government, is the gradual consuming corruption, which is spreading and carrying stockjobbing, Land jobbing and every species of speculation into our Legislature, state and national."[75] After intense debate, in July 1836 Jackson issued an executive order, the Specie Circular, declaring that one could only purchase public lands in gold or silver, as a means of regrounding material lands in material monetary exchanges rather than in speculations. Here, we return to the notion of speculation's roots as abstract and purely fictional, the opposite of what land and goods represented. In his farewell address in 1837, Jackson argued that

> these ebbs and flows in the currency and these indiscreet extensions of credit naturally engender a spirit of speculation injurious to the habits and character of the people. We have already seen its effects in the wild spirit of speculation in the public lands and various kinds of stock which within the last year or two seized upon such a multitude of our citizens and threatened to pervade all classes of society and to withdraw their attention from the sober pursuits of honest industry.[76]

Jackson casts himself as the defender of "honest industry" against the "wild spirit of speculation" that was rampant in the United States.

John Tyler assumed office five years later with a promise to resolve the ongoing problems that Jackson identified but had failed to stem. In his State of the Union address in December 1842, Tyler contended that "a vast amount of what was called money" had been "thrown upon the country," leading to "the spread of a speculative mania all over the country." Americans now had to borrow from "European capitalists, who were seized with the same speculative mania which prevailed in the United States," Tyler lamented.[77] And yet, just two years later, Tyler concluded (with overconfidence) that, because of his policies, "trade and barter, no longer governed by a wild and speculative mania," now "rest upon a solid and substantial footing."[78] A shift has taken place: Washington and Adams saw speculators as individual or small-group threats because they were unvirtuous; Tyler, a half century after Benjamin Rush's discursive breakthroughs, saw speculation as a widespread epidemic that his supreme powers alone could eradicate.

Spirit and mania, however, were not enough to recharacterize speculation: there were "panics" on top of and integrated into them. The *Oxford English Dictionary* notes that *panic* was first used to mean a "condition of widespread apprehension in relation to financial and commercial matters" in the late 1750s; it then picks up as a categorizing term in the 1820s.[79] (*Panicmonger* arrives in the economic world in the 1840s.) From the Greek god Pan, "panic" signals a seizure of terror so overwhelming one loses rational capacities.[80] The first session of the twenty-third U.S. Congress was called the "Panic Session" when it convened in December 1833 to address credit shortages and coinage problems that had plagued Jackson's first term. The Panics in England in 1836 and the United States in 1837 were proclaimed the results of "speculative manias," thereby creating a new interplay between the concepts of mania and panic. During the Panic of 1837, we see the phrase "mania for speculation" repeated endlessly.[81] The boundless desire for future wealth had trapped Americans in cycles of speculative manias, bubbles, and panics that would doom its future.

WITCHES, HOAXES, AND ALCHEMICAL SPECULATION

With this, we have firmly in place the enduring figuration of speculative manias, a topic that has yielded countless studies of speculation in

American culture. But we need to pay special attention to a particular study from this moment—one that looked at speculation as a maniacal spirit, and at the panics in the United States and England, as a prompt for tracing speculation across a *longue durée*. The Scottish journalist Charles Mackay produced in 1841 a study of speculation that would become even more monumental than any of Rush's. Mackay's *Memoirs of Extraordinary Popular Delusions* was arguably the first attempt at a full, panoramic history of speculation as a broad-based phenomenon, and its focus is more on the practices and the concept than the term itself. The enormously popular book, whose initial (and ongoing) influence is difficult to overstate, went through multiple editions and was expanded to *Memoirs of Extraordinary Popular Delusions and the Madness of Crowds* in 1852. Mackay goes chapter by chapter through a range of events that he groups together as crowd-driven mad behaviors. An incomplete list includes tulipomania, John Law, the Mississippi Bubble, the South Sea Bubble, alchemists, prophecy, fortune-telling, magnetism, hair and beards, crusades, witches, slow poisoners, haunted houses, popular follies of great cities, admiration of thieves, duels and ordeals, urban slang, and relics. Mackay aims to draw an ever-expanding, often incongruous line around speculative manias and to encircle them within human history's most infamous moments of prognostication, divination, occultism, and mass irrationality. He thereby associates speculation—which Smith had defended, on certain grounds—with exactly the kinds of "poison[s] of enthusiasm and superstition" that Smith warned against. Such themes were common for Mackay: he was also a poet and, in the previous year, had published *The Hope of the World, and Other Poems* (1840), in which he meditated on the "bad passions," the "evils of Intolerance and Ambition," and the "sad folly" that "blind[ed]" humanity.[82]

Speculation here has lost nearly any connection to contemplative or reflective observation and instead signals humanity's least measured considerations. The element of scientific conjecture and experimentation has been swallowed by recourse to divination and hoaxes, and the destruction that speculation brings reaches from medieval mythologies to modern financial gambles. But Mackay insists that we should "not, in the pride of our superior knowledge, turn with contempt from the follies of our predecessors. The study of the errors into which great minds have fallen in the pursuit of truth can never be uninstructive."[83] Speculation, for Mackay, is a type of madness, but one that is evidentiary and useful in its trail of mistakes.

Mackay sees the speculator figure in the multiple forms that we have now encountered: he inhabits "men of all ranks, characters, and conditions: the truth-seeking but erring philosopher; the ambitious prince and the needy noble, who have believed in it; as well as the designing charlatan, who has not believed in it, but has merely made the pretension to it the means of cheating his fellows, and living upon their credulity."[84] By placing faith in these figures and by following their reliance on ancient and modernized forms of divination and augury, "whole communities suddenly fix their minds upon one object, and go mad in its pursuit; that millions of people become simultaneously impressed with one delusion, and run after it, till their attention is caught by some new folly more captivating than the first."[85] Here again, speculation instantly translates from the one to the many in madness. Mackay then pinpoints "three causes [that] especially have excited the discontent of mankind; and, by impelling us to seek for remedies for the irremediable, have bewildered us in a maze of madness and error. These are death, toil, and ignorance of the future."[86] That is, humans speculate because they fear the inevitability of death, because they are lazy and do not want to work for their fortunes, and because they seek predictive knowledge about the future.

Specifically, they want to benefit financially in the future, and that desire sends them into madness. Regarding the Mississippi and South Sea Bubbles, Mackay argues that "visions of boundless wealth floated before the fascinated eyes of the people in the two most celebrated countries of Europe. The English commenced their career of extravagance somewhat later than the French; but as soon as the delirium seized them, they were determined not to be outdone."[87] We are back to speculation's roots in mediation between the seen and the unseen, now juxtaposed temporally: the "vision" of future wealth, seen only in one's mind, prompts the practice of speculation in the real-world present. Mackay ultimately contends that "every age has its peculiar folly; some scheme, project, or phantasy into which it plunges," so that the cycle of manias and speculative fevers is unstoppable.[88] His book merges theories of speculation as madness with contemporaneous theories of the crowd and of mob psychology, and while it relies on some heavily distorted and questionable evidence, it remains an indispensable chapter in the history of speculation.[89] It provided for the first time a synoptic taxonomy, vocabulary, and schematic plan for understanding speculative behaviors across deep time. Its portrait of speculation, which capitalized on the term's changes over the preceding half century, was quickly and memorably ingrained.

SPECULATING AMERICA, AGAIN

With speculation now given a historical and contemporary characterization as a madness tied to capitalism and its risks (and potential hoaxes), and flourishing specifically in the American political and financial experiment, the American transcendentalists could reread their country's speculation and weave together a number of the threads we have seen thus far in our history. And they could do so through their specific renovation of British Romanticism, too. Emerson praised Coleridge for taking a view "from a specular mount" in order to attain "universal knowledge," and saw him as "a restless human soul bursting the narrow boundaries of antique speculation and mad to know the secrets of that unknown world, on whose brink it is sure it is standing."[90] Which is to say, Emerson reinterprets Coleridge as an advocate of *speculation*, rather than of *imagination* (a term whose power faded after the 1820s), and Emerson saw in him some element of celebratory mania that appealed to him in his own attempt to move beyond the scientific, materialist empiricism that prevailed in the New England of his day.

This also gave Emerson a way to distinguish an American view of speculation even further, to venerate rather than fear it, and to combine several threads of speculation newly in operation. Emerson observed that "the so-called 'practical men' sneer at speculative men, as if, because they speculate or *see*, they could do nothing."[91] But on the contrary, speculators, for Emerson, find a divine union of the material and the immaterial, just as "prayer is the contemplation of the facts of life from the highest point of view," but grounded in material facts.[92] This faculty applies equally to the economic realm, for Emerson. He writes that "wealth has its source in applications of the mind to nature," and that God and nature provide the invisible hand that maintains a natural, organic equilibrium in all human affairs, including economy.[93]

Emerson therefore argues in "Compensation" (1841) that "a perfect equity adjusts its balance in all parts of life," while the "dice of God are always loaded." Projectors, he asserts, chase after imbalances and never have "the smallest success," because divine nature always restores a balance.[94] What becomes of speculators and projectors, then? Emerson argues in "Wealth" that

> this *speculative* genius is the madness of few for the gain of the world. The projectors are sacrificed, but the public is the gainer. Each of these idealists, working after his thought, would make it tyrannical, if he could. He is met and antagonized by other speculators, as hot as he. The equilibrium is preserved by these counteractions, as one tree keeps down another in the forest, that it may not absorb all the sap in the ground.[95]

The *failures* of speculators, much as we saw in the previous century's acceptance of the useful failures of projectors, are evidence of a divine, balanced order. Speculators, as "monomaniacs," attempt to exploit uneven situations but end up providing the necessary equilibrium, reconciling the two minds of speculation for Emerson. The ugliness and catastrophes of speculative manias are thereby sanitized as valuable, indicative failures (we might recall Treasury Secretary Paul O'Neill's infamous comment in 2002 that the collapse of Enron evinced "the genius of capitalism"). To see America as a country of "projects," as Emerson did, was to legitimize such failures as creating the "future" that the country represented, thereby encircling together what indeed seem like polar antagonists in speculation's manic state in the 1840s.

Even as he departed from Emerson on key points in natural philosophy, Henry David Thoreau took this notion yet farther and sums up where this chapter ends, arguing, "We may believe it, but never do we live a quite free life, such as Adam's, but are enveloped in an invisible network of speculations—Our progress is only from one such speculation to another, and only at rare intervals do we perceive that it is no progress.—Could we for a moment drop this by-play—and simply wonder—without reference or inference!"[96]

Building "castles in the air," as he puts it in *Walden* (1854), is to be celebrated; as Jennifer J. Baker explains, it is a validation of "the Romantic mind's creation of the world, making more palpable the tendency of these writers to emphasize the social consequences of speculation."[97] Whereas the English, for Thoreau, can "speculate only within bounds," the success of the American experiment is that its citizens, "in more than one sense, can *speculate* without bounds."[98] Speculation is part of the character of the exceptional American experience, past, present, and future. It is no longer a threat to America's stability; rather, it *constitutes* stability and is a net public good. Together, Emerson and Thoreau seek to revive and restore a vision of speculation in America, and America as a speculative enterprise, that could redeem the concept from the negative connotations it acquired in the preceding half century.

Where Rush could see nothing but mad frenzy in speculation, and where Mackay could only understand it through hoaxes and divination, two of the greatest apologists for the American experiment saw its putatively damaging effects as ideally suited to the new country. What if America's future, then, were embedded in a model of natural, organic growth, of which speculative madnesses, like hurricanes or earthquakes, were necessarily active components? The federalist John Sergeant told

Congress in 1819 that "the youthful energy of our happy country" has produced "speculators of many kinds.... The variety is infinite, and in no country upon earth greater than in this. Every thing about us invites to speculation."[99] And much later, in 1932, the historian of finance Aaron M. Sakolski conceded, with language that recalls where this chapter began, that "America, from its inception, was a speculation. It was a speculation to Columbus. It was considered a speculation by the kings of Spain, France and England."[100] But surely this embrace of speculation as magically always there in America was too simple and, in fact, politically naive. Thoreau confesses, it turns out, only a few lines after the bullish claim quoted above, that his positive evaluation of "what makes the United States government, on the whole, more tolerable" applies only "for us lucky white men."[101] If speculation were part of American projections of futurity, its relationship to the specific bodies that it inhabits as a mania or spirit cannot be taken for granted. Nor can we overlook the rapidly changing technologies and instruments that, over the course of the nineteenth century, reshaped how speculation functioned both as an economic practice and as a concept more broadly.

5

SPECULITIS, OR THE TECHNOLOGIES OF PROPHECY

> *While the ways of making money are many and varied, the most successful, and that in which the largest fortunes have been accumulated, can be told in one word, SPECULATION. In a measure we are all speculators, whether we buy merchandise which we expect to sell at a profit, houses and lands which we hold for an advance, or stocks, bonds and grain. But of all commodities, stocks and grain pay the greatest profit. . . . No long, tedious waits . . . before you realize a profit, . . . but a constant and rapid change in values, registered daily on the "Ticker."*
>
> —"HOW TO GET RICH," ADVERTISEMENT IN
> *THE HARVARD ADVOCATE* (1894)

In 1908, a new magazine called *The Ticker* announced its diagnosis of a madness that was afflicting America: "speculitis." This addiction to speculation, named as if it were an inflammation of speculation itself, was not the same manic state that Benjamin Rush pinpointed just over a century prior. Rather, as the financial writer Reyam Ora asserted, speculitis was gambling for gambling's sake in financial markets—with no knowledge of how markets move, with no real interest in owning the underlying assets, and with only blind luck. Instinct-driven wagers and base impulses that belonged in casinos and alleys now threatened the national economy. But what distinguished this modern mass speculation was the fact that it was readily accessible to ordinary people, by way of a tiny yet powerful machine: the ticker. This instrument, invented in 1867, had become synonymous, over the preceding four decades, with a mode of speculating itself. It churned out an endless stream of data that diminished the very centrality of human contemplation in the speculative process. Instead, the ticker overwhelmed and benumbed minds with seemingly prophetic, coded information, leaving people to speculate in a mechanically induced trance.

Clearly, "speculitis," like so many other permutations of speculation, was not simply a financial activity. It was a theory of human behavior, of how we consider evidence, of how we project futures, and much more. In this case, it represents the intersection of several conceptual and practical threads of speculation with a particular new technology that set the stage for yet more battles for who controlled the definition of *speculation* and what that control entailed. In this period of American history, those battles went into universities, professions, and even the Supreme Court.[1] More than anything, the battles staked claims concerning the politics of information itself—especially machine-generated information—and what it meant to craft information mastery into expertise in future forecasting for an entire society or nation. We can see, Ora asserted, that the only cure for the addiction to speculitis was to "combine experience with . . . knowledge," in order to speculate "properly."[2] "Proper" speculation, though, was paradoxically defined as an individual mastery of the mysterious and undefinable essence of speculation itself. In other words, what made speculation a rampant disorder was not any kind of contagious infection or spirit, but—reaching back to speculation's roots in scientific experimentation—the way that nonhuman data could not be processed adequately by human minds, and instead left human bodies to respond affectively. In rapidly expanding stock and commodity exchanges, and in semi-illicit bucket shops too, ticker speculation was making more fools than fortunes, and the only antidote to its effects was *better* speculation—which, unfortunately, no one could quite define other than retroactively. But information mastery, with its charts and its language of predictive "cycles," became the promised path to this utopian future.

A seismic shift in the Anglo-American "information infrastructure" took place thanks to the ticker and its associated financial mechanisms, one that has imprinted itself on speculation into the present.[3] Information became a new type of engine for speculations of many types, prompting instruments like the futures contracts and the abstractions of commodities markets that radically dematerialized speculation even further. The bifurcations in speculation that we have seen emerging thus far split yet again, now among putative experts and nonexperts, or those with access and education and those without it. As we follow the ways in which technology, information, and the late nineteenth-century professionalization movement reckon with speculation, we'll finally be able to contextualize the rise of speculative fiction in this same moment as the twin product of these same forces. Speculation now becomes inextricable from the technologies, information, and socioeconomic risks that create multiple possible futures. The contingent knowledge it produces along the way, and the personas and social types associated with its production, become crucial to the contours of American modernity. Thus, across the period from roughly the 1870s through the 1920s, a common dynamic recurs many times expertise and instinct, abstraction and concreteness (or sometimes embodiment), data-supported prediction and natural "cycles" all battle to determine what the next phase of techno-futurism will look like in the speculative landscape of American life.

A PROPHETIC MACHINE

The ticker was the instrument of a massive data revolution that enduringly reshaped the velocity and immateriality of speculation. The oracle-like tabletop machine spit out prices and quotes with seemingly boundless energy. For the first time, data generated by a machine in real time, about a character per second (analog information, not computational), was the basis for speculation, both financial and cognitive. Here, speculation appeared the farthest thing from deliberate contemplation in solitude. The temporal and spatial *durées* that information had traveled for millennia seemed to dissolve before one's eyes. Functioning through the expanding system of telegraph lines, the ticker quickly took on a hierophantic quality that linked it to the spheres through which Charles Mackay had understood speculation: it was a modern version of the Fates, telling the predetermined prophecies of humanity through an unending line of information on tape. (And to *telegraph* something, in this moment, took on the connotation of "to signal what is coming.") The ticker spoke a language that combined the abbreviated forms of telegraphy with the recondite coded language of stock quotes to emit "magic words," as one writer called them, that foretold the future of entire economies.[4]

The spread of these magical machines was astounding. The Gold and Stock Telegraph Company had 25 tickers in service in 1867; by 1878, that number had grown to 1,342.[5] An estimated 23,000 tickers were in use by 1905. Especially with the addition of telephones, in 1876, anonymous and distant speculation was now possible, as was crossing continents, thanks to new transatlantic cables.[6] A financial writer argued in 1903 that there is "no better proof . . . of the universality of speculation" than the ubiquity of the ticker.[7] Private tickers became more common, too, as speculators hoped to corner a new market in information itself. Initially, many had understood its forerunner, the telegraph, as having *reduced* the opportunities for speculation that had previously thrived on the information asymmetries inherent in the delayed delivery of information. But in this chapter in the history of the "cultural life of information," the ticker ultimately increased the opportunities for real-time (and often manipulated) speculation.[8] All this contributed to a "radical abstraction and reconfiguration of the visual experience of the market," for whereas previous markets relied on information, newer markets "increasingly became markets *in* information. Participants came to regard markets less as places to trade tangible things and more as the flow of quotations printed by the ticker and posted on distant blackboards."⁹

Furthermore, to participate in markets (however loosely defined) no longer required fighting for space on trading floors and in pits, nor even the privileges of masculinity and whiteness, creating an expanded democratic element to speculation. (Only a tiny percentage of Americans owned stocks before the 1920s, it's worth recalling.) Brokerage houses, commodities exchanges, and saloons all used tickers, as did bucket shops, those ersatz brokerages where commoners could gamble on the prices of stocks without every actually owning them—we'll return to this democratic element in the next chapter.¹⁰ But the development marks a clear dividing line in this new transformation of speculation: more and more people *could* speculate in many markets, and on many objects and ideas, in more potentially volatile ways. A far-reaching and well-conditioned response, then, was to translate the "mystical" and "magical" elements of the ticker into a language requiring "expertise" and "study" to master and understand—a kind of expertise that could only be gained by educated white men. To knowingly *interpret* the ticker, it was claimed, required one to master pricing data and futures markets in order to become learned fortune-tellers. A grassroots publishing industry quickly arose to issue guides on how to read its product—ticker tape. By 1886, the archive of data in the ticker tape was being rained down as confetti for parades: the value of this material text was by definition ephemeral, making it useless detritus shortly after it seemed to determine an entire market's fate.

But more telling are the highly stylized and metaphorical accounts of the ticker's revelations and of the powers of male "ticker speculators" and "tape speculators," for whom reading was something of an addiction to mechanized data consumption. The journalist Julius Chambers recorded in his novel *On a Margin* (1884):

> The discovery of America is usually regarded as a rather important historical and commercial event; but to the new estate of man that grows rich without toil the invention of the "stock ticker" outshines the achievement of Columbus. This machine has an overmastering

power for good or evil. It is the most gigantic engine that ever was created to serve the speculative purposes of man.... [Everyone] recognized its future potency, its universality, and the volume of its voice before he had watched it a fortnight.[11]

Chambers also records the tale of an experienced broker: so "expert had his ear become that he could read...the music of the ticker... without looking at the tape."[12] The broker was, in the words of another novel of the period, "the humble interpreter of a dark and Delphic oracle, of which the ticker was the mouth-piece."[13] Some tape readers, as in Edwin Lefèvre's popular roman à clef *Reminiscences of a Stock Operator* (1923), even became frustrated at the slight delay between the action on the trading floor and the report of the tape and claimed that "the ticker beat me by lagging the market," to which he had an even more powerfully telepathic connection.[14]

The ticker also helped distinguish American speculation in the minds of many observers; it was never simply about the money-making element. One writer noted that "American dealers hover over, and intently watch the 'ticker' as it rapidly unwinds the tangled web of financial fate. They are therefore amazed to think how it can be possible that immense speculations are carried on in Paris without a 'ticker,' though such is the case," the French having rejected the technology at the time.[15] This distinction was double-edged and dangerous. A column from 1882 called "Another Victim to the 'Ticker'" records the sad fate of a clerk who was "converted...into a criminal and put...upon the high road to the penitentiary" by "stock speculation. He listened for the 'ticker' when it clicked and looked upon the tape as it unwound—a veritable tapeworm that has devoured the substance, pecuniary and moral, of thousands.... The 'ticker' beats the swift time of a march to destruction for every honest man who watches it in the hope of gain."[16]

We can get a sense of the ticker's all-consuming power of futuristic prediction through a brief glance at some contemporaneous accounts of brokers demonstrating how the ticker worked. In one of them, a trader

FIGURE 5.1 Illustration by William Robinson Leigh from *McClure's* magazine, November 1901. Two men stand by a ticker as it streams out tape, one of them gesturing with his hand. The caption reads, "I don't *think* it's going up; I *know* it's going up!," signaling the distinction between hunches and expertise that the ticker prompted.

Modernist Journals Project, modjourn.org, public domain.

kindly took hold of the tape which continually streams out from the "ticker," as the little wheel of fortune is called, which constantly records the rise and decline of stocks, and tried to explain all about it.... Ten, fifteen, or twenty [brokers] at a time would clutch at the tape, as it streamed out with its endless lines of quotations, and mutter to themselves, jabber at each other, swear like pirates, drop the tape, and dash away. Others would dart in, clutch the tape, swear or chuckle as their fortunes went, wheel about, give orders to their broker to buy or sell, as they prophesied the future of the market.[17]

The "click of the 'ticker'" thus becomes "the pulse and heart-beat of the nation," with an allusion to Boethius's Wheel of Fortune along the way.[18] Its language is its own, channeling a prophecy of the future through the "jabber" of traders. In the opening scene of Robert Grant's play *The Lambs: A Tragedy* (1883), a ticker is "in operation," with bulls and bears as choruses, while "in front, after the manner of the old Greek chorus, stand a group of speculators who have been sold out in former days, but still continue to shadow the tape as a chorus of shorn lambs."[19] The overwrought and ham-fisted drama, staged as a modern-day Greek tragedy, with strophe and antistrophe and choruses of bulls and lambs, features a constant refrain: "Ere on the tape the shrill recording 'ticker' / Has scored ten times its fate-abounding figures. / Ah, Destiny grim ruler of the ages, / What boots it to resist thee?"[20] The ticker itself was a literary topic and object, one that could be reworked to multiple purposes because of its multiform properties. Pointing to the ticker's serial, addictive power, an even stronger account in Charles Dudley Warner's *A Little Journey in the World* (1889) describes a familiar scene of speculators as bees swarming around the ticker. Warner writes that "the electric wire running up the stand quivers and takes the figure, passes it to all the other wires, transmits it to every office and hotel in the city, to all the 'tickers' in ten thousand chambers and 'bucket-shops' and offices in the republic,... electrifying the watchers of these boards, who begin to jabber and gesticulate and 'transact business.' It is wonderful."[21]

Warner uses *wonderful* in its quite literal sense to capture the awe at the rapidity and the expanse across which speculation now occurs as the new mode of future-creation. And this form of speculation also produces *more* (cognitive) speculation, as the bystanders silently speculate on what prompted this speculation, this "business of the higher and almost immaterial sort." Warner's narrator insists, however, that this is "not gambling," nor is it "a lottery," but rather, the ticker creates a "temple" in which "a fortune may be made here in a day or lost here in a day, but that a nod and a wink here enable people all over the land to ruin others or ruin themselves with celerity."[22] The ticker changed the *speed* of market changes and, more broadly, of American economic life, even at the level of patterns of consumption. Massive fluctuations and serial panics with broad effects became the norm, not the exception, thanks to the velocity it brought. This modern technological instrument of futurity had become a determining force in speculation that was even more anonymous, abstract, distant, and inhuman than before. A machine augured a nation's fate in an abstruse code that prompted gambles on the *idea* of objects more than on the objects themselves. Speculation seemed increasingly occult and recondite, all while it relied on information that was proclaimed to be knowable by precise study, by contemplation of its coded divination. It's not hard to see marks of our present moment in the patterns that emerged here.

TO MASTER THE FUTURE

The prophetic quality that the ticker seemed to possess points us to the second, interrelated revolution in speculation that took hold in the latter half of the nineteenth century, and which takes us to the heart of the aggressive legal and regulatory regimes around speculation in this era. An instrument of speculation now held a power not only to predict the future, but also—and even more consequentially—to enable an enormous number of individuals to gamble in ways that might *shape* and make economically viable (or not) that future. That is, gambling in backrooms or bucket shops, where expert study was no factor and no stocks were actually purchased, would mostly enrich or impoverish legions of bettors themselves. But anyone who had access to a ticker, whether they could understand its language or not, could conceivably influence futures contracts. These contracts and the "forwards" from which they grew were not new instruments in economic history, but they exploded in popularity and became nearly synonymous with the Chicago exchanges in the 1860s especially.[23] In an instant, ticker speculators could change how a nation consumed some of its staple commodities—now, six months from now, or both. Around these phenomena arose the need and desire for a hard science and defined vocabulary, one in which *speculation* was a critical term, where the economic future could be putatively known and projected with greater certainty: But how?

The booming market for futures first created another new subtype: the futures speculator, who bought and sold fictions of futurity without ever actually owning the goods in question when the contract matured. Regulators spent decades trying to parse exactly how and when a futures contract became a speculation or a gamble instead of an investment. As a federal report tried to argue in 1920, "The moment that the operator, after having sold his actual grain, fails to buy back his hedge in the future market, he is backing his individual judgment against the fluctuations of market prices and is speculating and no longer hedging."[24] Scott Sandage states it well in his account of how the idea of futurity itself as a potential commodity represents a microcosm of what capitalism promised in the nineteenth century: "Capitalism made a fetish of the future, seeing nothing better than profit except the prospect of more," once again turning the immaterial idea of profit into a prompt for chasing more profit.[25] The future could be priced and valued with yet another new set of speculative instruments, technologies, risks, platforms, and languages, much as computer programs do now.

The data of the ticker held out the hope that the future was more knowable, but it was unclear what would tame or naturalize the chaos of the data itself, or what actions the data would stimulate. After all, as

Samuel Butler put it in his satire of utopianism *Erewhon* (1872), "Who would plough or sow if he disbelieved in the fixity of the future? ... The future must be a lottery to those who think that the same combinations can sometimes precede one set of results, and sometimes another. If their belief is sincere they will speculate instead of working."[26] But across the latter part of the nineteenth century, as a response to the processes of abstraction, mechanized speculation, and contracted futurity, a rising professional class of purported experts—from ticker readers to newspaper columnists to university professors—devised means to theorize how the market futures operated. Ticker-tape data joined a host of new data sets produced by correlated revolutions in the late 1800s in the fields of statistics, probabilities, actuarial sciences, and financial analysis. Enough expertise and enough information, as the "speculitis" article claimed, could finally bring markets into equilibrium, such that they could be relied upon and predicted.

It was not enough simply to make these claims; to advance beyond this, economists needed their own established, professional science with a technical vocabulary. To fix *speculation* in economic taxonomy, and in securities regulations and government documents as well, became a new project. That is, the battles we have previously seen over the definition of *speculation* slowly started to move from dictionaries and philosophical treatises to courts and securities regulations. An early key figure here was the political economist William Stanley Jevons, who argued that "in minds of much intelligence and foresight, the greatest force of feeling and motive arises from the anticipation of a long-continued future," and that, therefore, the "power of anticipation must have a large influence in Economics," because "that class or race of men who have the most foresight will work most for the future."[27] In seeing that any economic decision involved "*some function of the future actual feeling and of the intervening time,* and [that] it must increase as we approach the moment of realisation," Jevons realized, "we are compelled to take account of the uncertainty of all future events."[28] How to account for this basic uncertainty—as old as time—in an era characterized by the promise of future-telling data? And how to account for speculation's role in creating that uncertainty when it failed to "equalise prices" and instead, in Jevons's words, "complicate[d] the action of the laws of supply and demand in a high degree, but does not in the least degree arrest their action or alter their nature?"[29] The future could be understood, mastered, and perhaps even predicted by the taming of data, these new authorities claimed.

But for all this reliance on the predictability that hard data and study promised, speculation could not completely sever its ties to a premodern world of divination and augury, and this reciprocal dynamic of science and chance that has been with speculation for so long would remain intact here. Thus, one of the first consequential theories propounded as a means of explaining the unknowable and potentially chaotic elements of the changing world of markets was that of economic "cycles" that were beyond any causal explanation. As Jevons put it, "industry is periodic," and its variances are "regular" like those of the sun and the tides; giving new significance to Shakespeare's use of *fortune*, Jevons quotes the famous lines from *Julius Caesar* (ca. 1599), "There is a tide in the affairs of men / Which, taken at the flood, leads on to fortune."[30] Jevons also tied changes in market prices for some commodities to solar patterns, and he infuses his account of economic behaviors with the naturalism of climate and seasonal cycles.[31] What fluctuates, for Jevons, in speculative spheres are ethereal, immaterial phenomena like hope and optimism, and collectively they rise and fall like a tide or a storm front. As Caitlin Zaloom explains, "For speculators, fate lies in the time gap between the present and the future."[32]

Figures like Roger Babson, Wesley Mitchell, and Samuel Benner became well-known economic forecasters who, like their weatherman peers, were seen as prophets. Guides like H. M. Williams's *Key to Wall Street's Mysteries and Methods* (1904) combined astronomy and weather forecasting. In his popular treatise *The Cycles of Speculation* (1909), Thomas Gibson argued that "the successful speculator requires four things: 1—A knowledge of values. 2—A knowledge of general conditions. 3—A knowledge of the machinery of speculation—and 4—Something besides." In short, as that fourth item indicates, speculation was both scientifically knowable and yet never fully graspable, always elusive and mystical. Gibson instead urges that "unseen future developments or, in some cases, hidden and submerged present truths... must be consulted" by the speculator.[33] Jamie L. Pietruska argues that "prediction became a ubiquitous scientific, economic, and cultural practice, and forecasts, accurate or not, offered illusions of control over one's future in what William Dean Howells recognized as the 'economic chance-world' of late nineteenth-century America."[34] Pietruska points to the irony that, while "crop estimates, weather forecasts, economic predictions, and the predictions of fortune-tellers [were employed] to uncover the significance of systematized forecasts as new forms of knowledge and risk management," the result was that "a search for predictability yielded just the opposite: acceptance of the uncertainties of economic and cultural life."[35]

The newly thriving industry of financial reporting and analysis aimed to prove the paradoxically scientific basis for theories of cyclicality and chance. A rising class of professionals believed that the mass of data could be structured into a solid predictive structure, even while never fully guaranteeing an elimination of aleatory elements. Firms like Moody's argued that one of the features that distinguished *speculation* from *investment* was that the former relied on gossip and hunches, the latter on empirical facts and dutiful study. Charts and graphs gave a striking visual component to their arguments, and mathematics gave them new formulas to employ in what one writer called "scientific speculation."[36] The forces of physics and pneumatics provided another set of metaphors.[37] The first newly titled certified public accountants were licensed in 1896 (making the cardboard-cutout Accountant in Conrad's *Heart of Darkness* [1899] a very recent type for the author to portray). But economists, like those who were now university professors with a clear disciplinary charge, or even those hired by corporations as analysts, still held that "investment is a science, and speculation is an art."[38] The latter, therefore, needed to be disciplined with more and more data, the hard lines of charts and firm predictions that science and its language promised.

Markets were endowed with an internal logic that worked naturally and organically with human behaviors to make them legible—past, present, and future. As Lisi Schoenbach writes, "This understanding of prediction, in which rationality, data collection, bell curves, and regression to the mean has replaced mere chance, and in which statistics and probabilities have become substitutes for luck, suggests a modern world in which contingency has been minimized and a managerial, organizational, and thoroughly institutional mind-set has become the dominant mode of engagement with an uncertain future."[39] But again, we must note that this "modern world" also included the career of the controversial astrologer Evangeline Adams, who gained massive popularity as a stock-advising fortune-teller with a devout following. The future may have been less enigmatic, but the paths to its knowability were not settled; the world of bureaucracies and institutions of business was not, perhaps, as disenchanted as Max Weber saw it.[40] Contrarily, Aaron M. Sakolski was among those in the 1920s who argued *against* the idea that statistics revealed anything terribly important in the face of the mysterious and unpredictable psychology of the collective imagination.[41]

The effect of statistics- and data-driven prophecy was profound, especially on the age-old human understandings of chance and fortune. A backbone of information helped legitimize speculation as grounded in fact, whereas gambling existed purely in the realms of luck and chance. Here we are back to the debates about speculation's opposition to practice; but now, ironically, chance had an army of hard numbers behind it that made it look like prophetic decision-making that influenced the course of a country's future. And, paradoxically, greater apparent control meant greater actual indeterminacy, and vice versa.[42] T. J. Jackson Lears likewise sees the self-made man and the con man as two sides of the same coin in the nineteenth century: mastery of the self was the antithesis of success by luck and chance, yet it was retroactively understood based on results.[43] This insight takes us back to the battles between divine providence and human control that Calvin fixated upon; in this later moment, William James especially became associated with philosophies of chance, contingency, and luck.[44]

The most sustained and powerful effort to synthesize and modify these divergent forces came in long-delayed governmental efforts to regulate *speculation*—to tame its wild, illegible elements and to validate the goods that it could deliver.⁴⁵ At the turn of the century, the economist Henry Crosby Emery became a leading voice in the defense of speculation, as distinct from gambling, insisting that the former depended on the mastery of information, data, and evidence. But the needed validation of speculation would eventually come from the Supreme Court. Oliver Wendell Holmes had noted as early as his "The Path of the Law" (1897) that "prediction" was a legitimate object of legal study, and that the body of the law itself was "systematized prediction."⁴⁶ In 1905, he issued a majority opinion in *Board of Trade of Chicago v. Christie Grain & Stock Co.* that effectively killed bucket shops and made market speculation legitimate, even if not always morally condoned, for the foreseeable future. Taking pages from both John Stuart Mill's and Emery's theories of speculation, Holmes argued that "people will endeavor to forecast the future, and to make agreements according to their prophecy. Speculation of this kind by competent men is the self-adjustment of society to the probable. Its value is well known as a means of avoiding or mitigating catastrophes, equalizing prices, and providing for periods of want."⁴⁷

We are all speculators, prophesying all the time, Holmes believes; we can't help it. But "competent men"—gendered experts, not "the weak" who "imitat[e]" these "strong" figures—can ensure that speculation has a natural, self-regulating quality to it.⁴⁸ Gambling *introduced* risks that were unnecessary; speculation attempted to bet on intrinsic, naturally occurring risks. The following year, Theodore Roosevelt opened his State of the Union address with the claim that "as a nation we still continue to enjoy a literally unprecedented prosperity; and it is probable that only reckless speculation and disregard of legitimate business methods on the part of the business world can materially mar this prosperity."⁴⁹ Whereas John Tyler had seen an engulfing "mania for speculation," Roosevelt now sees speculation as ultimately controllable and a part of the country's "legitimate" economic future. Against the argument that speculation produces nothing and is purely abstract, Holmes furthermore counters that most any speculation is not "for its own sake. It seems to us an extraordinary and unlikely proposition that the dealings which give its character to the great market for future sales in this country are to be regarded as mere wagers or as 'pretended' buying or selling, without any intention of receiving and paying for the property bought, or of delivering the property sold."[50] The fictional futures that cultural critics saw everywhere were, to Holmes's mind, an aberration, and the mass of information now available was a means to delimit speculation to the experts. The New York Stock Exchange, the Council of Grain Exchanges, and others agreed that, in Emery's Columbia University colleague Carl Parker's often-quoted words, the United States should work to ensure the "elimination from the field of speculation of those who are unfitted by nature, financial circumstances, or training to engage in it."[51] As an anonymous writer would put it in *The Outlook* in 1917, "Speculators are the risk-bearers of modern commerce and finance," and they therefore provide a "valuable service" by "merely attempting to profit by foreseeing the results of economic forces working in the markets."[52] A stable, secure future now existed in data that could be interpreted expertly and profited on by certain men who knew how to take what we would now call "calculated risks." Speculation, if naturalized, quantified, and crisply defined, could be validated in precise terms and entrusted to the hands of masterful white men.

Two issues of the *Saturday Evening Post* from May 1908 give us a glimpse into the stakes over the battles to define and find ways to affirm speculation in this moment. The first issue offers an extensive set of articles on "Wall Street Views of Speculation," the modern practices of usury, and the cornering of markets.[53] Then, in an issue appearing two weeks later, we see an ad for the "Carbo Magnetic Razor," which claims that there is "NO SPECULATION in buying a CARBO MAGNETIC RAZOR but an investment that declares a daily dividend of perfect satisfaction. . . . You can't lose."[54] A few pages later, we see the story of young Lord Stranleigh, who invests in railways, followed by another forum on Wall Street. The juxtapositions indicate, to the *Post*'s typical middlebrow reader, that speculation is far away from them, yet influences them daily. But next, an article declares that "everything is speculation. The discovery of America was a speculation. The American people are a people of speculators. The entire industrial progressiveness and aggressiveness of America are possible only because of the speculative spirit," which is the spirit of those who turn "dream[s] into practice."[55] But the author is adamant that "blind, senseless, tipster speculation—by all means let it be eliminated!"[56] In other words, *you*—reader—are a speculator, and speculation is fundamental to what you do. In fact, in a seamless transition, the Wall Street veteran Henry Clews then offers an opinion piece, "No Speculation Would Mean Socialism," which argues, in a renovation of Adam Smith, that "speculation is the basis of all enterprise. A man who has no speculative spirit in his composition will not take risks to enable him to do business in a large way." Clews believes that "to stop speculation would mean to invite Socialism which is devoid of individualism."[57] The issue continues with pieces such as "Speculation Necessary for Development" and "Human Nature in Selling Goods: Is the Salesman a Parasite?" Finally, the journal asks readers to submit their own stories of speculation for future issues—to speculate on the very future of the *Post*. Speculation, as we have seen for centuries now, is an inevitable temptation always to be guarded against, and yet somehow to be embraced; it is best left to the experts, yet it is available to everyone and impossible not to undertake. Morality is not the matter, but rather, the construction of the future—by whom, and by what instruments, and with how much use of our minds.

SPECULATORS, IN THE ABSTRACT FLESH

With these changes in the concept and practices of speculation came a reformation of the figure of the speculator, too, as yet another movement toward the increasing embodiment of speculation in America. Perhaps no period in American cultural history is more closely identified with the speculator than the Gilded Age. But these speculators are hardly sage readers of data calculating future risks. By contrast, Mark Twain and Charles Dudley Warner's 1873 novel that gave the period its name features numerous characters who dream their way into the "vapory realms of speculation" by scheming to make "oceans of money" through land swindles, mule breeding, diamonds, a "vast iron speculation," "sugar speculation," "hog speculation," and much more—not to mention some more traditional banking scams.[58] Their character Washington Hawkins is dazzled by Washington, DC, precisely because it was a "world of enchantment [that] teemed with speculation—the whole atmosphere was thick with it."[59] (As Twain himself quipped once after having lost fortunes on ill-advised speculations, "There are two times in a man's life when he should not speculate: when he can't afford it and when he can."[60]) One could argue that an equal frenzy for speculation in this moment appeared in texts *about* speculation. In 1929, the English writer Ralph Hale Mottram began his retrospective *History of Financial Speculation* with a summary of a plot formula he saw everywhere: "He speculated and lost everything." Mottram then explores, in language now familiar to us, what "the word Speculation has meant, in the worn but not necessarily debased currency of the English tongue in which it has been chiefly handled."[61] Here, Mottram sees an explosion of books as the culprit in devaluing speculation all over again.

Conservative estimates point to 250 to 300 "economic novels" in the US alone between 1870 and 1900, and that is likely an undercount.[62] And this is to say nothing of another genre that was thriving in the late 1800s: financial periodicals and guidebooks, which often promised objectivity and sober advice, or even a short course in professional investing.[63] The outbursts of literature on the topic were significant enough to cause critics, reviewers, and writers all around the world in this moment to document a trend that seemed remarkable to them. Speculators certainly abound in literature from this era: think of Henry James's *The American* (1877), Charles Chesnutt's "The Goophered Grapevine" (1887), Twain's *A Connecticut Yankee in King Arthur's Court* (1889), Edith Wharton's *The House of Mirth* (1905), Theodore Dreiser's *The Financier* (1912), or any number of Frank Norris's novels. And of course, America was not alone: we could point in this period also to Giovanni Verga's *I Malavoglia* (1881), Benito Pérez Galdós's *La desheredada* (1881), Julián Martel's *La bolsa* (1891), Émile Zola's *L'argent* (1891), Thomas Hardy's *The Mayor of Casterbridge* (1886) and *Tess of the d'Urbervilles* (1891), Narcís Oller's *La febre d'or* (1892), Joseph Conrad's

Nostromo (1904), and Harley Granville-Barker's *The Voysey Inheritance* (1905).[64]

The effect, both in literature and across the economic cultures that developed in the moment, was that the cultural typology of the speculator expanded and took on new forms, just as markets and technologies themselves did.[65] With such expansion and change came more disgust and distrust of speculators, just as the professional class of economists and regulators sought to credential them. Cedric B. Cowing has charted the intense vilification of speculators that seemed to be on every tongue across the second half of the nineteenth century, noting that *speculator* became "more than ever a term of opprobrium; the physiocratic bias against those who produced no primary products was more bitterly asserted as the agrarian population shifted consciously to the defensive. The mysterious and remote commodity speculator seemed more of a parasite."[66] *Speculator*, in other words, functioned as a new abstracting category and not simply a term, with profound implications. Overlapping variations arrived, too, in a profusion of terms like *plungers*, *lambs*, *pikers*, and *jobbers*, as did animalistic representations of all stripes, typically to demonize speculators and their effects.[67] "Confidence men" (so named in 1849) also preyed on the anonymity enabled by mass urban crowds and by the increasing urban/rural divide in the United States, as the nameless titular figure of Herman Melville's *The Confidence-Man* (1857) showed.[68]

The speculator thus was appearing in varied guises: a small-town swindler, a land surveyor, a wheat trader, a metropolitan (in many cases, Jewish) banker, even as a speculator in eggs or theater tickets. The age-old fraudster, gambler, and forestaller had both new clothing and new instruments, while figures such as the failed "business man" and the monopolist characterized a mid- and late-nineteenth-century skepticism and pessimism toward speculation's promises, all while more Americans themselves speculated.[69] The ubiquitous figure of the speculator was increasingly an internally variegated type: a configured representation of a set of ideas and practices. Meanwhile, antipathy toward speculators became a political rallying cry, especially for populists. And yet, here again, speculators and speculation were not univocally evil: the westward-moving Americans that John Steinbeck later depicted were also speculators and nomads looking for profit, while the farmers that L. Frank Baum and Frank Norris sought to protect from venomous speculators were themselves speculators, too.[70] They were everywhere, the central protagonists of modern finance-driven capitalism and not the figures Adam Smith had to recharacterize: But who were they? That is, a dialectical and somewhat paradoxical tension became apparent in the late nineteenth century and transformed this moment in the history of speculation. Speculators were both abstract figures and living, named people.[71] They were ideological stand-ins and identifiable humans: immaterial and yet always material. They could be male or female, as we have seen in the two previous chapters, and the processes by which they became both abstract and concrete were part and parcel of the changes in how speculation was being understood as a concept. Boethius and Benjamin Rush, as it were, had been modernized by speculation's intersection with the technologies and instruments of contemporary markets.

The simultaneous abstraction and concreteness thus characterized the signature speculative domain from roughly 1865 to 1905: commodities. Therein we find an uncanny return to questions about the materiality of speculation that preoccupied thinkers for millennia, and this turn in the conceptual history of speculation captures a great deal of foregoing intellectual energy when we combine it with the history of the ticker in this moment. Whereas speculation had been condemned primarily in moralistic terms for centuries, a new logic began to prevail in the late 1800s, one that was sourced in the abstracting power of speculation as a bet on the immaterial qualities of material goods. Commodities were (and remain) at once everyday consumable goods—corn, oil, cotton—and speculative objects for financiers who will never consume, touch, or use them, needing them instead only for their conceptual functions, we might say. In an instance of what Marx called the "double form" of the commodity (use-value and exchange-value), wheat—a staple grain for millennia—was by the late 1800s also a wildly fluctuating commodity. As Jonathan Levy notes, for instance, "In 1888, American farmers harvested 415 million bushels of wheat . . . [while]

some 25,000 trillion bushels of wheat sold in futures contracts in the United States... were set off, never delivered."[72] What exactly *was* being traded? Where was the wheat, in the end? Furthermore, as Frank Norris's novels famously illustrated, farming was now subject both to the weather patterns and mismanagement that had always affected it and to the vicissitudes of risky, seemingly immaterial bets and trades made far away by unknown persons, creating what was popularly called, in an updated version of Defoe's "Air-Money," "wind wheat." ("The world's food should not be at the mercy of the Chicago wheat pit," says Charles Cressler in *The Pit* [1903], after he sees his "immense fortune vanish... like a whiff of smoke," in a speculation.[73]) Speculators were the purest gamblers in the most solid and sustaining commodities.

Many legal and moral arguments against speculation in this moment thus were grounded in questions of materiality and ontology: "investments" delivered tangible goods and assets, or dividends and cash, whereas "speculation" traded only ideas and in a world of imagination untethered from hard reality, especially when executed via tickers.[74] Speculation was a double sin: a sin of idleness and a sin against materiality, now committed by unindividuated persons through their bets on imaginary future outcomes. (An advertisement in the popular magazine *McClure's* from 1905 captured this common logic by asking: "Have you idle money?—EMPLOY it—Get interest and safety. Don't speculate. Be content with fair interest."[75]) Invested money *works*, whereas speculative money tries to cheat its way into the future.[76] Or, as Urs Stäheli theorizes it, speculation "convert[s] its economic referents into a play of self-generated signs, abstracted from the 'real' values previously considered to underwrite the substance of economic operations" in a market that exhibits a constant "process of rigorous self-referential abstraction."[77] That is, the value of material goods could consist only in what the wildest, most "subjective" financiers were willing to pay for it, all in a game of self-reference removed even from the putative rationality of *homo economicus*. Money can produce the idea of more money, which is then gambled on an unknown future asset, which can then generate more money, and so on ad infinitum, never fearing that the underlying asset could run out, as grains necessarily could and would.

The consequences of these processes for the extended considerations of speculation were clear to a number of theorists, especially in the Marxist tradition.[78] Just as these topics surfaced in naturalist and Gilded Age novels, abstraction, double abstraction, and meta-abstraction also became important theoretical underpinnings of the aesthetics of modernism, postmodernism, and more, both for figures at the turn of the twentieth century and into the present. What we can note here is that even aesthetic movements *as such* in this time became new kinds of speculative objects.[79] That is, speculation had long been a part of aesthetic production, whether in the cognitive sense (speculative contemplation leads to creative works) or in the financial sense (the wealthy had commissioned art "on spec"). But the new velocity, volume, and nature of commodity speculation that the late nineteenth and early twentieth century witnessed had analogous effects on how aesthetic movements themselves appeared to coteries and general publics alike. For instance, as Laura Meixner recounts, impressionist paintings arrived in the US precisely at the moment in 1889 of a raging debate on whether and how to tax aesthetic objects. (The United States had slapped 30 percent tariffs on imported art in retaliation for a ban in France on U.S. pork.[80]) French painters saw Gilded Age collectors as what we would now call angel investors and convinced them to gamble on culture and prestige, thereby making art a speculative good in new ways. Impressionism—that hazy, ethereal, speculative brand of painting—thus arrived in America as a speculative commodity that, to the surprise of many, also commented on its own speculative qualities through its depictions of commodities like wheat or even urban real estate.

The same was true several decades later as the modernist movement rose to prominence. In 1916, the new journal *Art World* lamented in a pair of editorial headlines that "Modernism and Politics Play Havoc with Art." Readers were warned not to follow the path of "art speculators and corrupt dealers" who had been "misled by the noise made in the press by the modernistic party in Paris," where buyers "gambled on the future value of their creations as they might gamble in wheat and pork."[81] One could purchase contracts for corn futures, that is, and in the next room over, effectively purchase art futures. The degraded condition that modernism represented occurred in the overlapping spheres of modern markets, where art auctions in France operated like commodities exchanges in Chicago, and vice versa—and where media hype and insider whispers drove wild fluctuations in both price and prestige. The editors of *Art World* could only have recoiled a few years later when a leading British art critic urged speculators to "BUY modern Pictures and Make MONEY," arguing that they were actually a safe investment "for the collector of moderate means who wants oil paintings that are cheap now and likely to increase in value."[82] Claude McKay's *Harlem: Negro Metropolis* (1940) made even more explicit links between the New Negro movement in Harlem and the soaring real estate prices of the neighborhood, noting that "even solid real estate values were affected by the fluid idealistic art values of Harlem."[83] Taking such logic to an extreme, creators like Joyce, Duchamp, and Proust tried to become versions of speculative objects themselves, asking patrons to place wild bets on them.[84] Here, as economics and aesthetics entwined across this period, *speculation* seemed to express anew its age-old tensions between idea and practice, materiality and immateriality, abstract and concrete, present and future brought upon by a technological and media ecology revolution.

THE SPECULATIVE FICTIONAL FUTURE

With these historical and conceptual pieces in place—developments in commodities markets, the ticker and other technologies of futurity, the new languages of prophecy and prediction, the threats and dangers of gendered nonexpertise, the increasing traction of economics as a science, and the many fictional plots involving economic abstraction—we can now plot a critical new turn in *speculation* in the late nineteenth and early twentieth centuries: *speculative fiction*. Both popular mythology and the *Oxford English Dictionary* credit the science fiction writer Robert Heinlein with defining that term in 1953, when he claimed that "the term 'speculative fiction' may be defined negatively as being fiction about things that have not happened"—a definition he laid out after having used the term for at least half a dozen years already.[85] That may be so, but in fact the turn of the century had already witnessed the consistent attachment of *speculation* to this well-known and well-defined genre of writing. A literary review from 1902, for instance, writes of H. G. Wells that "in his 'Anticipations,' [Wells] has set rolling the ball of speculation as to the future. There are now other Richmonds in the field. Speculating amongst them are some speculating largely upon the future of literature. Jules Verne, the writer of many speculative stories, comes to the front with the prediction that the time will come when the novel will be altogether supplanted by the newspaper."[86] Several years later, a magazine refers to Wells's "speculative novels" as a well-established characterization.[87]

It should not surprise us, then, that a great number of works of speculative fiction from the late 1800s and early 1900s hinge crucially on plots and readings of financial speculation of some type, much like the many titles we saw in the previous chapter. That is to say, the "speculative" as applied to them is meant to be polysemous. This is true of many of Jules Verne's works, including *The Castles of California* (1852), *From the Earth to the Moon* (1865), *The Begum's Millions* (1879), *The Will of an Eccentric* (1900), and *Paris in the Twentieth Century* (written in 1863, published in 1994), in which economic speculation is often a central motive. In this final novel, we even see "literature" created from stock market quotations. This pattern is apparent, too, in Wells's *Tono-Bungay* (1908): as Nicky Marsh writes of that novel, "The counterfeit illusory money produced and required by speculation in the novel undermines and replaces the sanctity of gold, upon which Britain's exhausted old order had depended. Teddy Pondevero's participation in the rapid expansion of an unsubstantiated form of commercial speculation eventually destroys the very thing—gold and the class system— that made it possible."[88] And, in many other contexts, the nature of speculation by this time fosters much wordplay in these novels. In Wells's *The Time Machine* (1905), when the Time Traveller returns and fears his story will be doubted, he is forthright: "I cannot expect you to believe it. Take it as a lie—or a prophecy. Say I dreamed it in the workshop. Consider I have been speculating upon the destinies of our race until I have hatched this fiction."[89]

Even in the more biological, naturalist vein of speculative fiction, we see a similar pattern and even a fixation on *speculation* as a term. In Edward Bulwer-Lytton's *The Coming Race* (1871), the economic world has been regulated to the point that "there are no hazardous speculations, no emulators striving for superior wealth and rank," and as a corollary, "all theological speculations, though not forbidden, have been so discouraged as to have fallen utterly into disuse."[90] Edward Bellamy's *Looking Backward* (1887) imagined a future year 2000 in which government planning had eliminated all insecurity and contingency in human affairs, including the threats of speculation. Or, to make the point on another kind of literal level, from a few decades later: Thomas Temple Hoyne starts his career as an economic writer and publishes *Speculation: Its Sound Principles and Rules for Its Practice*, in 1922. Here he asserts a defense of speculation as a viable and meaningful mode of future creation. By 1934, he is a futuristic-dystopian novelist who publishes *Intrigue on the Upper Level* (1934), a book about Chicago in 2050 A.D. in a desolate, divided world run by speculators. We often think of the spate of speculative fiction in this era as responding to advances in machine technology, and thus feeding the origins of science fiction's version of futurity in particular.[91] But the catch is that we rarely see those technologies at work: the fantastic but barely described Time Machine of Wells's novel is a perfect example. Speculative ideas themselves—the futuristic forecasts that underlie speculation—*are* the technologies.

Speculation is by now far from belonging to an immanently human domain, as it had been for centuries, and instead is initiated by machine technologies through which futures come into being, even machines as simple as a ticker. And, as we saw above, the world of future speculation that late nineteenth-century speculative fictions are recasting was *already* performing multilayered abstractions and dematerializations in the present. There are several ways we can understand the relationship between economic speculation and speculative fiction, but perhaps most useful for our purposes here is the idea that authors are taking two key elements of speculation from the 1860s and 1870s—its being machine-driven and the future-projective power of speculative abstraction—and converting them into technological futures via theories of risk.[92]

The swelling genre of speculative fiction, in the end, did not *need* to establish itself with "hard science," not even the kind of science in which economics itself was gaining traction. In fact, a number of other emergent domains of knowledge production were in this same moment partnered with established hard sciences also called "speculative." In particular, the fields where the scientific revolutions of the early 1900s were most pronounced were routinely labeled "speculative," such as what is now generally called "theoretical physics," and they shared much overlap with the genre of speculative fiction. As Stephen Ross notes, "speculation" was actually the "default mode of research" in fields like early psychoanalysis.[93] There, Freud's theories were commonly deemed "speculative" because their insights were not based on directly observable (in this case, external) empirical data. Einstein himself declared that there can be "no empirical method without speculative concepts and systems."[94] Max Planck said of Einstein's theories in 1909 that "this new conception of the idea of time makes the most serious demands upon the capacity of abstraction and the projective power of the physicist. It surpasses in boldness everything previously suggested in speculative natural philosophy."[95] One needs very little speculative power to imagine what validation a speculative fiction writer would find in such a statement. Speculative fiction has tapped and popularized *speculation*'s history to push back against the power of mastery and deterministic prophecy, to instead recall the term's invocation of the unknown chances of futurity. In that, it mingles with the world of human-created risks, pervasive mass speculation, and the social consequences of speculation as a condition of collective life.

Tickers had altered the way humans thought and interacted with one another to create the future, and had thereby altered what "speculators" themselves had become. And tickers' effects raised new questions of social access and inequality. In one account from 1887, we read that, in countless homes, "fathers and sons, or mothers with a son or daughter, just taking an eye-opener in the great world of business, stand side by side at the tickers. If fortune favors for the moment, they laugh and cackle and build castles in the air. More often they are depressed with gloom, or, if women, wring their hands in terror as they see their money disappear. What a school to initiate the young into the mysteries of gambling!"[96] Furthermore, the wide and cheap availability of tickers made them staples of the thriving bucket-shop industry. In 1879, the *Chicago Tribune* declared of bucket shops that "no broker is necessary, any person, man or woman, boy or girl, white, black, yellow or bronze can deal directly."[97] But bucket shops were known to be full of deceit: "The fraud, cheat and swindle are so transparent that it seems to be a libel upon common intelligence to admit that these establishments do an immense business every day."[98] Women who are "wives and mothers of families in comfortable financial condition"—not at all "desperate or questionable condition"—have fallen prey to them, too, it turns out.[99] Newspaper accounts reported that "women . . . gamblers" now "feverishly eye the ticker" all day, losing sight of anything else.[100] And meanwhile, an educated class of white women, by the late 1920s, had become successful enough on Wall Street to become the first of what the writer Eunice Fuller Barnard profiled memorably as the "ladies of the ticker."[101] The social difference and necessity for critique around and through speculation would only grow, as will be seen when we turn to the ways in which the conditions of speculation itself become paramount.

6

THE LADY SPECULATOR

The female character is, in many respects, suited to a life of speculation. Speculation is founded on hope, and women are generally remarkably prone to hope. Speculation requires patience and fortitude, which are, or should be, both womanly virtues. Speculation derives its food from excitement, and women often feed on excitement. Speculation comes from fancy, and women are much given to fancy. Women of a certain type, are naturally, or by education, inclined to speculate in stocks.
—WILLIAM WORTHINGTON FOWLER,
TEN YEARS IN WALL STREET (1870)

Manias, frenzies, fevers, panics, hysterias: the discourse of the embodied passions that we saw transform *speculation* several times has a series of gendered implications.[1] The same is true of the discourse of mastery and competence that led to entrusted expertise for forecasting the future through speculation. And Thoreau was explicit about the privileges of speculating as a white man. All this is part of the broader story of women and speculation. At the onset of the financial revolution, male investors and writers bemoaned the fickle inconstancy of "Lady Credit" and nicknamed the Bank of England the "Old Lady of Threadneedle Street." Daniel Defoe called Lady Credit "despotickly" in her "Actions," and held that "if you court her, you lose her, or must buy her unreasonable Rates," all the while accepting the risk that, in an instant, she could be "gone, and perhaps never come again as long as you live."[2] That is, even while economics was said to have sober, reasoned (male) judgment at its core, most everyone acknowledged that to gamble on stocks or on speculative ventures, one had to court the intemperate whims of opinion, fancy, and desire. In J. G. A. Pocock's words, "production and exchange" themselves were "regularly equated with the ascendancy of the passions and the female principle."[3] By speculating, men risked playing a game that was apparently feminized, and that could thereby feminize them in the process. We even find a similarly gendered pattern of thought in the recharacterization of speculation as a mindless, mob-like behavior. Charles Mackay's *Memoirs* features not only portraits of witches, female sorcerers, and bloodthirsty women crusaders, but also scenes centered on crazed "mob[s] of women," or "a number of hysterical women and weak-minded persons of all descriptions."[4] His expanded edition of 1852 added "the Madness of Crowds" to its titular topics, now drawing upon the emergent idea that, as Gustave Le Bon would put it, "crowds are everywhere distinguished by feminine characteristics."[5] In putatively different contexts, Ralph Waldo Emerson still noted that the clergy, or "speculative men," around him were constantly "addressed as women."[6]

Feminized men who speculate, women who speculate in mad mobs: these circumstances raised a set of questions for cultural commentators everywhere, questions that bear on the history of speculation that we have considered thus far. Were women—by their supposed intuitions or their inability to think dispassionately—actually *more* naturally "suited" to speculation, as the Wall Street ethnographer William Worthington Fowler claimed? Or would their susceptibility to passions and their weak powers of judgment make speculation a doubly disastrous practice for them? And what did women's purportedly privileged yet restricted access to the worlds of economic speculation mean for the concept of speculation? To answer these questions, we need to retrace some elements of the gendered history of speculation, then to chart how speculation took yet another dramatic turn. Not only were women seen to embody (literally) a number of the traits that men argued were endemic to speculating, they also lived in and pivotally shaped the worlds that *speculation* schematized as a connected set of ideations and behaviors.[7]

Male speculators are mostly easy to identify, and their roles in the cultural and political histories of this moment are typically visible. Female speculators have been less studied, yet their role animates this chapter in the history of the concept and practices of speculation. What we see at first glance is a rather narrow portrait crafted primarily by men, but with the aid of powerful female voices, too. When perceived as stepping into the fields of financial risk, women were typologized as impulsive, addicted, and sexually licentious, at once hyperfeminine and overly masculine. But *female speculators*, by the mid-nineteenth century, ultimately could not simply indicate economic, or specifically financial, women actors. At this point in our history, we have an astounding variety of speculations: divine, idle, immaterial, experimental, fanciful, impractical, practical, projective, gambling, plaintive, maniacal, individual, collective, and more. Women, and women writers in particular, have been refashioning speculation throughout its history, and that topic alone could fill another library. Once we start to unpack this history, we find a series of transformations by which *speculation* is expanded from the economic realm, largely through novelistic discourse, into a multifaceted, multifunctional term that lays the groundwork for the modes of social critique that remain significant well beyond women's thought and writing. This begins in the work of Eliza Haywood, Jane Austen, and George Eliot, where speculation is concerned not with moral judgment, medical diagnosis, psychological conditions, or national fortunes, even if it incorporates many elements of what preceded it. Instead, in this context the term assesses unequal social conditions and women's positions, especially in the imbalanced and asymmetrical "marriage speculations" of the nineteenth century, with the history of allusions to Calvinism and to mania all in tow.

The roots of this specific development in speculation are in the figure of the female gambler. Over time, the financialization of everyday life, especially as depicted in novels, became the grounds for transforming *speculation* into this potent watchword in critical thought. The term still looks toward the future, re-creating the life-shaping prospect of marriage into a reading of women's intellectual trajectories and of a minoritized position of speculation that resonates for multiple groups in the present. Thus, what began as a seemingly narrow economic consideration, with men fixated on the degraded bodies of women gamblers, actually opens up to the current aspirational, liberating model of reconsidering social circumstances through speculation. Rather than the expert men who were presumed to master information and balance the future, it was the challenging women—whether in novels or on Wall Street—who laid the groundwork for recasting the ideological, technological, and embodied effects of speculative futurity in contemporary capitalism. We can use this analysis, and all that it ties together, to rewind speculation's course through philosophical and financial modernity and finally arrive at the schisms and conflicts within the concept that define its present state.

GAMBLING WOMEN

Women had to speculate, but they did so at their own peril. If we return to the 1600s, and to the adjectives that most often accompanied *speculation* in Calvinist discourse (*idle* and *vain*), we can see immediately that they were also qualities that women were particularly admonished to avoid developing. Women, in short, were assumed to be overly susceptible to what speculation engendered, and they were even charged and jailed in the 1640s (if not earlier) for being "idle."[8] Texts like Bathsua Makin's *Essay to Revive the Antient Education of Gentlewomen*

(1673) featured stern warnings to women that "God... will take an account for every idle thought, will certainly reckon with those Persons that shall spend their whole lives in idle play and chat. Poor Women will make but a lame excuse at the last day for their vain lives."[9] The language of the burgeoning and often-contested cult of domesticity pointed clearly to the dangers of vanity, idleness, and undisciplined financial habits for women. Lady Masham warned in her *Occasional Thoughts in Reference to a Vertuous and Christian Life* (1705) that it was "very preposterous for a Woman to employ her Time in enquiries, or speculations not necessary for her," while Hannah Woolley's guide to womanhood, the *Gentlewomans Companion* (1675), advised married women about their husbands: "Be careful to manage what money he doth trust you with, to his and your own credit; abuse not the freedom you have of his purse, by being too lavish;... [nor] throw away that money in buying trifles, which shall evidence your vanity as well as luxury."[10] If women were especially vulnerable to all that speculation named, the controls on their imaginations and their spending alike had to be enforced severely.

But one thing is clear: women speculated everywhere, and their speculations operated both within and against the patterns of feminized-male behavior that dominated new markets. And women were in a variety of impossible situations: married women, for example, usually could not accrue debts of their own, yet had to assume their husbands' debts. They were bought and sold as sexual objects but could not own or trade upon their sexuality legally. They were expected to shop for and maintain a financially stable interior of the domestic unit, and the consumption-driven economy enabled them to influence markets with their purchasing power and habits, yet they were presumed ignorant of money matters.[11]

Men feared and lamented the effects of women as speculators, and thus we see their anxiety about what speculating women meant for the meaning of speculation per se. Allan Ramsay's "The Rise and Fall of Stocks" (1720) claimed that "stock-jobbing" and "project[ing]" appeals to "baith sexes, of a' sorts and sizes," but would turn women in particular into "harlots." The financial revolution, he claims, had made women into corrupt, money-hungry frauds; the desire for speculating spreads like a "pox," indeed like a venereal disease ("a clap"), transmitting through "banks built in the air."[12] Ramsay was not alone in his dire assessment; others feared that women's participation in the stock market would tempt them toward idleness and the neglect of their household duties. Joseph Addison had warned in the *Spectator* that "Publick Credit" was "a beautiful virgin seated on a throne of gold" who would "wither into a skeleton" upon learning of bad economic news.[13] Women were blamed for the South Sea Bubble because they accounted for a large percentage of the stock's subscribers (which was, we recall, understood as a mode of gambling).[14] Jonathan Swift's poem "The Journal of a Modern Lady" (1728) wondered about the "superstitious whims" that "fill a female gamester's pate."[15] With similar language, Alexander Pope bemoaned the imagined woman "Fufidia," a thieving personification of interest rates equated to a "pox," and he lamented during the South Sea stock's rise that "the ladies are much richer than I" while arguing that "ev'ry Woman is at heart a Rake."[16] One writer asked bluntly, "What will not a female gamester do for money?," while the priest and author William Dodd asked, "Who in their right senses would take a Female Gamester to their family and embraces?"[17] (Dodd himself, we might note, was a debtor, gambler, and forger who would be hanged in 1777.) Men could not bear either the mental or (imagined) bodily effects of women speculators.

Yet, in the new markets of the late 1600s and early 1700s, women—especially unmarried women—faced fewer barriers to participation than one might expect, even if the regimes policing their behaviors as investors, speculators, gamblers, and many other types of financial actors were strict once they began.[18] John Carswell and Catherine Ingrassia have both shown that women owned around 20 percent of most major bond and bank funds in this period.[19] In particular, Ingrassia notes, "Women held 16.6 percent of Bank [of England] stock in 1709, a percentage that rose steadily to 20.7 percent in 1724 and 25.4 percent in 1744."[20] By the 1840s, nearly half of all public creditors were women, who were also major investors and speculators in canal and railway schemes. Few of them were married, and most were spinsters or widows, or "feme sole" traders.[21] And in the mid-1800s, a stream of investing guides specifically for women appeared. The pattern was similar in the United States. Original bank subscriptions were around 5–10 percent women-owned in the early republic, with government bonds at a similar rate, and both grew steadily over time.[22] Women generally held 10–15 percent of bank stocks, and in some banks, that number was as high as 38.5 percent, while some bond-holding proportions were even higher.[23] The newspaper coverage of scripomania in Philadelphia mentioned women investors consistently, while the legislator William Findley of Pennsylvania wrote of the Bank of the United States and the American financial system just after the exposure of William Duer's scheming that "even the speculating ladies complain of having been injured by their dependence on the success of this plan, for ladies were then speculators."[24] Reports from the Paris Bourse similarly accounted for the means by which "imagination was lost in regions of imaginary riches," so much that "dexterous female speculators, tormented by the desire of gaining," were now found everywhere.[25] Feminists like Mary Astell argued that women were the more prudent managers of money—a familial role that they increasingly took on during the first industrial revolution.[26] All these financial risks were considered *gambles* to some degree, and when they were taken by women, they were deemed speculations (rather than "investments") in many cases.

How did speculation transform women, then? In *The Guardian*, Joseph Addison and Richard Steele worried at length, in very typical language, about the "ill consequences which Gaming has on the bodies of our Female adventurers": "Hollow Eyes, haggard Looks, and pale Complexions, are the natural indications of a Female gamester. . . . In short, I never knew a thorough-paced Female gamester hold her beauty two winters together."[27] The bodily destruction that gaming brought about, such moralists argue, is intensified in women. They decay rapidly, their bodies unable to withstand the inherently ravaging effects of what we'd likely now recognize as gambling addiction—here imagined as gaming in general. Spending money on nothing, nonproductively, is idle self-destruction. Thomas Mortimer's revised *Every Man His Own Broker* (1781) even argued that "ignorance, joined to a propensity for gaming, become of late years a female passion, renders [women] dupes of Stock-jobbing brokers."[28] *The Guardian* warned that "the man that plays beyond his income pawns his estate; the woman must find out something else to mortgage when her pin-money is gone: the husband has his lands to dispose of, the wife her person."[29] Some women were suspected of witchcraft when their financial gambles paid off.[30]

The consequences of speculation as a mania that we saw before seem fully concentrated in women's lives as financial risk-takers. But even key figures in the history of feminism agreed at least partially with the predominant social admonitions. Eliza Haywood feared that gaming and stock speculation had, especially since the South Sea Bubble, put England and its women on a path to ruin.[31] Mary Wollstonecraft—the daughter of a failed speculator, and one-time romantic partner of the speculative debtor Gilbert Imlay—affirmed "the baleful effect of extensive speculations on the moral character," and she claimed that "virtue is not to be acquired even by speculation, much less by the negative supineness that wealth naturally generates."[32] Conduct manuals warned women to "lay no wagers with gentlemen, and have no philopenas with them.... No delicate and refined female ever bets at all. It is a very coarse and masculine way of asserting an opinion or a belief; and always reminds gentlemen of the race-course, or the gaming-table."[33] And yet courts, casinos, and clubs often welcomed them with tacit approval, and the games leveled their odds and negated any value of expertise or insider knowledge that men could wield.

The famed diarist Harriet Arbuthnot offers a window into the prevailing mentalities of this milieu in March 1825, just before a panic that year would become nearly fatal to the Bank of England:

> The House & the whole country seem now completely occupied with the different speculations set on foot in the City. There are companies set on foot of all kinds, such as Mexican, Peruvian, Brazilian mining companies; & such is the rage for speculation & the abundance of money from the high price of the funds, that large premiums may be gained upon any speculation that is brought out.... Many of these Companies will no doubt end in smoke & many foolish persons will

be ruined; . . . [by] this speculating mania, [because] all the companies are bubbles invented for stockjobbing purposes & [and] there will be a *general crash*. . . . I am very fond of these speculations & shd *gamble* greatly in them if I could, but Mr. Arbuthnot does not like them & will not allow me to have any of the American ones as their value depends upon political events.[34]

For Arbuthnot, the opprobrium of speculation's ties to gambling is something to embrace. The "rage" and "mania" for speculation that she sees around her *is* the future she wants to help shape, one in which these frenzied spirits can be harnessed and trammeled for purpose and profit.[35] Like Emerson, she envisions a public good in speculations—rise or fall—and she links these South American speculations to "political events" and their inherent volatility. Gambling, as we have seen and as Arbuthnot again indicates, was at once illicit and socially accepted (even fashionable), immoral and benignly amusing, depending on a variety of shifting contexts, and despite sensationalist accounts of the "Faro ladies" in the 1790s, for instance.[36] Gambling's social milieus required a level of trust and security, just as the world of private credit and stock markets did; gambling also threw a light upon the elements of chance, luck, fortune, control, providence, and a host of irrational and untamable forces that bore upon daily life in the wake of the financial revolution.

Arbuthnot *wants* to be the female gamester that was robustly warned against and condemned—and she was not alone in that desire. She only runs into a wall when her husband disapproves. On the conceptual level, Arbuthnot sees financial, behavioral, and intellectual autonomy as one unit, all bound together by the polyvalence of *speculation*, a term she is now turning back *against* the many castigations and warnings that had employed it against women. Arbuthnot seems to want to participate in the mania, to harness its fever for her own fortune, and she is only thwarted by a patriarchal marriage system and its hierarchies of financial decision-making. (If she were a spinster, that is, she could gamble more freely.) What she voices here reverberates when we plot it against the developments in literature across more than a century.

THE FEMALE GAMESTER AND THE NOVEL

Given what she articulates, Arbuthnot would also have been the perfect heroine or narrator for a novel in her moment. Diaries like hers were not public, and financial journalism was dominated by men, but the novel offered women a new space to communicate and adapt such "plots." Women's speculations motivated many novels and informed the vocabulary of plot, character, and readership in crucial ways. A number of scholars have examined the shared fundamental premises of novels and of investments, speculations, and gambles, relying as they all do on notions of faith, credulity, and unknown future prospects.[37] More specifically, Catherine Gallagher has reassessed the ties among reading, women's social circumstances, and the senses of *speculation* that we have been tracing within this matrix of texts and concepts.[38] The rhetoric of speculation and the more general language of novels as a whole often overlapped.[39] The term *adventure*, for instance, appears in the titles and subtitles of many works in the mid-1700s, at which time it was also a close relative to *project* and, later, *speculation*. The symbiotic relationship between speculators—especially women speculators—and a novelistic tradition ranged from the traveling merchant at the outset of Margaret Cavendish's *The Blazing-World* (1666) to Bathsheba Everdene in Hardy's *Far from the Madding Crowd* (1874). And beyond novels in particular, we can see instances like Aphra Behn's identification, via her initials, with her character Angellica Bianca, a prostitute who must sell herself, as a proxy for women's work within the new domains of commercial literature.[40]

The "female gamester," whom a number of scholars have recently studied, was therefore equally as pronounced a figure in novels as she was in the markets, encapsulating the "speculative" qualities described above. Jessica Richard follows Frances Burney's Cecilia, for instance, through her series of "private credit relationships," observing that "the female gambler displays a passion for play that is physically disfiguring, her absorption in play supplants her attention to lover, husband, or children and her play inevitably leads her to pay her play debts with sexual favors."[41] Similarly, Defoe's figuration of Lady Credit in his financial journalism has much in common with his protagonists Moll Flanders and Roxana. In an exemplary moment in *Moll Flanders* (1722), the passage of time in the narrative discloses the fictional inflation of the value of real estate as if "air-money" were operating upon it: as she learns the art of scamming, Moll Flanders realizes that she can "turn . . . [her] Tale" and inflate the value of plots of land or plantations in Virginia or in Ireland.[42] Defoe's heroine embodies the economic world of the Projecting Age, all in service of Defoe's effort to make the novel simultaneously a mode of economic writing.

Male characters and narrators in novels of the first half of the 1700s, moreover, often refer to their romantic pursuit of a woman as a "project." Novelists like Mary Davys filled their books with "Projects," too. Thus, a figure like the titular character in Sarah Fielding's *The Adventures of David Simple* (1744) confesses, all in one fell swoop, to a series of failed schemes in which he attempted to manipulate a "Set of *Sharpers*," played at the *"Gaming-Table,"* "endeavoured to cheat" a "Gentleman," failed to pay debts, and hatched a "Scheme" to "follow Women, for their *Money*, instead of their *Persons*," before he eventually became "weary of this *Project*."[43] In Defoe's *Roxana* (1724), however, his narrator is blunter: the novel is filled with suitors who make a "Project of coming to-Bed to me," which Roxana—who was carried as an infant from France to England alongside *"French* Brandy, Paper, and other Goods"—turns herself into her own speculative project by arguing "that the Favour of Lying with a Whore was equal, not to the thousand Pistoles only, but to all the Debt I owed him, for saving my Life, and all my Effects."[44] Here, Defoe's novels, both written just after the South Sea Bubble, bring to fictional life a version of the figure of a mercurial, unstable Lady Credit, not in the new economic sectors opened up by the financial revolution but in the markets for marriage and sex. Pocock identifies the Roman goddess Fortuna as the often-invoked ancestor of Lady Credit, who had to be tamed and mastered by men; it is in this vein that Defoe calls Roxana in his subtitle "the Fortunate Mistress." Defoe aimed to have it both ways: women themselves could be excellent and upright projectors and speculators, were they not limited by barriers of education and access. Roxana, as both speculator and commodity herself, notes that men "raise the

Value of the Object which they pretend to pitch upon, by their Fancy"; it is only by their own fault that men "purchase their own destruction."[45]

But all the while, women writers had been building a tradition of "speculation" in multiple genres that would eventually flourish in the nineteenth-century novel *through* but *beyond* the female gamester figure, and here we can start to sense the conceptual turns at play. A foundational starting point is Eliza Haywood's periodical *The Female Spectator* (1744–1746), whose very title announced its challenge to Addison and Steele (see chapter 2). Part of its bold statement is a declaration in the first issue—with the same language of spectatorship, speculation, and spying that we saw in *The Spectator*—that "it is highly proper I should acquaint the town, that to secure an eternal fund of intelligence, spies are placed, not only in all the places of resort in and about this great metropolis, but at *Bath, Tunbridge,* and the *Spaw*, and means found out to extend my speculations even as far as *France, Rome, Germany,* and other foreign parts, so that nothing curious or worthy of remark can escape me." Haywood's idea was that a panoptic female spectator would uncover "all the secrets of *Europe*," too, as if she had "the power of invisibility" to become an unseen watcher.[46] She explained in a later issue, too, that "as the principal design of these speculations is, therefore, to correct those errors in the mind, which are most imperceptible, and for that reason the most dangerous, such examples are not set down but with a view of shewing how the want of a proper way of thinking in our youth involves our whole future lives in misfortunes, which frequently no reflection can afterwards retrieve."[47] Like Addison, she links speculation and mental correctives to a sense of futurity and fortune—the idea that right seeing (visual comprehension) is a key to future good favor of some type. She continued by arguing that the "power of contemplation and reflection" is what "chiefly distinguishes the *human* from the *brute* creation," and that humans had privileged access—no matter their condition—to "divine contemplation."[48] Haywood is recuperating a sense of speculation and contemplation as paired faculties that combine the sensorial (visual) and the cognitive to access truths and insights beyond the phenomenal world—and, in this case, unique to a *female* vision.

In such work, Haywood is synthesizing multiple traditions of women's speculative and contemplative thought that contemporary scholars have traced from Julian of Norwich and St. Teresa of Ávila to Mary Wollstonecraft and Virginia Woolf. We can see how writers like Margaret Cavendish, for instance, created figures like the titular heroine of her play *Lady Contemplation* (1662), who is solitary and lost in imaginative worlds. Cavendish consistently championed "contemplation," and she laid out its role in the cognitive chain in her *Sociable Letters* (1664): "Contemplation brings Consideration, Consideration brings Judgment, Judgment brings Reason, Reason brings Truth, Truth brings Peace; also Consideration brings Conception, Conception brings Fancy, Fancy brings Wit, and Wit brings Delight."[49] And like Defoe, Haywood put her arguments into novel form in various ways, as when the eponymous protagonist Betsy Thoughtless is skeptical of the "designs" that Miss Flora "pretended in this project, though of what nature it could be was not in [Betsy's] power to conceive."[50] Betsy herself, however, spends her time "ruminating on projects, which had neither virtue nor generosity for their patrons."[51] Speculation and projection became important figurative concepts for authors, too. Anne Radcliffe's *The Mysteries of Udolpho* (1794) is both full of "projects" and highly symbolic "projecting rock[s]" in several pivotal scenes, a conceit Radcliffe also employs with cliffs and precipices in *A Sicilian Romance* (1790).[52]

In time, more female characters began operating at once as speculators (of the type Haywood outlined) and projectors (as gamesters), embodying the multiplicities of speculation in this moment and moving beyond what might appear to be the narrow figure of the female gamester. And this was taking place, as we recall from chapter 3, during a period of intense linguistic transformation of the term *speculation* and its particular new interplay with gambling and capitalism. We can see this in an illustrative scene featuring the titular heroine of Burney's *Camilla* (1796), who comes into a sudden fortune as an heiress and immediately becomes an example of what Andrea Henderson calls a "generous, imaginative speculator."[53] She finds herself surrounded by games, gambling, and lotteries from the very start. Camilla observes a game of chess between Sir Sedley Clarendel and General Kinsale that puzzles her until she starts to comprehend the role of speculation in it. Clarendel spends "at least half an hour contemplating this very move" on which he is certainly going to be checkmated. The general asks him why he can "do no better," to which Clarendel responds that he was "thinking of other things, my dear General," and letting his mind wander—contemplate, speculate.[54] He explains that "those exquisite little moments we steal from any given occupation, for the pleasure of speculating in secret upon something wholly foreign to it, are resistless to deliciousness." When the general's wife demands that he "make [his] speculations public," he claims that he cannot oblige, for "to attempt the least description would be a presumption of the first monstrousness."[55] Now, *speculation* is performing triple labor: it is idle and airy contemplation, scheming (albeit to no avail), and gaming, if not outright gambling. A loose network of women writers, rather than fearing speculation's multitudes as Christopher Anstey did, are finding literary purpose in it to reconfigure social relations and stimulate social critique. The presumed threats of women speculators were now rotating, around the term *speculation*, into commentaries on the implications of women's potential financial and intellectual independence.

Nowhere was this discourse clearer than in writing on marriage, which became the *point de repère* for gathering many strands of argument on and through speculation. Women, Catherine Gallagher writes, had to practice a suspension of disbelief while also holding in mind a certain sense of a plausible future reality that marriage would create, something that novels also demanded of them. Women needed, that is, "to be able to imagine what it would be like to love a particular man without committing themselves, for loving a man before he had proposed was still considered highly improper. As in courtship, so also in commerce," and in politics, in finance, in paper money, and beyond.[56] Women, in other words, had been speculators of another sort for millennia, though with little control. During and after the financial revolution, marriage became a new means of speculating. Putting the multiplicity of *speculation* into pragmatic advice, Maria Edgeworth and Richard Lovell Edgeworth first warn, in the opening chapter of their influential guide *Practical Education* (1798) of "the danger of the passion for gaming," and encourage parents to limit their children's exposure to games of chance. Then, they chide parents "who speculate on their daughters accomplishments" as a means to secure marriages to wealthier men: "But [parents] forget that every body now makes the same reflections, that parents are, and have been for some years, speculating in the same line; consequently, the market is likely to be overstocked, and, of course, the value of the commodities must fall. Every young lady (and every young woman is now a young lady) has some pretensions to accomplishments."[57]

Speaking baldly of the marriage market as an actual stock market, and squarely seeing marriage-age women as commodities of fluctuating value, the Edgeworths argue *not* against the logic of such an equation of marriage and stocks, but against *how* parents play what is an oversaturated market—a buyer's market for men, as it were. Likewise, they hope to instruct young men in how to be good speculators, for they note an "excellent essay on Projects" reveals that "calculation will shew what can be done, and how it can be done; and thus the individual, without injury to himself, may, if he wish it, speculate extensively for the good of his fellow-creatures."[58] Consonant with Emerson's argument regarding the madness of speculators, speculation in the hands of men is theorized as balancing out the ways that women as speculative objects skew the marriage market. Men here are not the seducers of Lady Credit, but rather, must be the rational buyers in a market where values fluctuate as wildly as they did with the South Sea stock. Furthermore, women were warned in Maria Eliza Rundell's widely read *New System of Domestic Cookery* (1802) that "many women are unfortunately ignorant of the state of their husband's income; and others are only made acquainted with it, when some speculative project, or profitable transaction, leads them to make a false estimate of what can be afforded."[59] This is dangerous, she notes, because once married, women are de facto co-speculators with their husbands. Speculation in marriage is neither a matter of willed contemplation nor an addictive phase; it is a forced life-circumstance that *makes* women both speculative objects and speculators—just not the kind that spinsters in bank stocks were. The novel would continue developing plots, narrative voices and devices, and a host of techniques devoted to working out the mechanics of this situation in the early nineteenth century especially, when the speculations of the marriage market would come to dominate several of the genre's conceptual frameworks.

A GAME OF SPECULATION

The fulcrum in this chapter of speculation's history, then, comes in the work of arguably the greatest author of the marriage-plot novel of the era: Jane Austen. Austen, herself the daughter of a successful wool merchant-speculator, draws an emblematic scene in *Mansfield Park* (1814) that comments upon the many conduct manuals, financial articles, and women's novels that preceded her own work. It features several characters gathered at a table to play cards—to gamble in a socially sanctioned atmosphere. Pressured into a "critical situation," to decide on a game, Lady Bertram defers and asks Sir Thomas Bertram to choose which game they will play: Whist—the standby of the leisure class—or a new game called "Speculation"?[60] This game of Speculation first appeared in the late 1700s, and it was one that Austen herself enjoyed so much that she composed a poem about it in one of her letters. It also involved mathematical skills, and for that, it became an object of study for players and for figures like the gaming authority Edmond Hoyle. Hoyle called it a "noisy round game" that relied on memory, patience, and an ability to "calculate[e] the probability of the trump [card] offered proving the highest in the deal then undetermined."[61] The game's name plays on the sense that one is speculating both on the future cards to be revealed and on the bidding war to purchase them, and the new association of speculation with cards surely solidified the concept's links to games of fortune and chance for Charles Mackay. In fact, *through* the game, the term *speculation* became a shorthand for the uncertain, unknown elements of chance, and from there, its metaphorical sense grew. As a popular "comic song" of the 1810s put it, each day one's life is "like a card":

> Only take the trouble just to call imagination,
> You'll find that life completely is a game of speculation. . . .
> Yes, life is a speculation from the cradle to the coffin: the boy speculates in marbles and tops; the lass of sixteen wishes to make a speculation of love, and when too late repents her speculation; the fond youth resolves on a desperate speculation—Gets married, and finds it is a speculation indeed.⁶²

This playfulness of speculation is quite telling: the song reads like a comic version of Mackay's understanding of speculation's deep imbrication in the history of dice games, fortune-telling, and prophecies, all apiece.

Austen taps into this growing polyvalent understanding of *speculation* as central to modern life, across a spectrum of cultural registers, to craft a reading of women, marriage, and property in this moment that we can tease out to see how much work *speculation* could now perform. Sir Thomas decides that the group will indeed play Speculation, and the scheming, charismatic Henry Crawford immediately realizes that he will not only be "in charge of all [Lady Bertram's] fame and fortune through the whole evening," but also that he has an opportunity to affect Fanny Price—to "sharpen her avarice, and harden her heart," though thus far he seems to be failing.⁶³ Fanny "had never played the game nor seen it played in her life," Austen writes, but the rest of the group insists "it was the easiest game on the cards"; Fanny then "feel[s] herself mistress of the rules of the game in three minutes."⁶⁴ The language by which Austen aligns the game of Speculation with the marriage market is clear, and quickly, the novel begins working out its own plot mechanics through the game. The conversation that ensues as the characters play the game concerns the upkeep, cost, and renovation of estates such as Thornton Lacey, including the would-be projector Henry's "scheme"—which indulges "agreeable fancies"—"to enhance the value of such a situation in point of privilege and independence beyond all calculation."⁶⁵ Meanwhile, in the card game, we find Sir Thomas making a "capital play" and Miss Crawford securing a "knave at an exorbitant rate" simply to make a point.⁶⁶ Finally, and rather abruptly, Austen notes of Mary Crawford that "all the agreeable of *her* speculation was over for that hour. It was time to have done with cards, if sermons prevailed; and she was glad to find it necessary to come to a conclusion, and be able to refresh her spirits by a change of place and neighbour."⁶⁷

Fanny's speculations are apparently limited both by the fast pace of the game and by others' conversational dominance. But beyond all the economic terms, Austen is also employing an enlarged sense of the form of *speculation* that we saw in Haywood: Fanny is a "female spectator," an internal observer and contemplator of a social milieu and its market dynamics in miniature before her. And if speculation is a practice of aiming to profit purely on amplified fictional value, it throws a highly unstable variable into the estate and dowry plots that Austen constantly picks apart. Its economic sense is powerful but conceptually impoverished. The novel features speculations ranging from Maria Ward's boost to her fortunes through marriage (recounted in the novel's opening lines) to Tom Bertram's gambling debts, to William Price's throwing away "speculations upon prize-money" on horse races. Amid all this, Fanny Price, the aptly surnamed woman speculator who nevertheless refuses to be enthralled by the game, manages not to have "*her* speculation" cut off abruptly or against her will; she achieves this by waiting out Edmund Bertram's dual realization of her "growing worth" and "mental superiority" at the end of the novel.⁶⁸ Austen's portrait of speculation seems to take every available sense of the word at the time—from contemplation to cards—and to spin them into one dense scene of studied social commentary. *Speculation*, as both concept and linguistic unit, allows women writers and characters to reorient and redress social asymmetries that disfavor them. Austen in particular reframes an understanding of speculation where women's roles are protected and rationalized, rather than conceding to stereotypes of speculators as unthinking, maniacal, feminized mobs. *Speculation* is an organizing sensibility here, and a term of analysis that women can own and repackage while taking up its deep semantic history, expanding it by way of their socio-philosophical interventions.

We can follow the ensuing course of *speculation*, both as a broad-based concept and as a discrete term, through women's writing by staying with its attachment to marriage across the widely noted mid-Victorian obsession with speculation in general. Here again, as in the 1780s and 1790s, the term becomes almost hyperliterary and overused in fiction. It arises in multiple references in fiction and even in legal texts through the 1840s and 1850s, as the "marriage speculation." Julia Pardoe's novel *Speculation* (1834) went through several editions, which Anna Bartlett Warner followed with *Speculation; or, The Glen Luna Family* (1854). The former centers on what one character also calls "matrimonial speculation—nay, don't frown, pardon me the word speculation; if it displease you, I am ready to substitute a smoother—and yet, in sober truth, all 'marrying and giving in marriage' is but a speculation at best: and you and I are but varieties of the exemplification of my theory; you and your high-born and portionless bride, and I and my less patrician, but better-dowried, widow."[69] The latter concerns a family headed by a father who is a philosophical speculator, lost in his thoughts, who foregoes the "wise proverb" of old to be "content, with what a man hath." Instead, the family endures "years of speculation, when money seemed as inexhaustible as the gold of California, and far more easily come by. No labour nor content now, the bargain of yesterday sold for five thousand dollars advance to-day."[70]

Before returning to women writers, we might also note the mid-nineteenth-century shift, broadly speaking, from inheritance and marriage-speculation plots to the classic plots of Victorian realist novels. In this vein, we find the familiar villainous and conniving financial speculators of Dickens, Trollope, and Thackeray, and again the word itself is key to unpacking what functions *speculation* performs in multiple registers. In the opening of *Nicholas Nickleby* (1839), the first words of dialogue concern what to do with a sum of money: "'Speculate with it,' said Mrs. Nickleby. "Spec—u—late, my dear?,'" Mr. Nickleby asks, skeptically.[71] Yet he does so, and the narrator explains, "Speculation is a round game; the players see little or nothing of their cards at first starting; gains *may* be great—and so may losses. The run of luck went against Mr. Nickleby. A mania prevailed, a bubble burst, four stock-brokers took villa residences at Florence, four hundred nobodies were ruined, and among them Mr. Nickleby."[72] There are numerous such examples in this novel; in others there are even images playing on what Anna Kornbluh has called the "semantic promiscuity" of *speculation*, as in the illustration "Mr. Melmotte Speculates" in Trollope's *The Way We Live Now* (1875).[73] And one could trace a line of wordplay on *speculation* across Elizabeth Gaskell's novels alone.[74] We even find playfully redundant titles such as the economic writer David Morier Evans's *Speculative Notes and Notes on Speculation, Ideal and Real* (1864).

But more pointedly, the intellectual lines of female speculation that this chapter has traced merge most fully in *Daniel Deronda* (1876), in which George Eliot, in her final novel, extends Austen's sense of *speculation*'s multiplicity, the notions of marriage speculation, and—returning to our previous chapter—the idea of speculative mania. We meet Eliot's heroine Gwendolen Harleth at the roulette table, where she is "occupied in gambling"—an updated female gamester—and with a mysterious expression on her face that Deronda cannot read. The losses are amplified when Gwendolen's mother, Mrs. Davilow, sends a letter informing Gwendolen that although she "know[s] nothing about business and will not understand" what has happened, her husband has lost a fortune in a failed business speculation, leaving the family "totally ruined."[75] Eliot's narrator explains that, as she processed these events, "Gwendolen was as inwardly rebellious against the restraints of family conditions, and as ready to look through obligations into her own fundamental want of feeling for them, as if she had been sustained by the boldest speculations; but she really had no such speculation, and would at once have marked herself off from any sort of theoretical or practically reforming women by satirizing them."[76] Rather than having her own "speculations," then, Gwendolen half-willingly becomes the object of marriage speculations, and of speculations *about* her suitability for marriage. Thus, Mrs. Davilow "could not be inwardly indifferent to an advent that might promise a brilliant lot for Gwendolen. A little speculation on 'what may be' comes naturally, without encouragement—comes inevitably in the form of images. . . . But then came the further speculation—would Gwendolen be satisfied with [Mr. Grandcourt]?"[77]

Even her suitor Mr. Grandcourt feels that "others speculated on him as a desirable match" for Gwendolen. Gwendolen finally speculates on herself and finds wealth by agreeing to marry the pushy Grandcourt. Deronda instead marries Mirah Lapidoth, whose father—a degenerate gambler—had planned to speculate upon *her* by selling her into marriage with a nobleman.

The narrative voice then develops further these entwined senses of *speculation* by noting, when referring to the idea that "people should construct matrimonial prospects on the mere report that a bachelor of good fortune and possibilities was coming within reach," that "such speculations might turn out to be fallacious"—with *speculations* here meaning both projective ideas and gambles on fortune.[78] Mrs. Davilow knows something of this: her second husband (Gwendolen's father) stole jewelry from her—though he technically owned it, due to the coverture laws that Eliot criticizes. She ultimately reaches back to Calvinist anti-chance theology and insists, though, that "we must resign ourselves to the will of Providence, my child," and not to speculative gambles. And yet, she defends Mr. Lassman's "great speculations" that cost the Davilow/Harleth family their savings because "he meant to gain"; his only mistake, she insists, was that he "risked too much." Gwendolen angrily resists: "It was his improvidence with our money, and he ought to be punished. Can't we go to law and recover our fortune?"[79] Completing the senses of *speculation* that Gwendolen both theorizes and embodies, from her speculative eyes when gambling to her marriage speculation and her readings of financial speculations, she finally has a "fit of madness" and "scream[s]" with "hysterical violence" at the sight of Grandcourt, her speculator.[80] Gwendolen is every form of the woman speculator at once—which leaves her prey to a maniacal fit that completes the circle.[81]

Gwendolen Harleth's fate, then, shines a light on several important novels in this tradition in which women *cannot* speculate for themselves, and on the language authors use to capture the implications of that circumstance. Kate Chopin—whose husband left her the substantial debts he had incurred before he died in 1882—thus has her heroine Edna Pontellier in *The Awakening* (1899) fall in love with Robert

Lebrun, who mysteriously flees to Mexico, "where fortune awaited him," on an unnamed speculative venture.[82] As Edna comes to her realizations about the state of her life and her future, Chopin writes that she "could see before her no denial—only the promise of excessive joy. She lay in bed awake, with bright eyes full of speculation," recalling the Shakespearian use of *speculation* in *Macbeth*. As she envisions and dreams of Robert "going to his business that morning," she is immediately dragged back to the reality of her failing marriage: a "letter also came from her husband, saying he hoped to be back early in March, and then they would get ready for that journey abroad which he had promised her so long,... thanks to his recent speculations in Wall Street."[83] Speculation—or the pretense of it—takes the man Edna desires away from her, leaving only her "speculation" as that which fills her eyes. Speculation also creates the financial stability that her husband has sought, far away, often against her will. Likewise, in the opening scene of Edith Wharton's *House of Mirth* (1905), Lawrence Selden is transfixed by Lily Bart because "she always roused speculation . . . [and] her simplest acts seemed the result of far-reaching intentions."[84] Lily can "rouse" speculation, but she must use Gus Trenor as her surrogate to make risky speculative bets on the market for her in hopes of erasing her gambling debts. Lily can only rely on a last-minute inheritance to pay off her debts before finally dying, just before Selden, a marriage speculator, had belatedly come to propose to her.

In such novels, *speculation* is a conceptual tether for a host of critiques that the line of writing from Austen to Eliot has helped concentrate, sharpening a concept that risked only portraying women as its wildest, most untamed representatives. It is an applied term with a resonant history that one can call up and employ across many registers, hardly the narrowed term that a concentration on women in markets had once made it. Women could be the speculators without "bounds" that Thoreau had idealized, though with solider grounding in lived reality than he granted, as the assessments of the speculative marriage markets across more than a century would attest. Speculation could be a tool for rethinking a host of new social *plots*, in a theme we'll see time and again, and what happens in novelistic plots and discourse would reverberate across real-world circumstances as it was picked up by readers, critics, cultural commentators, and analysts of all stripes.

We are left with an unresolved and quite potent tension: speculation, and in particular the notion of marriage speculation across a tradition of women's writing, ties together a host of connotative and denotative senses of *speculation* that we have tracked over time, all wound together toward the end of the nineteenth century. Yet in other discursive spheres, such as the male-dominated financial press and the lively print circuits of market ethnographies, the lady speculator was a passive figure, typed and troped. Speculation means little for her as a conceptual optic or platform for critique. In many ways, this tension updates and articulates the situation that Austen captured in her mise-en-scène, if we now fuse the real and fictional worlds—as was constantly happening here. The implications of this tension for thinking about gendered futurity, and about its possibility in a world of economically bound gender relations, help lay the groundwork for generations of feminist thought that would follow in the early twentieth century, from the New Woman movement to Virginia Woolf's economic theories, and much more.

THE RETURN OF THE LADY SPECULATOR

Unlike Lily Bart or Edna Pontellier, many women in the late 1800s and early 1900s finally *could* speculate in major markets, and the line of rhetoric developed in fiction helps us understand how they were read socially. That is, the movements for women's rights in this moment fundamentally shifted views of women as "speculators"—in stocks, in philosophy, in marital spheres, even in card games and gambling—in ways that Eliot and others registered and influenced themselves. As early as the 1870s, what were regularly called "lady speculators" were staples in the burgeoning publishing niche of Wall Street ethnographies, which themselves often included comparative scenes from other cities with booming exchanges, like Chicago, London, and Paris. All this meant that, in both reputable and disreputable sites, women were—in the words of William Worthington Fowler—both "frequent" and "daring speculators": "They encounter risks that would appall the stoutest Wall Street veteran, and rush boldly into places, where even a Vanderbilt would fear to tread." Returning to the language of speculative gambling as a disease, Fowler notes that "perhaps they may catch the infection from their brothers, or uncles," and adds that female speculators are often idle before they gamble: "wealthy ladies, who are their own mistresses, and have plenty of leisure time, might be expected, as they sit embroidering golden bees and butterflies, on black velvet, to have their thoughts turned upon stock-flyers, and to dream of new equipages, jewels, and silks, won out of stocks or gold. . . . [But there] are no more eager and venturesome speculators in stocks, than women."[85] Fowler sees women as arch-speculators—they are almost *too* naturally able, to their own detriment. He ties most every stereotypical characteristic of women to an improved ability to speculate, and he goes on to detail how women speculate in markets—often under men's names, and often when their husbands are traders.

The biggest problem, for him and many others, is that women are *not* experts. Thus, Fowler focuses at length on the Claflin sisters, Victoria and Tennessee, the "bewitching brokers" (as they were called) who had opened Wall Street's first brokerage house owned and operated by women, in 1870.[86] They operate by witchcraft, spells, and divination, as Charles Mackay had claimed of speculating women—not by way of data and study. They were masculinized and controlling, mysterious and charming, all sorts of tropes bundled together irrationally in the cultural imaginary. Victoria Claflin, who in 1872 boldly announced herself as the first female candidate for president in American history, exemplified the wide range of speculative practices that were bound together by this point: she had been a financially successful magnetic healer, an occultist, and a threatening radical in sociopolitical issues. She advocated for suffrage, women's rights to divorce and control of their own sexual freedom, and legalized prostitution. The Lady Speculator, too, differs dramatically from Lady Credit: she is active, with a seat at the table now, and she has newly powerful means

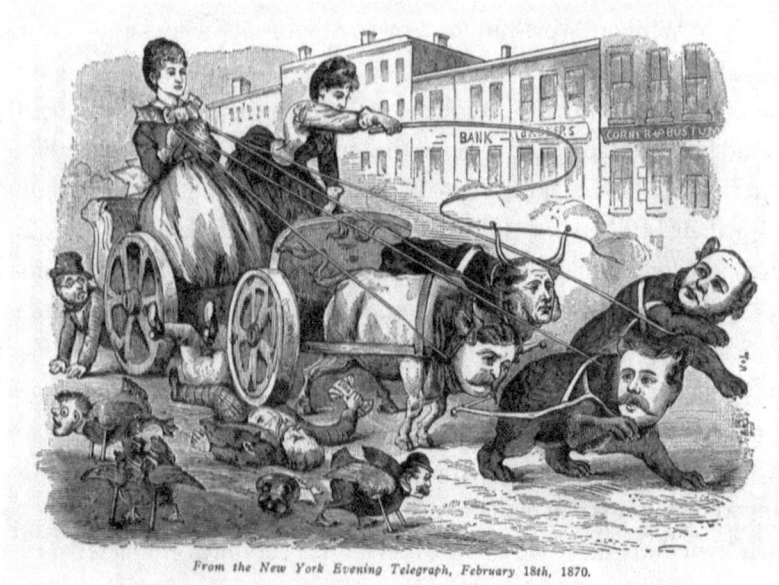

FIGURE 6.1 Cartoon of the Claflin sisters from *New York Evening Telegraph*, February 18, 1870. The caption reads, "The lady brokers driving the bulls and bears of Wall Street. Tennie C. holding the reins, Victoria the whip."

Public domain.

of entrancing men in their market interactions.[87] Once again, as in the early 1700s, this speculator is much more than a simple and ineffectual gamester.

Even while journalistic exposés highlighted how many women were harmed by speculative losses, and while moralistic commentaries voiced strident opposition, women rode this new wave on post–Civil War Wall Street. The *San Francisco Chronicle* and *New York Times* carried stories in 1875 on "speculating women" and their increasing numbers and power.[88] Indeed, at one point, women held 55 percent of AT&T's entire stock, and the Pennsylvania Railroad was nicknamed "the Petticoat Line" because of a similar proportion of women stockholders.[89] Flipping coverture on its head, Antoinette Brown Blackwell argued in the first issue of the *Woman's Advocate* in 1869 that "the good, faithful mother is not an idler, and though she may not be herself a money-maker, yet as partner in the matrimonial firm, she is justly fully entitled to an equal share in all profits."[90] "Exclusive offices for lady speculators" were created and advertised.[91] The American feminist reformer Caroline H. Dall's *The College, the Market, and the Court* (1867) even portrayed scenes such as a farmer's wife coming to "speculate in corn" in Chicago: "She said her husband had lost money several years in succession, and now she was going to try. By her first speculation, she made five thousand dollars; and this she put into competent hands, for re-investment. It gained her twenty thousand dollars."[92]

Thus it was that the popular sensationalist-adventure novelist Ouida (Maria Louise Ramé), in her *Friendship: A Story of Society* (1878), could sum up what came before her in a passage that captures the breadth of thought and activity for women speculators:

> The nineteenth century has some touch of all, but its own novelty of production is the female speculator[,] . . . whose favor can only be won by some hint in advance of the newspapers; . . . who starts banks, who concocts companies, who keeps a broker, as in the eighteenth century a woman kept a monkey, and in the twelfth a knight; whose especial art is to buy in at the right moments and to sell out in the nick of time. . . . The present age is blessed with the female financier, and must make the best of her, as it must of the rotten railways, the bubble banks, the choked-up mines, the sand-filled canals, the solitudes of brick and mortar, which it owes to her genius.[93]

The nineteenth century as defined by the "female speculator," who succeeds not by information and expertise, but by insider tips and instinct—she joins the line of women-owners who have shaped societies, built futures, and created bubbles of all sorts. The female speculator in this moment, then, was an embodied abstraction of a different sort than we saw above, one that could not be represented by a new abstraction imbued with the confidence of data and knowledge. Across the 1880s and 1890s, we find both assertions of the power of female speculator and regular, often sensationalistic reports of women speculators as "Female Plungers" and "Petticoated Sharks," with speculation depicted variously as an addictive drug and a vortex from which there was no escape. Soon they were deemed "Ladybulls," "Mud-Hens," or "Lady Financiers." Reports on the Panic of 1901 often pointed to the number of women involved and noted that they "furnished hysterical scenes and sensations."[94] Images of "panic-stricken lady speculators overwhelmed by the crash" circulated on both sides of the Atlantic.[95] Others dismissed the "lady speculator" as an "unfortunate person" sure to become a "victim" of the "fraud" that occurs daily on Wall Street especially.[96] The deprecations intensified in the coverage of Hetty Green, dubbed the "Witch of Wall Street," who made over a billion dollars in today's money as a currency speculator, and, as Laura Meixner notes, represented "for the public the feminine speculator irrational."[97]

The lady speculator became a well-outlined figure who, in turn, began to reshape the concept of speculation through means that women could not previously access, and here we can piece together more fully what that means retrospectively for the history of speculation before her. The attempts to restrain, regulate, and often condemn the woman speculator always conditioned, however, what this type could be. E. V. Smith's *Plain Truths About Stock Speculation* (1887) held that "it is a species of insanity which allures young and old of both sexes into the maelstrom" of speculation, and quickly, women "wring their hands in terror as they see their money disappear." He ultimately concludes that "they are women of good character, aside from the propensity to risk their present and future support on the game of chance," but that, "in speculation, as a rule, they are too impulsive and quick to jump at wrong conclusions."[98] Even a physicians' manual on insanity warned that "several instances are on record in which such patients have been induced to marry courtesans or other speculating women, in some instances thereby committing bigamy. The undue influence in such cases has the way prepared by the patient's forgetfulness of the fact of a previous marriage, or his moral deterioration."[99] (Furthermore, "psychotic patients" were "dangerous to society" because, among other things, "they may squander their property in insane speculation, absurd purchases, or in excesses."[100]) Meixner adds that "the social pathologies of female speculation" in particular were "medicalized" all over again, with theories abounding that speculation, as in the 1700s, caused women to age prematurely, develop "nervous ailments," and fall into states of hysterical delusion.[101] Could the lady speculator only exist, as a historicized entity, by inhabiting what men had cast upon her, and if so, what might be *done* with those typologies?

And so, in the early 1900s, the diagnoses and dismissals of women's speculation were turned on their heads. Feminists seized on the language H. H. Asquith used to defer action on the suffrage movement, which he said was "a contingent question in regard to a remote and speculative future."[102] What if those contingencies and that "speculative future" were to be *created*, brought into the present, in concrete form, just as in the scientific revolution? Thus we find publications like the feminist *Freewoman* continuing the thread of *speculation* as a feminist keyword and offering "Speculations on Sex War" that shifted the term toward activism, here and now.[103] (Meanwhile, anti-feminists condemned the "speculative intellectuals in the Woman Movement."[104]) Speculation, even and *especially* while it was cast aside, continued to have an applied social function, and Mabel Dodge tellingly titled her important essay praising Gertrude Stein's innovative writing method "Speculations." She noted that "out of the shattering of the petrifaction of today—up from the cleavage and the disintegration—we will see order emerging tomorrow," because of the projections of futurity in Stein's work.[105] Again, speculating women were building the future— for women. Virginia Woolf also used the term to describe her method of composition, and thereby to give a miniature statement of modernism's elevation of speculative thought, midway through *Orlando* (1928): "We have done our best to piece out a meagre summary from the charred fragments that remain; but often it has been necessary to speculate, to surmise, and even to use the imagination" in order to piece together her subject's (fictionalized) life.[106] For Woolf, speculation recovers the fulsome humanity and creativity of abstract ideation, against the imperatives of cold rationalization.

Women must not only reclaim speculation; they must also speculate widely and assertively. A generation of feminist figures became not only activists but also speculative investors in the arts (among them, perhaps most famously, Gertrude Stein), who believed that art, too, would reshape the future. The barriers many would-be women investors still faced on Wall Street made these cultural domains special alternative sites for speculative opportunities.[107] Harriet Shaw Weaver's sponsorship of James Joyce would fall into this class, as would, in a more complicated way, Charlotte Osgood Mason's of Zora Neale Hurston.[108] Looking back with some perverse pride on her role in Joyce's career, Adrienne Monnier, owner of La Maison des Amis des Livres, the bookstore opposite Sylvia Beach's Shakespeare and Company in Paris, confessed in 1938 that "we behaved ourselves rather badly. We made books objects of speculation; we made or let be made a *stock exchange* for books. . . . The artist has no worse enemy than the speculator."[109] As we saw above, speculation offers a double edge for wealth and advancement: it creates fabulous wealth and prestige for women like Monnier, yet it destroys those who practice it, destroys the art objects, and ultimately destroys artists themselves, too. It's a behavior and a deceit as much as it's a capitalist pursuit of an idea. Regardless, speculation is a means of cognitive socioeconomic intervention at the same time, and women must pursue it to create new, different futures. Applied speculation, of all forms, here counteracts the vulnerability that masterful men's speculation creates. *Speculation* names a new means of wresting control and expertise, represented by the female speculator as social critic and controller of the vehicles of multiform speculation.

Animating anew its mode of social critique, especially when tied to the arts, *speculation* as a term has recently been embraced as a mode of thinking otherwise from and resisting the risky, threatening, and inequitable conditions of the current moment, especially from positions understood as collectively vulnerable. As Gabriella Friedman writes, "Speculation evokes an extrapolative practice that articulates the repercussions of urgent global problems, a set of political tactics that shape worlds through activism, and an imaginative strategy that etches unexpected ways to organize social life"—all of which have seen speculative fiction play a significant role in their articulation.[110] Her sense of what "speculative studies" evokes in its approach to world-making as imaginative and activist resistance alike captures this powerful sense of the term.[111] We see this in Fred Moten's invocation of "speculative practice," Aimee Bahng's study of "decolonized" and "migrant" speculation, or in the critical methodology of a "speculative history" that Saidiya Hartman employs, too.[112] An anonymous collective at Duke University called "uncertain commons" produced the collaboratively written, charged manifesto *Speculate This!* in 2013, published quite fittingly in a free, open-access format. It aimed to give order and context to this sense of *speculation*'s power in and as critique of the present, refusing to cede the term fully to a system of global capitalism to whom "the future has been sold. . . . Projections of better tomorrows incorporate us in collective fictions."[113] Against this global schema, they propose to combine the "cognitive and economic" elements of speculation into one "potentiality."[114] In a similar vein, it's rather telling that, if we now live in a perceptual state of anticipated catastrophe, the past few years alone have seen no fewer than four academic studies, from distinct fields, precisely titled *Imagined Futures*.[115] The future *must* be continually imagined, the logic goes, as an act of resistance if nothing else, and imagined futures of the past must remain constant objects of historical inquiry. But the meaning of this potentiality, and of speculation's potency, in the age of risks beyond human comprehension and of computational and algorithmic trading that takes place without human intervention, is a question we must explore further in our final considerations.

CONCLUSION

Speculative Risks, Inhuman Imaginations

It is quite useless speculating on the Future, unless you want some particular Future. Then you obviously should speculate, and it is by speculations (of all sorts, unfortunately) that the Future is made.

—WYNDHAM LEWIS, *BLAST* (1915)

The modern welfare state is one of the major speculative projects of the twentieth century. Leftist movements in the early 1900s realized that the best way to mitigate the dangers of excess speculative risk by the wealthy and dominant classes was—quite ironically—through the power of speculative risk itself, collectivized and distributed across an entire society. Social insurance and social security programs modified and even inverted the financial tools of speculators to "plac[e] the burden and the risk upon many shoulders," so that individuals' risks are "lessened," as an advocate put it in 1914.[1] We are, therefore, *all* speculating on the futures and the risks of everyone else around us now. And more than anything else, this realization brings out what is the defining feature of speculation in the twentieth and twenty-first centuries, one framed clearly by the vulnerability and

CONCLUSION: SPECULATIVE RISKS, INHUMAN IMAGINATIONS   173

social critique we just addressed: its near-complete identification with the concept of risk. Speculation and risk have been entwined in important ways at least since the mid-1700s, but now the nature, scale, and ubiquity of risk have been enabled and altered conclusively by the transformations of the machine age. Speculation began as a supremely human mode of thinking; but in the present, we cannot understand speculation without machines of all types, from war technologies to computers. These machines create risks that might make the future possible or impossible, wealthy or impoverished, inhabitable or empty. We cannot speculate without them, and they cannot speculate without us. As they now "look through" with vision and minds that are neither theirs nor ours, we must take stock of how these machines register speculation and its projections of risk in our present.

SPECULATIVE RISK, THEN AND NOW

There are substantive differences between the risks of invading a neighboring village and those of the Chernobyl disaster. Or, more pointedly and in a shorter time frame, the changing risks of interconnected international currency markets have given speculation heretofore unthinkably powerful force and far-reaching effects. The South Sea Bubble ruined certain moneyed individuals and dented the stability of the new parliamentary state in the early 1700s. The depression of the 1930s, however, was global, and it triggered untold losses of wealth and even life, exacerbating rising totalitarian movements and fueling the march to what became world wars of unthinkable scale. Those wars showed how technologically advanced methods of mass murder brought unprecedented risks to every corner of the globe, culminating in the awful and awesome power of nuclear weaponry. Looking with acerbic despair at the ongoing Great War, Wyndham Lewis noted in 1915 that "the glorious future of War" was within reach through a combination of military technology and scientific expertise: "We might eventually arrive at such a point of excellence that two-thirds of the population of the world could be exterminated with mathematical precision in a fortnight."[2] Aerial bombardment and chemical weapons brought previously unknown terrors to average civilians in metropoles and in colonies. Automobile and airplane accidents became regular occurrences, highrises and bridges collapsed, while a world running on electricity meant that one could die in a horrifying new manner (as the electric chair would emblematize).

The import of these phenomena is captured succinctly in the theory of "risk society," which is most closely associated with the sociological work of Ulrich Beck and Anthony Giddens, and which bears on how we think about speculation in our day. "Risk society" theorists seek to understand how risk itself has changed across human history, and especially since the onset of the first industrial revolution. Modern "manufactured risks"—the shifting, never fully knowable consequences of technological innovation—are signatures of modernity, and with each new creation, a new threat arrives.[3] As Hannah Arendt succinctly put it, "Progress and Doom are two sides of the same medal."[4] Concepts like fortune and faith are pushed into the background as premodern formations; self-determination and mastery of the future are argued as scientifically and mathematically justified.[5] In a process that Beck calls "reflexive modernity," modernization in the industrial West becomes both its own theme and a self-perpetuating concept, with an endless and rarely stunted drive toward innovation, speed, and ubiquitous transformation that promises a better future.[6] Here, the speculative thought of scientists like Einstein had the most frightening real-world application imaginable in the development of the bomb.

An indicative feature of risk society is the possibility that one person's actions in a laboratory, a war room, or a financial exchange can affect the lives of millions in an instant—effects that, in the past, took more time and more coordinated infrastructure. The line between individual behavioral risks and existential, universal perils became increasingly blurry by the dawn of the twentieth century—so much so that some argued that it barely mattered, as in the threat of nuclear annihilation. Or, as John Maynard Keynes wrote of currency speculators in Germany after the war: "Nothing like this has been known in the history of speculation—so large and so widespread. Bankers and servant girls have been equally involved."[7] The impact of human activity around the planet had, by the turn of the twentieth century, nearly erased the boundaries between "acts of God" and self-induced catastrophes, throwing into relief a host of questions about the nature of collective agency and the instruments by which risk and peril are created. Increasing population density, increasingly scarce resources, and an increasing reliance on technology in everyday life intensified the power of such instruments. Every technology that brings safety also brings the potential for a new threat.

Risk merges most fully with speculation in this conceptual sphere by way of this shared restructuring of the future, which seems endlessly expansive yet always threatened to be foreclosed and doomed.[8] Risk, in Giddens's words, is a way of "organizing future time," an "attempt to break away from the past and confront an open future" through the "binding of time and space."[9] Or, as Elaine Freedgood writes, risk is "by definition a temporal problem; it exists only and always as a possibility, a future contingency."[10] Here, risk even begins to overtake the element of projected futurity that speculation has held for centuries. Beck adds that "wrestl[ing] with the side effects of successful modernization" necessarily means remaining in a state of *"anticipation* of the catastrophe," much as we saw with the temporal element of speculation's gambling qualities.[11] The economist Frank Knight's landmark thesis *Risk, Uncertainty, and Profit* (1921) used theories of probability and of existential unknowability to reframe speculation's articulation of risk. He called speculation "the most important instrument in modern economic society for the specialization of uncertainty, after the institution of free enterprise itself."[12] Speculation, in Knight's influential reading, was a means of packaging risk for the market, so that risk could be traded upon in innovative ways that were not inherent or intrinsic to it or its situations. Speculation becomes a container or vehicle for risk, a way to monetize and finance it, and like the "wind wheat" scenario, in which the commodity itself is unimportant, the risk, too, becomes secondary to the profitability of the speculation. Speculation, that is, helps risk monetize its own endangerment of the future—by way of its own mechanisms, with endless recursiveness. But at every turn, the system could collapse and the future could be rendered bleak due to what was risked, and the more we entrust to machine technologies, the more we amplify that risk of annihilation (a point many speculative fictions take as their premise). Speculation—to return to the matter of vulnerability and collectivity—can now come to feel like the anticipation of another triggering of the switch by which a certain technology brings about our doom.

SPECULATING MACHINES?

Manufactured risk pinpoints the role machines have played in exponentially scaling up the risks that humans create and pose to ourselves and our planet. But such theories of risk, and of risk society, have done little to consider a famous question, posed in an often-quoted article for the journal *Mind* in 1950 by Alan Turing: "Can machines think?"[13] That question might seem like the farthest provocation from our own story's origins in Boethius, but in fact, it brings us to our logical end point. The discussion that ensued from the question led to the formulation of the so-called Turing test, which probes the matter of exactly what kind of cogitation happens inside computational machines, and whether or not computers can successfully imitate and enact an activity long thought to be the exclusive preserve of humans. But Turing's rhetoric— specifically, his choice of *think* as his critical verb—actually is very much in keeping with the history of speculation that we have traced thus far: "thinking," for Turing, is a serious, higher-order "intellectual capacit[y]" and innate embodiment of "intelligence." Thinking is hardly controversial, almost never condemned morally nor dismissed as airy conjecture. In fact, Turing himself neatly cordons off "thinking" from "mere speculation," a phrase he uses to dismiss the first principal objection raised to his considerations.[14]

Turing's question points forward to the ways in which succeeding revolutions in information processing and artificial intelligence have

CONCLUSION: SPECULATIVE RISKS, INHUMAN IMAGINATIONS 177

brought us, it might seem, to a far extreme of speculation. Thus, we might reframe Turing's question in light of the history that this book has traced: "Can machines *speculate*?"[15] On the one hand, many would offer an immediate and emphatic "No." That is, if we consider the full breadth of future-making, risk-taking, and imaginative and contemplative thinking that has characterized *speculation* across time, we might consider computers incapable of that essence that separates speculation from programmed data-processing. The ticker was a *means* of speculation, one might argue, but speculation itself remains human at some fundamental level. But at the same time, computers already speculate in a variety of ways: they predict future events all the time, they gamble, and they abstract and dematerialize data collected from the phenomenal world. Experimental computational projects are routinely described as "speculative."

And from the start of the modern era of computing, both the theoretical and applied understandings of machines have pointed to their speculative potential. There is familiar language in a profoundly evidentiary document from the history of computation: Ada Lovelace's notes on Charles Babbage's Analytical Engine. Here, there is an acknowledgment that "those who incline to very strictly utilitarian views may perhaps feel that the peculiar powers of the Analytical Engine bear upon questions of abstract and speculative science, rather than upon those involving every-day and ordinary human interests," and thus "would be a barren and unproductive laying out of yet more money and labour; in fact, a work of supererogation."[16] But the engine's defense lay in that it held powers that "it may not yet be possible to foresee, but which would be brought forth by the daily increasing requirements of science, and by a more intimate practical acquaintance with the powers of the engine, were it in actual existence."[17] The engine, furthermore, would have "no pretensions whatever to *originate* anything," but would certainly have "indirect, and ... somewhat *speculative* ... consequence[s]" that no human mind could fully fathom in the present.[18]

Such postulates abound in the history of "thinking" machines. And the possibility—and typically, the dread—of intelligent and/or self-aware machines has prompted volumes of speculative and science fiction for well over a century. It was captured in an important early moment in Samuel Butler's article "Darwin Among the Machines" (1863), which speculated on the potential for machines to evolve; Butler later expanded and incorporated much of this into his *Erewhon* (1872). Fantasies from *2001: A Space Odyssey* to the *Terminator* series portray the darker, dystopian edge of humans' theoretical submission and surrender to machines (or we could even consider here the nonmachine policing of human speculation itself in Margaret Atwood's *Handmaid's Tale*). The title of Philip K. Dick's *Do Androids Dream of Electric Sheep?* (1968) points not just to the imagined sentience of machines but also to the ideational lifeworlds that they could possibly create.

A common point emphasized in work by scholars such as Donna J. Haraway and N. Katherine Hayles is that it is now difficult, if not impossible, to draw clear lines between human and machine.[19] Humans use machines to project the future worlds that we might inhabit, whether we are calculating our insurance premiums or studying maps of how climate change will in the coming decades affect the places we live. Computers—especially those that can process big data—are now the means of many forms of prediction and future-making. An innumerably vast number of speculative trades in contemporary markets are made by computers, of course, and function through algorithms, not through on-site human decisions in the moment—or, more precisely, they create "speculative regime[s] measured in nanoseconds."[20] Our smartphones and digital clouds are integral parts of our lifeworlds, and indeed are some of the most intimate parts of ourselves. Scholars have noted how our minds have offloaded the knowledge of trivia and facts, which were once the markers of a certain, often peculiar, personality type and mentality, to search engines and internet sources. And by the same measure, machines use constant human input and manipulation, from programming languages to value judgments, in order to generate future scenarios or execute trades, thereby continuing the endless feedback loop. Among the financial bets computers can now offer humans are not only stock or derivative investments, but wagers on when a stranger will die.[21] There's even a common term in computer science, *speculative execution*, that describes how a computer attempts to predict a function that will be needed in the future, and then performs a task in the present that will ideally make the predicted future action occur more efficiently. But it needs a human architect to guide it to and through the structure of this process.

Thus, we may be tempted to say that speculation has now been fully outsourced from minds to machines—or, as Michael Lewis put it in his startling account of high-frequency trading, "computers [have] entirely replac[ed] the people" in financial markets.[22] A recent article from *The Economist* struck a nostalgic tone in evoking the time when "investing was a distinctly human affair"—only some fifty years ago, in the early 1970s.[23] And it's true that not only do machines make trades and calculate the very risks that they take, they make entire markets. But here again, the human-computer interface is actually the key: hardly a large investment firm is now without "quants" who train the machines to perform in ways that will ideally maximize profits, and all use trading programs that draw on Monte Carlo and other simulations of future-time pricing and that "learn" as they process data over time. And because of this human-machine relationship at every level, to say that speculation is fully computational and mechanized, even in financial markets, is to let humans off the hook—and we've seen the dangers of such a move, as studies documenting bias and discrimination in algorithms and machine learning have documented.[24]

Likewise, to argue that machines will never be able to intuit, to have affects, to love, or to respond with a singular humanity (think of Proust's madeleine) risks holding on to a Romantic, preindustrial notion of creative originality as the truest marker of humanity. Many of the attempts to make machines creative have produced laughs and groans in equal numbers, like absurd recipes from data sets of flavors or comically irrational scripts generated by bots that "learned" formulas for writing. But that cannot be construed as evidence that machines are once and forever incapable of the range of speculation that that we have covered. (We could similarly ask whether animals can speculate, and we could point to arguments that they take risks and guard against external dangers, build for their own futures, dream and imagine, and so on.) In fact, we can't even be certain that, were they alive today, Aristotle or Boethius would categorically limit speculation to embodied, "natural" human minds—nor that they would consider artificial intelligence absolutely nonhuman.

There is a new fault line here, the most recent one in the history of speculation. Speculation is neither fully human nor fully mechanized, and thus its implications and consequences now must be rethought against the formations of agency that the ancient division between speculation and practice bequeathed the modern world. Humans and machines cannot speculate without one another, as the practitioners of social, applied, and critical speculation have shown to be true with devastating consequences. Does this leave speculation, in the present, in perpetual imbalance, in a tug-of-war between human minds and algorithms dependent on one another for their survival and futures? Will speculation further splinter between an even *more* computational, more technologized version developed for high-frequency, high-volume, high-dollar-amount trading, and a more humanistic and socially analytic version developed precisely to resist the effects of this mode of financial capitalism? That seems too stark a schism and too monolithic a portrait of modern America; but the number of contingencies, risks, conjectures, and uncertainties that we must ponder simply to project speculation's next course are overwhelming to human and machine alike at this moment. I write these final words amid a pandemic, after all. Maggie Koerth puts it well: not just every speculation, but "every decision is a risk. Every risk is a decision."[25] The world feels too precarious, we have all said many times, to speculate far into our futures, now.

Several years ago, I was preparing to teach Tom McCarthy's *Remainder* (2005), and when I returned to it for maybe a third or fourth reading, I lingered over a certain passage that, in retrospect, sums up much from the foregoing chapters. The unnamed narrator has received a lump-sum payment of £8.5 million as compensation for an unnamed

CONCLUSION: SPECULATIVE RISKS, INHUMAN IMAGINATIONS 181

trauma—something fell from the sky and hit him, and he can neither remember it nor (on the chance that he were to remember anything) speak about it, per his settlement. He has, in other words, experienced an infinitesimally small but calculable and real effect of risk in quotidian life: he has been injured by a piece of technology that gravity and/or human error brought down, against whatever combined human and machine powers had been holding it suspended in space. He eventually decides to speculate recklessly in tech stocks with his new fortune, but he doesn't quite understand how markets work. He asks his financial advisor, Matthew Younger, how he will become wealthier; Younger explains that "what really propels your investment upwards is speculation."

> "Speculation?" I repeated. "What's that?" . . .
> "When people buy shares, they don't value them by what they actually represent in terms of goods or services: they value them by what they *might* be worth, in an imaginary future."
> "But what if that future comes and they're not worth what people thought they would be?" I asked.
> "It never does," said Matthew Younger. "By the time one future's there, there's another one being imagined. The collective imagination of all the investors keeps projecting futures, keeping the shares buoyant. Of course, sometimes a particular set of shares stop catching people's imagination, so they fall. It's our job to get you out of a particular one before it falls—and, conversely, to get you into another when it's just about to shoot up." . . .
> "What if everyone stops imagining futures for all of them at the same time?" I asked him.
> "Ah!" . . . "That throws the switch on the whole system, and the market crashes. That's what happened in '29. In theory it could happen again. . . . But if no one thinks it will, it won't."[26]

Here, McCarthy reaches back to the sense of *speculation* as abstraction—the seemingly mystical process of turning the material into the immaterial, a process that preoccupies the narrator of the novel from start to finish. He also captures both the fundamental nature of speculative finance in the idea that the "collective imagination" is a life force, impalpable and unknowable yet fully real, and the even older sense of *speculation* as a means of projecting futures (which, in this case, never come into being).

McCarthy is attempting to write *through* the history and operations of speculation—of the financial instruments that project future wealth and then suspend those projections indefinitely. Instead of *matter* being sustained in the air (as the object that mysteriously fell on the narrator was not), we have an inversion in which the narrator and his advisor are trying to understand what keeps *ideas* sustained in a way that allows them to eventually turn into actual, material money, as profits). The central idea here—that "if no one thinks" something will happen, "it won't"—points to the "collective imagination" that speculation embodies. The power of groupthink, materialized in human actions and in trading algorithms, "keeps shares buoyant." Something that is convertible into material wealth, something that can be de-abstracted and that floats on the magic of collective human-machine ideation, can drop at any moment. The narrator finds a thrilling rush in speculating, in exposing his money; he ultimately calls another friend, Naz, and demands that he look up the word *speculation* in a dictionary for him: "'The faculty of seeing,' Naz read; 'observation of the heavens, stars, etc.; contemplation or profound study of a subject; a conjectural consideration; the practice of buying and selling goods. From the Latin *speculari*: to spy out, watch, and *specula*: watch tower....' 'Watch tower,' I said; 'heavens: I like that. You could see the heavens better from a watch tower. But you'd be exposed.'"[27] *Exposed* is the keyword here. If you look to the heavens, if you spy out to the future, you are exposed to the dangers and threats of both the present and the past, and that's the narrator's ultimate preference. The data and calculations that make modern risk management (the field obsessed with exposure) only exist in lived time. One is exposed to conjecture itself, to contemplation and its possibilities of futurity. The culmination of the novel is the narrator's staging of a bank robbery—the most concrete way of instantly gaining wealth, with no need for speculative abstraction or buoyancy. In the

CONCLUSION: SPECULATIVE RISKS, INHUMAN IMAGINATIONS 183

end, it's the endorphin rush and not the hard currency or wealth that the narrator cares about; he wants to rob a bank in order to experience robbing a bank. The novel concludes with him fleeing the robbery, on a plane suspended in the air, endlessly "banking" back and forth, suspended in time, stuck in the present with no future, even if we readers know that logically, the plane must eventually crash, like a market.[28] Perhaps it is the newest version of what Defoe called "air money."

Vladimir Nabokov wrote in the opening of his novel *Transparent Things* (1972), "If the future existed, concretely and individually, as something that could be discerned by a better brain, the past would not be so seductive"; but as long as it remains only "a specter of thought," we have only such imperfect tools as speculation offers us.[29] Or, as Ben Levisohn put it succinctly in a recent article, "The stock market is not a bubble. . . . Until it is."[30] The postulates we make, the risks we venture in collaborations with machines, are what make speculation itself both seductive and necessary for that abstract tomorrow, for making what might be—the bubbles, the chances, the specters of thought—into what is. Which, in the end, is all we have. Until we don't.

ACKNOWLEDGMENTS

Family first. Audrey, Aiden, Ella, and I all made this book together. We are a family of speculators. Speculators of very different types, but all speculators nonetheless. Writing this book has been my day job, and I hope I left that labor in my laptop at the right times. But together, speculation courses through our veins, never ceases. And for that, we are collaborators, and the questions we ask one another, the adventures of futurity that we create together, the tomorrows that we discover—these speculations are the wonders that fed the curiosity that made this book possible. Wonder itself is at the heart of our shared love. Ella's appreciation of my silly magic tricks inspired the cover, and she would like to say that she loves her family and friends. Aiden's questions to me about the topic of my book gave me the title, and he says that he loves sports and friends and family. Audrey remains the most loving person I know—lucky for us all—and as I composed this book, she successfully pursued multiple career speculations that I admire and love watching come to fruition. My family has all my love, and always will, throughout all the futures we could possibly imagine, and all the ones we will grow into together. And my larger family grew once again as this book grew into being, too. I could not be happier and prouder that it now includes Alice and Britt Rogers, Laura Rogers, Cordie and Tatum Dabbs, Meghan Frank and Britt Rogers, Brittain and

Frances Rogers, Patricia Horwitz, Debbie and Eric Nieman, and Tracy and Andy Drucker. I love all of you.

I began this book as an investigation of a relatively specific question about literature and finance in the 1920s; but like a speculative venture itself, it ballooned quickly and took me back to Boethius and Aristotle. One of the genuine pleasures of that process has been the contact it has stimulated with friends and colleagues who work in fields far-flung relative to my own. I had always admired their scholarship and been intrigued by the larger questions their fields tackled, but now I could ask them questions on which they were experts, and can even cite them in my own book. No doubt I've made some errors as I wandered far from my home fields, but those belong to me, not them. This same process brought me back into contact with fields and subjects I studied in high school (like Latin), in college (where I was a philosophy major before adding English), and in grad school (eighteenth-century political economy). It took me back, even, to the lessons of my teachers in Tupelo public schools and in Sunday school, where I first learned to think about how humans have used language to project futures. It helped me, I hope, to become a better listener to my father, who patiently taught me how to explore why markets move, all long before I knew how to connect that to the questions of human behavior that fascinate him. And similarly to my mother, who patiently taught me how to think about why tomorrow might matter differently to others than it does to me, and why the future one person projects is never simply singular. In ways I have tried to impart to my own kids, my parents taught me how to ask questions, and for that I'm eternally grateful. All along, as this manuscript percolated, I asked banal, quotidian questions of those around me (especially my kids), who didn't even know at the time that they were being interviewed for my book. All of you offered theories on futurity that shaped the way I thought about this book, and I'll never be able to account for all your contributions, but I hope you can see your fingerprints somewhere in here.

A great number of people answered a great number of questions for me along the way. They are (and surely I am forgetting some—I apologize): Jonathan Arac, Magalí Armillas-Tiseyra, Elizabeth Archibald,

Greg Barnhisel, María del Pilar Blanco, Kathleen Blee, Jim Bogen, Daniel Borzutzky, Grace Davie, Tommy Davis, Hoda El Shakry, Merve Emre, Jed Esty, Harris Feinsod, Baruch Fischhoff, Rachel Galvin, Geoffrey Glover, Randall Halle, Christina Hoenig, Jeanne-Marie Jackson, Hannah Johnson, R. A. Judy, Benjy Kahan, Tamar Krishnamurti, Anthony Lacenere, Sean Latham, Adam Lee, Jessica Levy, Jonathan Levy, George Loewenstein, Jenny Mann, David Marshall, Doug Mao, Ryan McDermott, Michael Meyer, Daniel Morgan, Amy Murray Twyning, Nadia Nurhussein, Jeff Oaks, Sophia Rosenfeld, Paul Saint-Amour, Scott Sandage, Lisi Schoenbach, Bécquer Seguín, Josh Smith, Mark Christian Thompson, Annette Vee, Jen Waldron, Rebecca Walkowitz, and Emily Wanderer. Some kind mentors from my past at Northwestern University were crucial: Helen Thompson helped me lift this project off the ground. Jeffrey Masten pointed me to the necessary philological resources that got the ball rolling for the early modern sections. Here at the University of Pittsburgh, Alyssa Quintanilla was an amazing researcher into the history of the term *speculation* in the 1700s. A Facebook post that asked for novels featuring speculation proved quite rich and useful. I did my best to shield Jules Law from being sucked into work on this project, but he persevered in his usual generosity, and once again, proved himself equally the incredible friend and reader. Joanne Diaz, as always, was more than one could imagine as an interlocutor and *amiga*. Abram Van Engen read more of this manuscript than any human should have, and was exceedingly generous and insightful. A pandemic interrupted a ritual of camaraderie with Abram, Greg Downs, Erik Gellman, Guy Ortolano, and David Smith, but it didn't interrupt our communications. Lots of them. I've asked each of them a million questions, on everything from Black history to Cambridge school historiography, and from Calvinism to insurance to Reconstruction, and everything in between. They've been incredibly helpful and patient—and I'm incredibly grateful—and as I write this, I look forward to being able to see them all again.

Audiences at Oxford University, Johns Hopkins University, University of Pennsylvania, Northwestern University, and Bowdoin College were receptive and generous in giving me feedback. The same is true for audiences and panelists at meetings of the Modern Language Association, Modernist Studies Association, Post45, American Comparative Literature Association, Society for U.S. Intellectual History, the Genealogies of Modernity seminar, and the Humanities Center at the University of Pittsburgh. This book was supported by the Vice Chancellor for Research's Special Initiatives Fund and a University Center for International Studies Faculty Fellowship at the University of Pittsburgh.

Even more fundamentally, this book was supported by my colleagues and the office staff here at Pitt. Over the course of writing this book, I became chair of my department, and even though that has limited the time I've had to write, it has ultimately benefited me as a researcher and, I hope, as an inquisitor. I thrive in and around the ideas and passions of others, which is why I entered this line of work, and to have the opportunity to work even more closely with them and their scholarly pursuits has been a real boon. To witness their work of pedagogy in the crisis of a pandemic has been awe-inspiring and humbling. And since I became chair, to witness the daily expertise and grace of professionals who handle our budgets, make sure our courses are staffed, and manage panicked faculty in an unimaginable moment has inspired my profound appreciation. My department is too large for me to name everyone here, but I hope that those who take the time to read some of this work will see our collaborations in it.

I benefited greatly from several generous reports by anonymous readers for Columbia University Press. And I benefited once again from working with Philip Leventhal, who took the time to work through this manuscript in exquisite detail with me. Monique Briones was supremely prompt and helpful, too. Stephen Twilley was a magnificent copyeditor, with an enviable eye for detail and ear for prose. The production team at the press reminded me once again why the press does such excellent work, start to finish. Ryan McGinnis once again proved a marvelous and insightful indexer. This book has been a labor of love, and I am grateful for the press's work to help me bring it into the world.

NOTES

I have followed scholarly conventions in modernizing orthography and capitalization in both English and Latin, including silently emending u/v, i/j, and vv/w. I have consulted authoritative and critical editions of most texts, but where no substantive differences exist, I have aimed to cite digital, public-domain, or otherwise readily accessible editions, such as mass-market paperbacks.

INTRODUCTION

1. Samuel Johnson, *A Dictionary of the English Language*, 2 vols. (London: W. Strahan, 1755), s.v. "speculate."
2. I borrow this phrase from Catherine Gallagher, "The Rise of Fictionality," in *The Novel*, ed. Franco Moretti, 2 vols. (Princeton, NJ: Princeton University Press, 2006), 1:347.
3. See Jonathan Levy, *Freaks of Fortune: The Emerging World of Capitalism and Risk in America* (Cambridge, MA: Harvard University Press, 2012); Jamie L. Pietruska, *Looking Forward: Prediction and Uncertainty in Modern America* (Chicago: University of Chicago Press, 2017); Ann Fabian, *Card Sharps, Dream Books, and Bucket Shops: Gambling in Nineteenth-Century America* (Ithaca, NY: Cornell University Press, 1990); David G. Schwartz, *Roll the Bones: The History of Gambling* (New York: Gotham Books, 2006); Jackson Lears, *Something for Nothing: Luck in America* (New York: Viking, 2003); Ian Hacking, *The Taming of Chance* (Cambridge: Cambridge University Press, 1990); Gerda Reith, *The Age of Chance: Gambling in Western Culture* (London: Routledge, 1999); Scott A. Sandage, *Born Losers: A History of Failure in America* (Cambridge, MA: Harvard University Press, 2005); J. M. Cocking, *Imagination: A Study in the History of Ideas*, ed. Penelope Murray (London: Routledge,

1991); Kevin Young, *Bunk: The Rise of Hoaxes, Humbug, Plagiarists, Phonies, Post-Facts, and Fake News* (Minneapolis, MN: Graywolf, 2017). See also Mary Poovey, *A History of the Modern Fact: Problems of Knowledge in the Sciences of Wealth and Society* (Chicago: University of Chicago Press, 1998); Alec Ryrie, *Unbelievers: An Emotional History of Doubt* (Cambridge, MA: Harvard University Press, 2019); Barbara Benedict, *Curiosity: A Cultural History of Early Modern Inquiry* (Chicago: University of Chicago Press, 2001); Michael North, *Novelty: A History of the New* (Chicago: University of Chicago Press, 2013); and Nate Silver, *The Signal and the Noise: Why So Many Predictions Fail—but Some Don't* (New York: Penguin Press, 2012).

In this book I use *idea* and *concept* nearly interchangeably; there are differences that matter greatly to philosophers and linguists, but such differences do not bear substantively on the matters at hand, and going into the weeds of taxonomy would distract us from the arc of the story here. The same is true for *meaning* and *sense* in their more distinctly semantic usages. For our purposes, it's enough to say that *meaning* is more denotative and *sense* more connotative, though as we will see, the sources I quote often mingle the two. There is also a certain irony here in my attention to speculation's reciprocity with the practices tied to it: it spends a large portion of its linguistic life signifying the opposite of *practice*. It's also impossible to discuss speculation in history without using, at times, some terms that are anachronistic but useful to modern readers, in order to trace the plot of this concept in terms that are intelligible in the present. Such a method, though, actually has important roots in the texts I examine.

4. See Urs Stäheli, *Spectacular Speculation: Thrills, the Economy, and Popular Discourse*, trans. Eric Savoth (Stanford, CA: Stanford University Press, 2013); and Stuart Banner, *Speculation: A History of the Fine Line Between Gambling and Investing* (New York: Oxford University Press, 2017).

5. Raymond Williams, introduction to *Keywords: A Vocabulary of Culture and Society* (Oxford: Oxford University Press, 2014), xxvii.

6. David Armitage, *Civil Wars: A History in Ideas* (New Haven, CT: Yale University Press, 2017), 20; emphasis in original. Armitage's debts to Quentin Skinner and, deeper in the background, to Nietzsche and Foucault, are well documented. On method, I owe a more specific debt to Sophia Rosenfeld's *Common Sense: A Political History* (Cambridge, MA: Harvard University Press, 2011), esp. 1–16; Darrin M. McMahon, "The Return of the History of Ideas?," in *Rethinking Modern European Intellectual History*, ed. McMahon and Samuel Moyn (Oxford: Oxford University Press, 2014), 13–31; McMahon and Samuel Moyn, "Introduction: Interim Intellectual History," in *Rethinking Modern European Intellectual History*, 3–12; and Martin Jay, "Historical Explanation and the Event: Reflections on the Limits of Contextualization," *New Literary History* 42, no. 4 (Autumn 2011): 557–71. Also in the background here is Arthur Lovejoy's focus on a single concept and its changes, but with a greater emphasis on context over idea itself. For methodological context, see John Hope Mason, *The Value of Creativity: The Origins and Emergence of a Modern Belief* (Burlington, VT: Ashgate, 2003); Ross Hamilton, *Accident: A Philosophical and Literary*

History (Chicago: University of Chicago Press, 2008); and *Conceptual History in the European Space*, eds. Willibald Steinmetz, Michael Freeden, and Javier Fernández Sebastián (New York: Berghahn Books, 2017).

7. Nor is there a singular moment when *speculation*'s meaning shifts dramatically from *x* to *y*, thereby altering everything that follows, making it a political or a secular category, as the case may be. Rather, a dialectical tension between received meanings and substantive revisions is at the heart of each chapter, as writers especially sought to expand and refashion *speculation*, much as they have over time with words like *state*, *subject*, and *fiction*. Because of this, I should first confess that writing speculation's history felt, at times, like trying to pin down a chimera as one animal: speculation is the kind of concept one can see anywhere and everywhere if attuned to finding it. But that's the beauty of its story. To attend to moments that are most evidentiary for the concept, both qualitatively and quantitatively, will require a broad brush at some points, at others a granular exploration of discrete contexts. And as someone whose work has always been comparative, I should also confess that working mostly in anglophone materials after the first part of chapter 1 in this book has felt somewhat incomplete to me, even while English has hosted an incredible amount of activity around my titular term (and surely there's another book to be written about what preceded Aristotle). But when I tried to start sketching and researching this book as judiciously comparative, I quickly realized that it would take another several volumes to make anything more than passing observations.

And the historical record is sometimes unclear or even contradictory: as we know from words and concepts like *queer*, not only are meanings never final, but also, it's not that hard to find counterexamples of attested uses in the same moment, or to see old and new meanings battling with one another on pressing cultural issues. For a good overview of the benefits and pitfalls of an updated version of philology, and why it must remain attuned to a broader sweep of culture than its traditional practices suggested, see Geoffrey Galt Harpham, "Roots, Races, and the Return to Philology," *Representations* 106, no. 1 (Spring 2009): 34–62.

8. David Armitage, "What's the Big Idea?," *History of European Ideas* 38, no. 4 (2012): 497.

9. Williams, introduction to *Keywords*, xxxiii; emphasis in original. Concepts, as Reinhart Koselleck characterized them, "are like joints linking language and the extralinguistic world" ("A Response," in *The Meaning of Historical Terms and Concepts: New Studies on* Begriffsgeschichte, ed. Hartmut Lehmann and Melvin Richter [Washington, DC: German Historical Institute, 1996], 61). See also Reinhart Koselleck, *The Practice of Conceptual History: Timing History, Spacing Concepts*, trans. Todd Samuel Presner et al. (Stanford, CA: Stanford University Press, 2002).

10. To follow a single word has become an "increasingly common" historiographical pursuit, as Emily Robinson notes, and one that has helped shine a light on the paths of terms like *progressive*, *altruism*, and *ghetto*, all of which have carried forgotten political charges (*The Language of Progressive Politics in Modern Britain* [London: Palgrave MacMillan, 2017], 10); see also Michael Freeden, *Liberal Languages:*

Ideological Imaginations and Twentieth-Century Progressive Thought (Princeton, NJ: Princeton University Press, 2004). In this vein, see also Thomas Dixon, *The Invention of Altruism: Making Moral Meanings in Victorian Britain* (Oxford: Oxford University Press, 2011); and Daniel B. Schwartz, *Ghetto: The History of a Word* (Cambridge, MA: Harvard University Press, 2019). The *Oxford English Dictionary* provides a rough guide to *speculation*'s history, but as we'll see throughout, its suggestion of a neat array of tightly connected variations in meaning, with major language-creators in English acting as demarcating signposts over time, is dramatically oversimplified.

11. There are already discrete histories of financial speculation. A sampling of these titles would include Edward Chancellor, *Devil Take the Hindmost: A History of Financial Speculation* (New York: Plume, 2000); Charles Kindleberger, *Manias, Panics, and Crashes: A History of Financial Crises* (New York: Palgrave Macmillan, 2011); John Kenneth Galbraith, *A Short History of Financial Euphoria* (New York: Penguin, 1994); Karen Ho, *Liquidated: An Ethnography of Wall Street* (Durham, NC: Duke University Press, 2009); Steve Fraser, *Every Man a Speculator: A History of Wall Street in American Life* (New York: HarperCollins, 2005); Marieke de Goede, *Virtue, Fortune, and Faith: A Genealogy of Finance* (Minneapolis: University of Minnesota Press, 2005); Alex Preda, *Framing Finance: The Boundaries of Markets and Modern Capitalism* (Chicago: University of Chicago Press, 2009); Jens Beckert, *Imagined Futures: Fictional Expectations and Capitalist Dynamics* (Cambridge, MA: Harvard University Press, 2016); and the various treatments of speculation in New Historicism, New Economic Criticism, and New Capitalist Studies dating back at least to the early 1990s.

It's easy to use speculation to characterize a period (say, the Roaring Twenties), or to use familiar qualities of an era to try to explain speculation's effects. Other books might follow speculation through periods of economic turmoil, in particular. I will discuss such studies across the course of this book. But the reality is that most any period in any Western nation after roughly the 1650s could be said to have been marked formatively by speculation. Certainly there was heightened economic anxiety after the Panic of 1837, that is, but there was also plenty of anxiety during the Roaring Twenties. Indeed, the dot-com bubble showed how rising markets and valuations cut both ways: speculation prompts both promises of future security and constant anticipatory anxiety over the bubble's potential burst. In the bigger picture, it's important to remember that, contrary to many characterizations of the economic past that we'll encounter in this book, there *never was* a long, uninterrupted period of economic stability in England or in America that was completely free of convulsions, highs and lows, panics and serial bankruptcies, and so on. Many Americans look back to the 1950s, for instance, as a period of calm, steady economic growth; but in the year 1950 alone, the Dow Jones average, to take just one indicator, rose and fell sharply by more than 10 percent twice in either direction during the Korean War. I aim to avoid overgeneralizations, then, about cultural responses to broad economic trends.

12. Woodrow Wilson, "On Being Human," *Atlantic Monthly*, September 1897, 329.
13. Christopher Anstey, *Speculation; or, A Defence of Mankind* (London: J. Dodsley, 1780), 5. Here, *speculation* presses upon our typical sense of context itself and its putatively explanatory power. There is a great deal of literature on the idea (and especially the limits) of context that bears on my approach here. For two examples with similarly broad range but different conclusions, see Christopher Lane, "The Poverty of Context: Historicism and Nonmimetic Fiction," *PMLA* 118, no. 3 (May 2003): 450–69; and Rita Felski, *The Limits of Critique* (Chicago: University of Chicago Press, 2015). On perception and context, a relevant overview is Daniel Kahneman's *Thinking, Fast and Slow* (New York: Farrar, Straus and Giroux, 2011).

1. THE MIRROR AND THE WATCHTOWER

1. Augustine, *De trinitate*, ed. W. J. Mountain, CCSL 50 (Tournhout: Brepols, 1968), 15.8.14. The Vulgate reads: "Nos vero omnes, revelata facie gloriam Domini speculantes, in eandem imaginem transformamur a claritate in claritatem, tamquam a Domini Spiritu" (*The Vulgate New Testament* [London: Samuel Bagster, 1872], 2 Corinthians 3:18). Some newer translations of the Greek, such as the New International Version, actually erase the reference to a mirror or reflection and read "contemplate the Lord's glory." Augustine's reading of this passage, in turn, prompted much commentary over the centuries; see, for example, Aquinas's treatment of it in *Summa theologica* 2.3.180, "Of the contemplative life." The plural of the Latin *speculum* is *specula*, which makes for more wordplay among Latin writers.
2. There is much to explore here, too, concerning Greek and Latin theories of visual perception and optics. See Olivier Darrigol, *A History of Optics from Greek Antiquity to the Nineteenth Century* (Oxford: Oxford University Press, 2012); A. Mark Smith, *From Sight to Light: The Passage from Ancient to Modern Optics* (Chicago: University of Chicago Press, 2015); and David C. Lindberg, *Theories of Vision from Al-Kindi to Kepler* (Chicago: University of Chicago Press, 1976). More generally, see also David Freedberg, *The Power of Images: Studies in the History and Theory of Response* (Chicago: University of Chicago Press, 1989); and Martin Jay, *Downcast Eyes: The Denigration of Vision in Twentieth-Century French Thought* (Berkeley: University of California Press, 1993). Interestingly, the *-skop* stem goes on to become a root for some ecclesiastical terms, such as *episcopal* and *bishop*. We will use the benefit of hindsight to sort through some of the stray ends and errant leads here, where some formations have become little more than relics of linguistic history, like the now-forgotten *speculable*.
3. See Eileen Reeves's work on the use of mirrors and telescope-like objects in military reconnaissance from ancient Greek and Rome to the early modern period, in *Galileo's Glassworks: The Telescope and the Mirror* (Cambridge, MA: Harvard University Press, 2008). See also Sabine Melchior-Bonnet, *The Mirror: A History*, trans. Katharine H. Jewett (New York: Routledge, 2001).

4. See the listing for *speculatio* and related terms in the University of Chicago's Logeion dictionary-search tool: http://logeion.uchicago.edu/index.html#speculatio. Secondary meanings include an entertaining spectacle or show, and the money paid to a night watchman, who could be a *speculator*.

5. There are over two dozen formations across Latin, too much to consider here: *specular, speculatrix, speculor, spectaculum*, and so on. Mark 6:27 mentions a *spekoulatór* as an executioner. I am taking methodological cues in the early part of this chapter from Erich Auerbach's "Figura," in *Scenes from the Drama of European Literature* (Minneapolis: University of Minnesota Press, 1984), 11–76.

6. Readings of the "glass" changed over time, sometimes alongside the changing technologies of creating reflective surfaces; see Maurice A. Hunt, *Shakespeare's Speculative Art* (New York: Palgrave Macmillan, 2011). James 1:23 also uses this term, which becomes *speculum* again in Latin, in the line, "For if any be a hearer of the word, and not a doer, he is like unto a man beholding his natural face in a glass" (KJV). And 2 Peter 1:16 calls followers of Jesus "eyewitnesses of His majesty" (KJV), with the Greek term *epoptai* translated in the Vulgate as *speculators*.

7. *Vulgate New Testament*, 1 Corinthians 13:12. The rabbinical tradition uses a term Hebraized from Latin here: אספקלריה (*aspaklaria*), which indicates a prophetic vision in the Jewish mystical tradition. See Elliot R. Wolfson, *Through a Speculum That Shines: Vision and Imagination in Medieval Jewish Mysticism* (Princeton, NJ: Princeton University Press, 1994).

8. Augustine, *Enarrationes in Psalmos* 101, ed. Eligius Dekkers and Jean Fraipont, CCSL 40 (Turnhout: Brepols, 1990), sermo 2.4.

9. Hilary of Poitiers also gave *speculatio* for "Zion"; for more on this, see Annette Volfing, *The Daughter Zion Allegory in Medieval German Religious Writing* (New York: Routledge, 2017), 5–14. See also Ellen Scully, "Jerusalem's Lost Etymology: How Augustine Changed Latin Eschatology," *Vigiliæ Christianæ* 70 (2016): 1–30. The etymology of ציון (Zion) in Hebrew is still disputed.

10. See Hannah Arendt, *The Human Condition* (Chicago: University of Chicago Press, 1958). Arendt traces how these categories evolved and, sometimes, broke down in Greek and Roman life, and Augustine's role in redefining them. The distinctions among them were never cut and dry and have been debated for millennia now, but on the whole, theoretical philosophy (the summit of *theōria*) has been understood as concerned with universal truths that do not depend on time and space, whereas practical philosophy concerns contingent truths produced by human action. Theoretical knowledge, furthermore, is an end in itself, truth known for the sake of knowing truth. For an overview, see Jennifer Summit and Blakey Vermeule, *Action versus Contemplation: Why an Ancient Debate Still Matters* (Chicago: University of Chicago Press, 2018); and Steven Shapin, *Never Pure: Historical Studies of Science as if It Was Produced by People with Bodies, Situated in Time, Space, Culture, and Society, and Struggling for Credibility and Authority* (Baltimore: Johns Hopkins University Press, 2010). The typical reading here is that the Greeks prized contemplation, the Romans action, and medieval Christianity went back to contemplation again, before

1. THE MIRROR AND THE WATCHTOWER 195

Protestantism and the scientific revolution elevated action. A first-century-CE title ascribed to Philo, for example, was *De vita contemplativa*. The discursive shift from *theōria* to *contemplativa* in Latin that Arendt points out was possible because Cicero and Seneca influentially used forms of *contemplari* when translating Aristotle into Latin (see Cicero, *De officiis* 1.154 and 3.1, for example); the less common Greek *spekula* does not have the place in Aristotle that *theōria* does, either.

11. Boethius had grown frustrated with the now-lost Latin translation of Porphyry's *Isagōgē* by Marius Victorinus, which he had used for his initial commentaries; he later used his own translation as the source of his commentary. Boethius also passes on the Vulgate's many uses of *specula* and *speculator*, which offered him a number of potential conceptual pathways to develop his expansive sense of *speculatio*; he goes directly to Aristotle.

12. Boethius offers some explanations of his translations of Greek philosophical terms—though not *theōria*—in *Contra Eutychen et Nestorium*, chap. 3, in Boethius, *Theological Tractates and The Consolation of Philosophy*, trans. H. F. Stewart, E. K. Rand, and S. J. Tester, Loeb Classical Library 74 (Cambridge, MA: Harvard University Press, 1973), 84–90. On some of Boethius's other translations of Aristotelian philosophical terms, especially as mediated by his readings of Cicero, see Victorino Tejera, *The Return of the King: The Intellectual Warfare over Democratic Athens* (Lanham, MD: University Press of America, 1998), 162–65.

13. For parallel Greek, Latin, and English versions of the *Isagōgē*, see http://www.logicmuseum.com/wiki/Authors/Porphyry/isagoge/parallel#cite_ref-1. For a modern English translation with notes, see Porphyry the Phoenician, *Isagoge*, trans. Edward W. Warren (Toronto: Pontifical Institute of Mediaeval Studies, 1975). On Boethius as a translator, see Edmund Reiss, *Boethius* (Boston: Twayne, 1982), 33–34. For a timeline and bibliography of Boethius's commentaries and retranslations, see John Magee and John Marenbon, "Appendix: Boethius' Works," in *The Cambridge Companion to Boethius*, ed. Marenbon (New York: Cambridge University Press, 2009), 303–310.

14. Boethius, *In Isagogen Porphyrii commenta*, ed. George Schepss and Samuel Brandt (Leipzig: G. Freytag, 1906; repr., New York: Johnson Reprint, 1966), 8. *Poiēsis* was not a subject of philosophy, thus this dyad.

15. See Martin Heidegger, "Science and Reflection," in *The Question Concerning Technology, and Other Essays*, trans. William Lovitt (New York: Harper & Row, 1977), 163–165; and Rodolphe Gasché, *The Tain of the Mirror: Derrida and the Philosophy of Reflection* (Cambridge, MA: Harvard University Press, 1986), 42–43. The Latin *theoria* had also emerged around the fourth century CE as a common translation. Boethius complained, meanwhile, that the Latin tongue as a whole did not match the vocabulary and the semantic range of Greek's abstract concepts. See *Contra Eutychen et Nestorium*, chap. 3.

16. Boethius, *In Isagogen Porphyrii commenta*, 7.

17. See Thomas Christensen, "Music Theory in Clio's Mirror," *Music in the Mirror: Reflections on the History of Music Theory and Literature for the Twenty-First*

Century, ed. Andreas Giger and Thomas J. Mathiesen (Lincoln: University of Nebraska Press, 2002), 1–19.
18. Boethius, *De institutione musica* 1.15, in *De institutione arithmetica libri duo, De institutione music libri quinque* (Leipzig: B. G. Teubneri, 1867), 200; all translations mine unless otherwise noted. Calvin M. Bower gives it as "Concerning the sequence of subjects, that is, of speculations," in Boethius, *Fundamentals of Music*, trans. Bower, ed. Claude V. Palisca (New Haven, CT: Yale University Press, 1989), 21.
19. Boethius, *De institutione musica* I.15, 224; cf. Boethius, *Fundamentals of Music*, 51.
20. Boethius, *De trinitate*, in *Theological Tractates and The Consolation of Philosophy*, 24. See "An Overview of the Structure of Rhetoric" [*Speculatio de cognatione rhetoricae Boethii*], trans. Joseph M. Miller, in *Readings in Medieval Rhetoric*, eds. Miller, Michael H. Prosser, and Thomas W. Benson (Bloomington: Indiana University Press, 1973), 69–78. A brief text attributed to Boethius is also titled *Speculatio de cognatione rhetoricae*.
21. See James Shiel, "Boethius' Commentaries on Aristotle," in *Aristotle Transformed: The Ancient Commentators and Their Influence*, 2nd ed., ed. Richard Sorabji (New York: Bloomsbury, 2016), 377.
22. Cf. Aristotle, *Topica*, trans. Boethius (Turnhout: Brepols / Aristoteles Latinus Database, 2011), book 1, chap. 11, p. 16, para. l, line 22 [see Bekker 104b for original]; book 1, chap. 18, p. 28, para. l, line 21 [Bekker 108b]; and book 6, chap. 6, p. 128, para. l, line 5 [Bekker 145a].
23. See Henry Chadwick, *Boethius: The Consolations of Music, Logic, Theology, and Philosophy* (Oxford: Clarendon Press, 1981), 131–132. For more context, see *A Companion to Boethius in the Middle Ages*, ed. Noel Harold Kaylor Jr. and Philip Edward Philips (Leiden: Brill, 2012). See also *Five Texts on the Mediæval Problem of Universals: Porphyry, Boethius, Abelard, Duns Scotus, Ockham*, ed. Paul Vincent Spade (Indianapolis, IN: Hackett, 1997).
24. Boethius, *The Consolation of Philosophy*, trans. P. G. Walsh (Clarendon Press: Oxford, 1999), 4. Boethius writes, "Harum in extrema margine Π Graecum, in supremo vero Θ, legebatur intextum." The Loeb translation is available online: https://www.loebclassics.com/view/boethius-consolation_philosophy/1973/pb_LCL074.393.xml. Parallel texts of several translations can be found here: https://www2.hf.uio.no/polyglotta/index.php?page=fulltext&view=fulltext&vid=216&mid=0.
25. See John Marenbon, "Introduction: Reading Boethius Whole," in *Cambridge Companion to Boethius*, 7.
26. Boethius, *Consolation*, trans. Walsh, 71. The Latin reads, "Et: 'O,' inquam, 'ueri praeuia luminis quae usque adhuc tua fudit oratio, cum sui speculatione divina tum tuis rationibus inuicta patuerunt, eaque mihi etsi ob iniuriae dolorem nuper oblita non tamen antehac prorsus ignorata dixisti.'"
27. On Boethius's faith, see Chadwick, *Boethius*, 248–49.
28. "humanas vero animas liberiores quidem esse necesse est cum se in mentis divinae speculatione conservant, minus vero cum dilabuntur ad corpora, minusque etiam, cum terrenis artubus colligantur." Boethius, *Philosophae consolatio*, 5.2, ed. Ludwig Bieler, CCSL 94 (Turnhout: Brepols, 1957), 90.

1. THE MIRROR AND THE WATCHTOWER   197

29. "Qui cum ex alta providentiae specula respexit, quid unicuique conveniat agnoscit et quod convenire novit accommodat." Boethius, *Consolation*, trans. Walsh, 91; Boethius, *Philosophae consolatio*, 4.6, ed. Bieler, 81.
30. Boethius, *Philosophae consolatio*, 5.6, ed. Bieler, 103.
31. G. R. Evans, *Old Arts and New Theology: The Beginnings of Theology as an Academic Discipline* (Oxford: Clarendon Press, 1980), 91.
32. Evans, *Old Arts*, 99. Marcia L. Colish also describes a slow-moving "revival of speculation" and speculative theology that gained steam in the eleventh century (*Medieval Foundations of the Western Intellectual Tradition, 400–1400* [New Haven, CT: Yale University Press, 1997], 265). Dale Coulter adds that "*Speculatio* denotes an imaginative construction of reality that is more than merely hypothetical, in which one supposes what may be the case" ("Contemplation as 'Speculation': A Comparison of Boethius, Hugh of St. Victor, and Richard of St. Victor," in *From Knowledge to Beatitude: St. Victor, Twelfth-Century Scholars, and Beyond: Essays in Honor of Grover A. Zinn, Jr.*, ed. E. Ann Matter and Lesley Smith [Notre Dame, IN: University of Notre Dame Press, 2013], 205). See also Marcia L. Colish, *The Mirror of Language: A Study in the Medieval Theory of Knowledge* (New Haven, CT: Yale University Press, 1968). We see the *speculative/practical* language elsewhere in titles like Jean Gerson's *De mystica theologia speculativa* and *De mystica theologia practica* (ca. 1402).
33. See Evans, *Old Arts*, 91–100. See also, on the connections between speculation and mapping, Marcia Kupfer, "Reflections in the Ebstorf Map: Cartography, Theology, and *Dilectio Speculationis*," in *Mapping Medieval Geographies: Geographical Encounters in the Latin West and Beyond, 300–1600*, ed. Keith D. Lilley (New York: Cambridge University Press, 2013), 119–120.
34. For more context, see Richard Kroner's *Speculation and Revelation* trilogy of studies.
35. Evans, *Old Arts*, 92–93.
36. Dale M. Coulter, *Per Visibilia ad Invisibilia: Theological Method in Richard of St. Victor (d. 1173)* (Turnhout: Brepols, 2006), 35.
37. Quoted in Coulter, "Contemplation as 'Speculation,'" 217.
38. Andreas Speer explains that "Aquinas distinguishes between contemplation (*contemplatio*) in the true sense, by which one contemplates God as such, and speculation (*speculatio*), by which one sees the divine in created things like in a mirror ('in speculo inspicit')," in "Contemplation and Philosophy: A Historical and Systematic Approach," in *Contemplation and Philosophy: Scholastic and Mystical Modes of Medieval Philosophical Thought; A Tribute to Kent Emery, Jr.*, ed. Roberto Hofmeister Pich and Speer (Leiden: Brill, 2018), 90. See also Olga Taxidou, *Tragedy, Modernity, and Mourning* (Edinburgh: Edinburgh University Press, 2004), 34–35; and Françoise Dastur, "Tragedy and Speculation," in *Philosophy and Tragedy*, ed. Miguel de Beistegui and Simon Sparks (New York: Routledge, 2000), 77. *Speculabilia* followed as a Latin term for ideas that exist without regard to phenomenal matter.
39. In fact, for Jerome, the terms *speculatio* and *contemplatio* had been synonymous, if not interchangeable: in his book of Hebrew names, for instance, he gives the Latin of

Masefa/Massefath (watchtower) as "speculatio vel contemplatio," in Jerome, *Liber interpretationis hebraicorum nominum*, ed. Paul Anton de Lagarde, CPL 581 (Turnhout: Brepols, 2010), s.v. "masefa/massefath."

40. Sara Ritchey, *Holy Matter: Changing Perceptions of the Material World in Late Medieval Christianity* (Ithaca, NY: Cornell University Press, 2014), 35.

41. Henry Osborn Taylor, *The Medieval Mind: A History of the Development of Thought and Emotion in the Middle Ages*, 2 vols. (London: Macmillan, 1914), 2:108. See Mary Carruthers, *The Craft of Thought: Meditation, Rhetoric, and the Making of Images, 400–1200* (Cambridge: Cambridge University Press, 1998). See also Ritamary Bradley, "Backgrounds of the Title *Speculum* in Mediaeval Literature," *Speculum* 29, no. 1 (January 1954): 100–115. There were also the Modists, who penned "speculative grammars" such as the *Tractatus de modis significandi seu Grammatica speculativa*, by Thomas of Erfurt in the early 1300s. The long-standing journal of medieval studies founded in the twentieth century, of course, is named *Speculum*.

42. There is even more to say here about the mirrors of the soul and of God, and about speculation and contemplation's connections to mysticism; for an overview, see Jeffrey F. Hamburger, "Speculations on Speculation: Vision and Perception in the Theory and Practice of Mystical Devotions," in *Deutsche Mystik im abendländischen Zusammenhang: Neu erschlossene Texte, neue methodische Ansätze, neue theoretische Konzepte*, ed. Walter Haug and Wolfram Schneider-Lastin (Tübingen: Max Niemeyer Verlag, 2000), 353–408. On specular vision more specifically, see Barbara Newman, "What Did It Mean to Say 'I Saw?' The Clash between Theory and Practice in Medieval Visionary Culture," *Speculum* 80, no. 1 (January 2005), 1–43; and Herbert L. Kessler, "Speculum," *Speculum* 86, no. 1 (January 2011): 1–41. More generally, see also Suzanne Conklin Akbari, *Seeing Through the Veil: Optical Theory and Medieval Allegory* (Toronto: University of Toronto Press, 2004).

43. Dale Coulter writes that "*speculatio* [was] a contemplative reflecting upon the created world, which itself mirrors the divine Artist" ("Contemplation as 'Speculation,'" 206).

44. For an overview of these contexts, see Mary Catherine Davidson, *Medievalism, Multilingualism, and Chaucer* (New York: Palgrave Macmillan, 2010).

45. We must also be wary of the myth of Chaucer as creator of what became modern English, and within that myth, of the nationalist-monolingualist story of English's dominance. Christopher Cannon has shown that, even in terms of bringing French into English, Chaucer was not the first and arguably not the most important figure for England. See *The Making of Chaucer's English: A Study of Words* (Cambridge: Cambridge University Press, 1998); see also Simon Horobin, *Chaucer's Language* (New York: Palgrave Macmillan, 2007); *Multilingualism in Later Medieval Britain*, ed. D. A. Trotter (Rochester, NY: D. S. Brewer, 2000); and Marion Turner, *Chaucer: A European Life* (Princeton, NJ: Princeton University Press, 2019). Chaucer's close friend John Gower, for instance, authored works for similar audiences, at least one each in Latin, Anglo-Norman, and English.

46. On Chaucer as a translator, see Tim William Machan, *Techniques of Translation: Chaucer's Boece* (Norman, OK: Pilgrim Books, 1985); and Charles Muscatine, *Chaucer and the French Tradition: A Study in Style and Meaning* (Berkeley: University of California Press, 1957).
47. See *Chaucer's Boece and the Medieval Tradition of Boethius*, ed. A. J. Minnis (Cambridge: D. S. Brewer, 1993). Chaucer worked from Jean de Meun's recent Old French translation of the *Consolation* and with Nicholas Trevet's Latin commentary on the text.
48. Chaucer, *Boece*, in *The Riverside Chaucer*, ed. Larry D. Benson (Boston: Houghton Mifflin, 1987), 398.
49. Chaucer, *Boece*, 440.
50. Jean de Meun's translation here reads, "Mais les ames humaines couvient il que elles soient plus franchez quant ells se gardent ou regart de la *divine pensee*, et moins franchez quant elles descendent es corps, et moins encores quant ells son enlaciees et comprisez des members terriens" (V. L. Dedeck-Héry, "Boethius' De Consolatione by Jean de Meun," *Mediaeval Studies* 14 [1952]: 259; emphasis added). There is some uncertainty about which sections in texts attributed to Jean de Meun were by other translators; see *Sources of the Boece*, ed. Tim William Machan (Athens: University of Georgia Press, 2005). Another Old French translation from this time (translator unknown) renders it: "Mais les ames tant plus sont franches, quant plus s'eslievent sur les corps par contemplacion ... et moins quant ells s'entendent au corps" (*Le livre de Boece de consolacion*, ed. Glynnis M. Cropp [Geneva: Librairie Droz, 2006], 242–43). Some of these translations are combined versions from multiple translators. See also Denis Billotte, *Le vocabulaire de la traduction par Jean de Meun de la Consolatio Philosophiæ de Boèce* (Paris: Honoré Champion Éditeur, 2000).
51. Chaucer, *Boece*, 458. It's unclear whether the Latin text that Chaucer consulted had *speculatione* or *speculacione*; both orthographies were common at this time, and the title of Boethius's text varied in medieval transcriptions, too.
52. According to an exacting analysis by Joseph Mersand, Chaucer brought over more words from Romance languages per line in *Boece* (and used them for 17 percent of the whole text) than in most of his other writings. See Mersand, *Chaucer's Romance Vocabulary* (New York: Comet Press, 1939), 151–155; and the relevant chapters in Kaylor and Phillips, *Companion to Boethius in the Middle Ages*.
53. Here again, there is much more to say about medieval and early modern vision and optics than I could possibly address. See, e.g., Stuart Clark, *Vanities of the Eye: Vision in Early Modern European Culture* (New York: Oxford University Press, 2007); Ritchey, *Holy Matter*; and Eileen Reeves, *Evening News: Optics, Astronomy, and Journalism in Early Modern Europe* (Philadelphia: University of Pennsylvania Press, 2014); Peter Nolan, *Now Through a Glass Darkly: Specular Images of Being and Knowing from Virgil to Chaucer* (Ann Arbor, MI: University of Michigan, 1990); and Rayna Kalas, *Frame, Glass, Verse: The Technology of Poetic Invention in the English Renaissance* (Ithaca, NY: Cornell University Press, 2007).
54. Chaucer, *Boece*, 468.

55. *Boethius: De Consolatione Philosophiae*, trans. John Walton, ed. Mark Science (London: Oxford University Press, 1927), 290.
56. See *Queen Elizabeth's Englishings of Boethius*, ed. Caroline Pemberton (London: Kegan Paul, 1899), 104, https://babel.hathitrust.org/cgi/pt?id=hvd.hngeda&view=1up&seq=9.
57. The *Oxford English Dictionary*'s taxonomy of the various forms of *speculation* in the 1400–1500s is overly and somewhat artificially tedious; several of them capture the same sense, while others were not yet developed fully enough to be differentiated as the *OED* has them.
58. Reginald Pecock, *The Reule of Crysten Religioun*, ed. William Cabell Greet (London: Oxford University Press, 1927), 469.
59. See the associated quotations in *Middle English Dictionary*, s.v. "speculāciǒun," accessed May 18, 2017, https://quod.lib.umich.edu/m/middle-english-dictionary/dictionary/MED42048/track?counter=1&search_id=4717386. Speculative comes into English around the same time, too—at least based on existing records and apparent frequencies. Most of these senses and usages would become obsolete in a few centuries' time.
60. See Linne R. Mooney, "A Middle English Text on the Seven Liberal Arts," *Speculum* 68, no. 4 (October 1993): 1049.
61. Thomas Elyot, *The Dictionary of Syr Thomas Eliot Knyght* (London: Thomas Berthelet, 1538; Ann Arbor, MI: Text Creation Partnership, 2008), n.p., http://name.umdl.umich.edu/a21313.0001.001. Elyot's uses of the term were retained in others' expansions of his work in 1584 and 1587. John Rider's *Bibliotheca scholastica* (1589) has *speculation* as "speculatio, contemplatio" and "inspectus," a synonym for *contemplate*. For John Bullokar (*An English Expositor*, 1616), *speculation* is "the inward knowledge, or beholding of a thing." The *Ortus vocabulorum* (1500) has similar definitions and is more limited, with *speculum, specula, speculator*, and not *speculatio*. But the financial sense is still far away; the practice of cornering markets and forestalling was well established in the medieval era, but what we would now call a "speculator" was called an "ingroser" or "engrosser" in the 1400s. There were even accidental and circumstantial connections to finance, as in the title of Thomas Bell's *The Speculation of Usury* (1596). Bell's title refers to his ideas (speculations) on usury. This is another topic altogether—as is usury—that I cannot treat here, and on which there is a wealth of literature. For an overview, see John H. Munro, "The Medieval Origins of the Financial Revolution: Usury, *Rentes*, and Negotiability," *International History Review* 25, no. 3 (September 2003): 505–62; and Robert S. Lopez, *The Commercial Revolution of the Middle Ages, 950–1350* (Englewood Cliffs, NJ: Prentice-Hall, 1971). For a sketch of the theological debates on these topics, see Odd Langholm, *Economics in the Medieval Schools: Wealth, Exchange, Value, Money, and Usury According to the Paris Theological Tradition, 1200–1350* (Leiden: Brill, 1992).
62. John Florio, *A Worlde of Wordes, or Most Copious, and Exact Dictionarie in Italian and English* (London: Arnold Hatfield, 1598; Ann Arbor, MI: Text Creation Partnership, 2007), n.p., http://name.umdl.umich.edu/A00991.0001.001. By the early 1600s,

we have *speculate* as a transitive and then an intransitive verb, but the noun and adjective predominated in the 1400s and 1500s.

63. Thomas Adams, *A Commentary or, Exposition Upon the Divine Second Epistle Generall...* (London: Richard Badger; Ann Arbor, MI: Text Creation Partnership, 2014), 16, http://name.umdl.umich.edu/A00665.0001.001.

64. John Wycliffe, "Of Many Martris" (sermon 74), *Select English Works of John Wyclif*, ed. Thomas Arnold, 3 vols. (Oxford: Clarendon Press, 1871), 1:241. Wycliffe does not use any version of *speculatif* or *speculacioun* for the same lines in Corinthians that Augustine contemplated; instead, he writes, "We seen now bi a myrour in derknesse" and "trensfourmyd into the same ymage."

65. See also the instances in John Lydgate's *Troy Book*, ed. Henry Bergen (London: Oxford University Press, 1935), 118; and Lydgate, *The Pilgrimage of the Life of Man* (Philadelphia: J. B. Lippincott, 1904), 496.

66. The works of David Lindsay, Thomas Cooper, and again Thomas Elyot use these and other phrases.

67. Edmund Bunny, *A Booke of Christian Exercise* (London: Ninian Newton and Arnold Hatfield, 1584; Ann Arbor, MI: Text Creation Partnership, 2005), n.p., http://name.umdl.umich.edu/A09069.0001.001.

68. Paracelsus, *A Hundred and Fouretene Experiments and Cures...* (London: Vallentine Sims, 1596; Ann Arbor, MI: Text Creation Partnership, 2005), n.p., http://name.umdl.umich.edu/A08904.0001.001.

69. See Daniel R. Smith, "Nature," in *Encyclopedia of Martin Luther and the Reformation*, ed. Mark A. Lamport, 2 vols. (New York: Rowman & Littlefield, 2017), 2:549.

70. John Calvin, *Of the Life or Conversation of a Christen Man...*, trans. Thomas Broke (London: John Daye and Wyllyam Seres, 1549; Ann Arbor, MI: Text Creation Partnership, 2005), n.p., http://name.umdl.umich.edu/A17689.0001.001.

71. *Vain* still primarily signified "empty, worthless, void," from the Latin *vanus*, which Calvin used; the secondary sense of "narcissism" developed in the 1400s, more around *vanitas/vanity*.

72. John Calvin, *The Institution of Christian Religion* (London: Reinolde Wolfe and Richarde Harison 1561; Ann Arbor, MI: Text Creation Partnership, 2003), 1.12.1, http://name.umdl.umich.edu/A17662.0001.001. Calvin's most important English translator was the virulently anti-Catholic Thomas Norton; see Michael A. R. Graves, *Thomas Norton: The Parliament Man* (Cambridge, MA: Blackwell, 1994), 26–29; and Bruce Gordon, *John Calvin's "Institutes of the Christian Religion": A Biography* (Princeton, NJ: Princeton University Press, 2016), 58–60.

73. Calvin, *The Sermons of M. John Calvin...*, trans. Arthur Golding (London: Thomas Dawson, 1577; Ann Arbor, MI: Text Creation Partnership, 2005), n.p. http://name.umdl.umich.edu/A17705.0001.001. He warns in this same text against "wandering speculations" and "over hygh speculations."

74. Calvin, *Institution of Christian Religion*, 1.2.2.

75. Calvin, *Institution of Christian Religion*, preface, section 4.

76. Calvin, *Institution of Christian Religion*, 1.15.4.

77. Calvin, *Institution of Christian Religion*, 1.16.2; 1.5.10–11. Calvin was not alone in his sentiments here. As Lorraine Daston writes, "Antipathy to fortune [in the seventeenth century] united Protestant and Catholic, mechanical philosopher and Cambridge Platonist, Hobbesian with Christian virtuoso" ("Fortuna and the Passions," in *Chance, Culture, and the Literary Text*, ed. Thomas M. Kavanagh (Ann Arbor, MI: Michigan Romance Studies, 1994), 26.

78. For more on the dangers of idleness, see Kasey Evans, *Colonial Virtue: The Mobility of Temperance in Renaissance England* (Toronto: University of Toronto Press, 2012), 160–202 passim.

79. The Latin quotations are from *Institutio christianæ religionis* (1561 ed.); the French are from *Institution de la religion chrétienne* (1560 ed.). Other French terms include *froide spéculation, spéculations oisives, spéculation maigre, légères spéculations, spéculations volages*, and *une folle spéculation et inutile*.

80. Calvin explained, "God in himself is invisible, but since his majesty shines through in all of his works and creatures, men must acknowledge him in them—for they clearly make known their creator. Thus the Apostle [Paul] in his epistle to the Hebrews, calls the world a mirror or representation of invisible things" (*Iohannis Calvini Commentarius in Epistolam Pauli ad Romanos*, ed. T. H. L. Parker [Leiden: Brill, 1981], 29). Calvin even played on *specula* in his Latin, as in "*secula dicit esse specula, seu spectacula rerum invisibilium*." Cf. a dictionary entry for "*Speculum electionis*": "mirror of election; ... a term used by Calvin in describing Christ as the one in whom individual election can be known and assurance of salvation can be found," in Richard A. Muller, *Dictionary of Latin and Greek Theological Terms, Drawn Principally from Protestant Scholastic Theology*, 2nd ed. (Grand Rapids, MI: Baker, 2017), 340.

81. See David C. Steinmetz, "The Theology of John Calvin," in *The Cambridge Companion to Reformation Theology*, eds David Bagchi and David C. Steinmetz (Cambridge: Cambridge University Press, 2004), 113; see also Philip Benedict, *Christ's Churches Purely Reformed: A Social History of Calvinism* (New Haven, CT: Yale University Press, 2002), 245.

82. John Knox, *An Answer to a Great Number of Blasphemous Cavillations...* ([Geneva]: John Crespin, 1560; Ann Arbor, MI: Text Creation Partnership, 2003), 75, http://name.umdl.umich.edu/A04920.0001.001.

83. Calvin, *Institution of Christian Religion*, 1.13.14. The phrase does not appear in any of the several medieval corpora that I have been able to search.

84. Philip Sidney, *Astrophil and Stella*, sonnet 18, in *Selected Writings*, ed. Richard Dutton (Manchester: Carcanet Press, 1987), 37; transcription modified. Sidney amplifies his use of *vain* in his translation of Psalms 39: "They are but shades, not true things where we live; / Vain shades and vain, in vain to grieve" ("The Psalms of David," *The Complete Poems of Sir Philip Sidney*, ed. Alexander B. Grosart, 2 vols. [1873], 2:287).

85. Joseph Hall, *A Common Apologie for the Church of England...* (London: [William Stansby], 1610; Ann Arbor, MI: Text Creation Partnership, 2004), 140, http://name.umdl.umich.edu/A02522.0001.001; George Abbott, *An Exposition upon the Prophet Jonah...* (London: Richard Field, 1600; Ann Arbor, MI: Text Creation Partnership,

2003), 384, http://name.umdl.umich.edu/A16485.0001.001. Around the same time, the astrologer John Harvey speaks against "any idle fansie, vaine speculation, or forged invention" (*A Discoursive Probleme Concerning Prophesies*... [London: John Jackson, 1588; Ann Arbor, MI: Text Creation Partnership, 2006], n.p., http://name.umdl.umich .edu/A02779.0001.001). We find these in, among many others, *The Faerie Queene* (1590/1596), *A Christall Glasse of Christian Reformation* (1569), *The Passions of the Mind in General* (1601), and *The Anatomy of Melancholy* (1621). Even in putatively far-flung contexts, as Mary Poovey notes of the early modern origins of double-entry bookkeeping, similar phrases arise: "Since the relation between numerically rendered data and systematic knowledge had yet to be theorized, early modern efforts to assign cultural authority to numerical representation always had to negotiate the animus directed against whatever representational practice went under the epithet of 'mere conjecture' or 'sheer speculation'" (*A History of the Modern Fact: Problems of Knowledge in the Sciences of Wealth and Society* [Chicago: University of Chicago Press, 1998], 77).

86. Calvin, *Institution of Christian Religion*, 1.14.4.
87. Calvin, *Institution of Christian Religion*, 3.11.5. I am grateful to Abram Van Engen for many clarifying conversations on Calvinism here. For more, see Van Engen, *Sympathetic Puritans: Calvinist Fellow Feeling in Early New England* (Oxford: Oxford University Press, 2015).
88. "The Second Royal Injunctions of Henry VIII, 1538," *English Historical Documents*, ed. David C. Douglas, 10 vols. (New York: Oxford University Press, 1967), 5:812. On iconophobia in the history of images more generally, see Freedberg, *Power of Images*.
89. Calvin, *Institution of Christian Religion*, 1.11.8. See Carlos M. N. Eire, *The War Against the Idols: The Reformation of Worship from Erasmus to Calvin* (New York: Cambridge University Press, 1986).
90. Thomas Becon, *A Comfortable Epistle*... (Strasbourg: [J. Lambrecht?], 1542; Ann Arbor, MI: Text Creation Partnership, 2004), n.p., http://name.umdl.umich.edu /A06710.0001.001. See also the Scottish Quaker Robert Barclay's often-reprinted *Apology for the True Christian Divinity*..., first published, in Latin, in 1676, which speaks against the "Idle Worships, Idolatries, and numerous Superstitious Inventions among the Heathens" (London[?]: s.n., 1678; Ann Arbor, MI: Text Creation Partnership, 2005), 269, http://name.umdl.umich.edu/A30895.0001.001.
91. See David D. Hall's exploration of "practical divinity," in *The Puritans: A Transatlantic History* (Princeton, NJ: Princeton University Press, 2019), 109–143.
92. Samuel Clarke, *The Marrow of Ecclesiastical History*... (London: T. V., 1654; Ann Arbor, MI: Text Creation Partnership, 2005), 637, http://name.umdl.umich.edu /A33335.0001.001.
93. Westminster Assembly, *The 1647 Westminster Confession of Faith* (Crossville, TN: Puritan Publications, 2011), 61. And William Burkett explained further in 1716 that "Christianity is not a Speculative Science, but a Practical Art of Holy Living," and therefore "the Bible was not given us meerly for a Theme of Speculation, but for a Rule of Life" (*The Poor Man's Help*... [1716], 103, accessed April 13, 2017, Early American Imprints, series 1).

94. Richard Steele, *An Antidote Against the Distractions*... (London, 1667; Ann Arbor, MI: Text Creation Partnership, 2003), n.p., http://name.umdl.umich.edu/A61386.0001.001.
95. John Davis, *Seismos Megas. Or Heaven & Earth Shaken* (London: T. C., 1655; Ann Arbor, MI: Text Creation Partnership, 2008), 294, http://name.umdl.umich.edu/A81992.0001.001.
96. Henry Vaughan, *A Sermon Preached at the Publiquf [sic] fast*... (Oxford: Leonard Lichfield, 1644; Ann Arbor, MI: Text Creation Partnership, 2005), 9, http://name.umdl.umich.edu/A64750.0001.001.
97. For a broader history, see Mark Valeri, *Heavenly Merchandize: How Religion Shaped Commerce in Puritan America* (Princeton, NJ: Princeton University Press, 2010).
98. *For the Colony in Virginea Britannia: Lawes Diuine, Morall, and Martiall, &c.* (London: Walter Burre, 1612), 57, 24. This is not to conflate English Calvinism and the Puritan movement. There were plenty of English Calvinists who differed from their Puritan contemporaries in either emphasis or degree.
99. Counsel for Virginia, *A True Declaration of the Estate of the Colonie in Virginia*... (London: William Barret, 1610; Ann Arbor, MI: Text Creation Partnership, 2008), 67, http://name.umdl.umich.edu/A14518.0001.001.
100. Pierre de la Primaudaye, *The French Academie*... (London: Edmund Bollifant 1586; Ann Arbor, MI: Text Creation Partnership, 2007), 12, http://name.umdl.umich.edu/A05094.0001.001.
101. Calvin, *Sermons of Master John Calvin, upon the Booke of Job*, trans. Arthur Golding ([London]: [Henry Bynneman], 1574; Ann Arbor, MI: Text Creation Partnership, 2007), n.p., http://name.umdl.umich.edu/A69056.0001.001.
102. James 2:18, in Daniel Mace, *The New Testament in Greek and English* (London: J. Roberts, 1729). To see Mace's translational variant in context, compare here: https://studybible.info/compare/James%202:18. Later, some versions of Timothy 2:23 have the Greek ζητήσεις (*zétésis*) as "speculations."
103. Samuel Johnson, *A Dictionary of the English Language*, 2 vols. (London: W. Strahan, 1755), s.vv. "practical" and "theoretical."
104. Jonathan Edwards, *Practical Sermons: Never Before Published* (Edinburgh: M. Gray, 1788), 5, https://catalog.hathitrust.org/Record/008975283.
105. Edwards, *Practical Sermons*, 6.
106. *The Works of the Reverend John M. Wesley*, ed. John Emory, 7 vols. (New York: B. Waugh and T. Mason, 1833), 1:155.

2. EXPERIMENTING ON THOUGHT

1. *Oxford English Dictionary Online*, s.v. "speculation," accessed January 29, 2020.
2. My sense of this topic is influenced by Joanna Picciotto's insightful account of the early modern reinterpretation of knowledge creation as an active and productive mental labor, both in experimental philosophy and experimental literary texts. See

2. EXPERIMENTING ON THOUGHT 205

Labors of Innocence in Early Modern England (Cambridge, MA: Harvard University Press, 2010). I take the point that all the "revolutions" of this era were a set of incremental changes more than anything else, but for our purposes here, the characterization is solid enough to proceed.

3. *The Novum Organum of Sir Francis Bacon*, trans. M. D. (London, 1676; Ann Arbor, MI: Text Creation Partnership, 2003), 7, http://name.umdl.umich.edu/A28309.0001.001. There is a great deal of scholarship on the links between Reformation theology and natural philosophy. For an overview, see Peter Harrison, *The Bible, Protestantism, and the Rise of Natural Science* (Cambridge: Cambridge University Press, 1998); Amos Funkenstein, *Theology and the Scientific Imagination* (Princeton, NJ: Princeton University Press, 1986); and Steven Matthews, *Theology and Science in the Thought of Francis Bacon* (Aldershot, UK: Ashgate, 2008). See also Jennifer Waldron's notion of "enchanted empiricism," in *Reformations of the Body: Idolatry, Sacrifice, and Early Modern Theater* (New York: Palgrave Macmillan, 2013), 22. The questions of mind-body dualism and the materiality of cognition that arise in this chapter are too large to treat adequately here.
4. Though there are exceptions here, too: *contemplatio* is translated as "speculation" at times in the *Novum organum*.
5. *The Twoo Bookes of Francis Bacon* (London: [Thomas Purfoot and Thomas Creede], 1605; Ann Arbor, MI: Text Creation Partnership, 2003), 26, 27, http://name.umdl.umich.edu/A01516.0001.001.
6. *Twoo Bookes of Francis Bacon*, 111.
7. *Novum Organum of Francis Bacon*, 2.
8. *Twoo Bookes of Francis Bacon*, 21.
9. On the role of imagination here, see J. M. Cocking, *Imagination: A Study in the History of Ideas*, ed. Penelope Murray (London: Routledge, 1991), 268–69.
10. See Lorraine Daston and Peter Galison, *Objectivity* (New York: Zone Books, 2007).
11. *Novum Organum of Francis Bacon*, 6.
12. Francis Bacon, *The Instauratio Magna, Part II: Novum Organum and Associated Texts*, trans. and ed. Graham Rees and Maria Wakely, *The Oxford Francis Bacon*, vol. 11 (Oxford: Oxford University Press, 2004), 3. The title *Novum organum* was an allusion to Aristotle's *Organon*, which had dominated medieval natural philosophy, and which Bacon sought to supersede. Joyce Appleby overstates the case when she claims that "speculation about unknowable and imponderable subjects began to wither" after Bacon; in fact, the methods and means simply kept changing (*The Relentless Revolution: A History of Capitalism* [New York: Norton, 2010], 97).
13. *Twoo Bookes of Francis Bacon*, 27. On the same page, Bacon reads them through older cosmological associations, too: "a Conjunction like unto that of the two highest Planets, *Saturne* the Planet of rest and contemplation; and *Jupiter* the Planet of civile societie and action."
14. *Novum Organum of Francis Bacon*, 7, 8.
15. See *Novum Organum of Francis Bacon*, 21; *Twoo Bookes of Francis Bacon*, 32. The best outlines of Bacon's categories and taxonomies are Peter R. Anstey's; see

"Francis Bacon and the Classification of Natural History," *Early Science and Medicine* 17 (2012): 11–31; "Experimental versus Speculative Natural Philosophy," in *The Science of Nature in the Seventeenth Century: Patterns of Change in Early Modern Natural Philosophy*, ed. Anstey and John A. Schuster (Dordrecht: Springer, 2005), 215–42; and Anstey and Albert Vanzo, "The Origins of Early Modern Experimental Philosophy," *Intellectual History Review* 22, no. 4 (2012): 499–518. The distinction between "speculative" and "operative" masonry seems to have emerged around 1717, too.

16. See Anstey, "Francis Bacon," for a fuller sketch. Bacon's *De augmentis scientiarum* is a reworked and extended Latin version of the *Advancement of Learning*, paralleling it in structure but with plenty of new content.
17. *Two Bookes of Francis Bacon*, 32. In this work, Bacon began, in Joanna Picciotto's words, to "redeem … curiosity from its association with original sin: associated with investigative labor rather than appetite, the first sin became the first virtue" now that it had a potential object and purpose (*Labors of Innocence*, 3).
18. Bacon, *Of the Dignity and Advancement of Learning*, in *The Works of Francis Bacon*, 15 vols., ed. James Spedding, Robert Leslie Ellis, and Douglas Denon Heath (London: Longman, 1858), 4:382.
19. *Novum Organum of Francis Bacon*, 15.
20. Digital versions of Bacon's works in Latin are available at *The Works of Francis Bacon*, ed. James Spedding, Robert Leslie Ellis, and Douglas Denon Heath, 15 vols., Online Books Page, http://onlinebooks.library.upenn.edu/webbin/metabook?id=worksfbacon.
21. Francis Bacon, *The New Organon*, in *Works of Francis Bacon*, 8:101; translation modified. *Experience* and *experiment* crossed a good deal in the mid-1600s, when both terms were shifting; for Bacon, the former was accidental perception, the latter driven by tests. On *experiment* in these contexts, especially with regard to literature, see Karen L. Edwards, *Milton and the Natural World: Science and Poetry in* Paradise Lost (New York: Cambridge University Press, 1999); Martin Jay, *Songs of Experience: Modern American and European Variations on a Universal Theme* (Berkeley: University of California Press, 2005); and John Rogers, *The Matter of Revolution: Science, Poetry, and Politics in the Age of Milton* (Ithaca, NY: Cornell University Press, 1996).
22. Francis Bacon, *New Atlantis and the Great Instauration*, 2nd ed., ed. Jerry Weinberger (Malden, MA: Wiley Blackwell, 2017), 30–31.
23. See, for instance, Abraham Cowley's *A Proposition for the Advancement of Experimental Philosophy* (1667).
24. John Sergeant, *The Method to Science* (London: W. Redmayne, 1696), available at http://tei.it.ox.ac.uk/tcp/Texts-HTML/free/A59/A59232.html.
25. Jacques Savary des Brûlons, *The Universal Dictionary of Trade and Commerce*, 2 vols. (1751), n.p., accessed February 13, 2017, Eighteenth Century Collections Online; John Knox, "On Predestination," in *The Works of John Knox*, 6 vols., ed. David Laing (Edinburgh: James Thin, 1895), 5:116.
26. Isaac Newton, quoted in Anstey and Schuster, *Science of Nature*, 232.

27. Isaac Newton, *Opticks*, 4th ed. (London, 1730), 380, https://babel.hathitrust.org/cgi/pt?id=uc2.ark:/13960/t3ws8zp9j&view=1up&seq=3.
28. Quoted in Richard S. Westfall, *Never at Rest: A Biography of Isaac Newton* (Cambridge: Cambridge University Press, 1980), 862.
29. Mary Poovey, *A History of the Modern Fact: Problems of Knowledge in the Sciences of Wealth and Society* (Chicago: University of Chicago Press, 1998), 218.
30. Robert Boyle, quoted in Stephen Shapin and Simon Schaffer, *Leviathan and the Air-Pump: Hobbes, Boyle, and the Experimental Life* (Princeton, NJ: Princeton University Press, 1985), 331.
31. Quoted in Anstey and Schuster, *Science of Nature*, 218. See also Alexander M. Schlutz, *Mind's World: Imagination and Subjectivity from Descartes to Romanticism* (Seattle: University of Washington Press, 2009); and Jenny Uglow, *The Lunar Men: Five Friends Whose Curiosity Changed the World* (New York: Farrar, Straus and Giroux, 2003).
32. Thomas Browne, *Christian Morals*, in *Thomas Browne: Selected Writings*, ed. Kevin Kileen (Oxford: Oxford University Press, 2014), 756–57. More mystically inclined figures like Johannes Kepler elsewhere praised and valued speculation because of its appeal and approach to the kinds of universal harmony he theorized; Michael Faraday would later use the term in many of his titles, too.
33. William Oughtred uses the phrase "practical speculation" in his *Mathematicall Recreations* (1653), when instructing the reader on how to conduct experiments on an aeolipile, an early steam engine.
34. Thomas Sprat, "Epistle Dedicatory," *The History of the Royal-Society of London* . . . (London: T. R., 1667; Ann Arbor, MI: Text Creation Partnership, 2003), n.p., http://name.umdl.umich.edu/A61158.0001.001.
35. Sprat, *History of the Royal-Society*, 339, 341.
36. Sprat, *History of the Royal-Society*, 257.
37. Sprat, *History of the Royal-Society*, 340, 257.
38. Richard Allestree, *The Causes of the Decay of Christian Piety* (London: R. Norton, 1667; Ann Arbor, MI: Text Creation Partnership, 2004), 1, http://name.umdl.umich.edu/A23697.0001.001.
39. Sprat, *History of the Royal-Society*, 77, 25.
40. Sprat, "An Advertisement to the Reader," *History of the Royal-Society*, n.p.
41. Russell McCormmach, *Speculative Truth: Henry Cavendish, Natural Philosophy, and the Rise of Modern Theoretical Science* (Oxford: Oxford University Press, 2004), 3.
42. Charles Darwin, *On the Origin of Species* (London: John Murray, 1859), 1.
43. Joseph Priestley, *Experiments and Observations Relating to Various Branches of Natural Philosophy*, 6 vols. (London, 1779), 1:7.
44. Thomas Hobbes, *Leviathan* (London: Andrew Cooke, 1651), 105, 193.
45. To be sure, the speculative and the practical remained mostly distinct categories in the late 1600s, and the vocabulary attached to them is critical to what happens next. Thus we see that chapter 1 of book 1 of John Locke's *Essay Concerning Human*

Understanding (1690) is titled "No Innate Speculative Principles"; chapter 2 is "No Innate Practical Principles." The former are principles such as noncontradiction, which don't require particulars to demonstrate; the latter are principles such as the Golden Rule, which require contingent human circumstances and applied judgment to define. Whether speculation was being dismissed from or finding a place in the new science, "speculative knowledge," as it was known, kept a semiautonomous space for itself, too. David Hume followed the same division in his *Treatise of Human Nature* (1740). Speculative philosophy pointed more broadly to knowledge that can't be proven with tests, syllogisms, or propositions about contingent states of affairs, and as Hume noted, "Speculative sciences do, indeed, improve the mind; but this advantage reaches only to a few persons, who have leisure to apply themselves to them. And as to practical arts, which encrease the commodities and enjoyments of life, it is well known, that men's happiness consists not so much in an abundance of these, as in the peace and security with which they possess them" ("Of Parties in General," in *David Hume on Morals, Politics, and Society*, ed. Angela Coventry and Andrew Valls [New Haven, CT: Yale University Press, 2018], 155). See also Jules David Law, *The Rhetoric of Empiricism: Language and Perception from Locke to I. A. Richards* (Ithaca, NY: Cornell University Press, 1993).

46. See P. G. M. Dickson, *The Financial Revolution in England: A Study in the Development of Public Credit, 1688–1756* (London: Macmillan, 1967). For a synopsis, see Larry Stewart, "Measure for Measure: Projectors and the Manufacture of Enlightenment, 1770–1820," in *The Age of Projects*, ed. Maximillian E. Novak (Toronto: University of Toronto Press, 2018), 370–89.

47. J. G. A. Pocock, *The Machiavellian Moment: Florentine Political Thought and the Atlantic Republican Tradition* (Princeton, NJ: Princeton University Press, 2016), 425. See also John Brewer, *The Sinews of Power: War, Money, and the English State, 1688–1783* (London: Unwin Hyman, 1989); Deborah Valenze, *The Social Life of Money in the English Past* (New York: Cambridge University Press, 2006); Bruce G. Carruthers, *City of Capital: Politics and Markets in the English Financial Revolution* (Princeton, NJ: Princeton University Press, 1996); Stephanie Kuduk Weiner, *Republican Politics and English Poetry, 1789–1874* (New York: Palgrave Macmillan, 2005); and Carl Wennerlind, *Casualties of Credit: The English Financial Revolution, 1620–1720* (Cambridge, MA: Harvard University Press, 2011).

48. J. G. A. Pocock, "The Mobility of Property and the Rise of Eighteenth-Century Sociology," in *Virtue, Commerce, and History: Essays on Political Thought and History, Chiefly in the Eighteenth Century* (New York: Cambridge University Press, 1985), 112.

49. J. G. A. Pocock, "Modes of Political and Historical Time in Early Eighteenth-Century England," in *Virtue, Commerce, and History*, 98. See also Peter de Bolla, *The Discourse of the Sublime: Readings in History, Aesthetics, and the Subject* (New York: Blackwell, 1989); Colin Nicholson, *Writing and the Rise of Finance: Capital Satires of the Early Eighteenth Century* (New York: Cambridge University Press, 1994); and

James Thompson, *Models of Value: Eighteenth-Century Political Economy and the Novel* (Durham, NC: Duke University Press, 1996).

50. See John Carswell, *The South Sea Bubble* (Dover, NH: Alan Sutton, 1993), 8.
51. Uniting the languages of science and mind, Mr. Moneywise in William Chetwood's comedy *The Stock-Jobbers* (1720) tells Sir John Wealthy of a scheme he is hatching with a woman: "My Experience join'd to her Imagination, may work Wonders" (*The Stock-Jobbers; or, The Humours of Exchange-Alley* [London: J. Roberts, 1720], 4–5). There is more here to say about the language of wonder—in *Gulliver's Travels*, too—than I have space to treat. For an overview, see Sarah Kareem, *Eighteenth-Century Fiction and the Reinvention of Wonder* (Oxford: Oxford University Press, 2014).
52. Carswell, *South Sea Bubble*, 131; Helen J. Paul, *The South Sea Bubble: An Economic History of Its Origins and Consequences* (New York: Taylor and Francis, 2013), 23.
53. Pocock, *Machiavellian Moment*, 461.
54. Daniel Defoe, *The Anatomy of Exchange-Alley* (London: E. Smith, 1719), 23.
55. Defoe, *Anatomy of Exchange-Alley*, 23.
56. Daniel Defoe, *Review of the State of the British Nation*, June 11, 1709. See Sandra Sherman, *Finance and Fictionality in the Early Eighteenth Century: Accounting for Defoe* (New York: Cambridge University Press, 1996); John Vernon, *Money and Fiction: Literary Realism in the Nineteenth and Early Twentieth Centuries* (Ithaca, NY: Cornell University Press, 1984); Margot C. Finn, *The Character of Credit: Personal Debt in English Culture, 1740–1914* (Cambridge: Cambridge University Press, 2003); and Bram Dijkstra, *Defoe and Economics: The Fortunes of 'Roxana' in the History of Interpretation* (New York: St. Martin's Press, 1987).
57. Daniel Defoe, *An Essay Upon Projects* (London: Cockerill, 1697), 1, https://babel.hathitrust.org/cgi/pt?id=c00.31924013175868&view=1up&seq=10.
58. Ben Jonson, *The Divell Is an Asse* (London: I. B., 1616; Ann Arbor, MI: Text Creation Partnership, 2005), 14, http://name.umdl.umich.edu/A04633.0001.001. See also John Taylor's *The Complaint of M. Tenter-Hooke the Projector* (1641).
59. The often-quoted English preacher Thomas Scott attacked the schemers who would "invent such projects, as may undo the publique for their private and inordinate desires," and who "live in this world as *in a market [and] imagine there is nothing else for them to do, but to buy and sell, and that the only end of their creation and being was to gather riches, by all meanes possible*" (Scott, *The Belgicke Pismire...* [London (i.e., Holland), 1622; Ann Arbor, MI: Text Creation Partnership, 2006], 28, 34, http://name.umdl.umich.edu/A11774.0001.001). See also the anonymous account *The Projectors Down-Fall, or Times Changeling. Wherein the Monopolists and Patentees Are Unmasked to the View of the World* (1642), or playwright's John Wilson's *The Projectors* (1665). See also Michael McKeon, "Civic Humanism and the Logic of Historical Interpretation," in *The Political Imagination in History: Essays Concerning J. G. A. Pocock*, ed. D. N. DeLuna (Baltimore, MD: Owlworks, 2006), 59–99; and Jean-Christophe Agnew, *Worlds Apart: The Market and the Theater in Anglo-American*

Thought, 1550–1750 (Cambridge: Cambridge University Press, 1986), on the entwined languages of arts and markets in this period. In *The Tempest* (1610–1611), Prospero's sprite Ariel stops the deadly plot that Antonio and Sebastian concoct, "For else [my master's] project dies." Prospero then opens the final act with the declaration, "Now does my project gather to a head." But he closes the play in lament, asking in his epilogue that the audience

But release me from my bands
With the help of your good hands:
Gentle breath of yours my sails
Must fill, or else my project fails,
Which was to please.
(*The Tempest*, in *The Norton Shakespeare*, ed. Stephen Greenblatt, Walter Cohen, Jean E. Howard, and Katharine Eisaman Maus (New York: W. W. Norton, 1997), 2.1.295; 5.1.1; epilogue, lines 9–12.

60. David Hume, *Essays: Moral, Political, and Literary*, ed. T. H. Green and T. H. Grose, 2 vols. (London: Longman, Green, 1875), 1:371, https://books.google.com/books?id=z5M3AQAAMAAJ.
61. Defoe, *Essay Upon Projects*, 20.
62. Defoe, *Essay Upon Projects*, 24, 25.
63. We can note here, too, that once again, *contemplation* rarely surfaces in discussions of finance and carries almost none of the airy, abstract connotations that make it so flexible and adaptable for the intersecting ideas at play. And *contemplation* remains quite stable in its senses in comparison to *speculation*.
64. Respectively, Michael Geddes, *The Church-History of Ethiopia* (London, 1696; Ann Arbor, MI: Text Creation Partnership, 2014), 37, http://name.umdl.umich.edu/A42562.0001.001; John Gauden, *Hiera Dacrya . . .* (London: J. G., 1659; Ann Arbor, MI: Text Creation Partnership, 2008), 425, http://name.umdl.umich.edu/A42483.0001.001; John Wilkins, *Sermons Preached . . .* (London, 1682; Ann Arbor, MI: Text Creation Partnership, 2004), 269, http://name.umdl.umich.edu/A66062.0001.001.
65. Daniel Defoe, *Review*, October 22, 1706.
66. Daniel Defoe, *The Chimera* (London, 1720; Ann Arbor, MI: Text Creation Partnership, 2007), 4, http://name.umdl.umich.edu/004834057.0001.000.
67. Samuel Johnson, "The Adventurer," in *The Works of Samuel Johnson*, 12 vols. (London: T. Longman et al., 1796), 3:223.
68. Defoe, *Essay Upon Projects*, 15.
69. Defoe, *Essay Upon Projects*, 35, 16.
70. Defoe, *Essay Upon Projects*, 13, 14.
71. See David Alff, *The Wreckage of Intentions: Projects in British Culture, 1660–1730* (Philadelphia: University of Pennsylvania Press, 2017). See also Patrick Brantliger,

2. EXPERIMENTING ON THOUGHT   211

Fictions of State: Culture and Credit in Britain, 1694–1994 (Ithaca, NY: Cornell University Press, 1996), 48–87.

72. Andrea Finkelstein, *Harmony and the Balance: An Intellectual History of Seventeenth-Century English Economic Thought* (Ann Arbor, MI: University of Michigan Press, 2000), 61.

73. See Jürgen Habermas, *The Structural Transformation of the Public Sphere*, trans. Thomas Burger (Cambridge, MA: MIT Press, 1991), 42–43. See also Lee Morrissey, *The Constitution of Literature: Literacy, Democracy, and Early English Literary Criticism* (Stanford, CA: Stanford University Press, 2008), 87–95. For an overview of criticism of this theory, see Anthony Pollock, "Neutering Addison and Steele: Aesthetic Failure and the Spectatorial Public Sphere," *ELH* 74, no. 3 (Fall 2007): 707–34. There is some "speculation" in *The Tatler*, too, but not as much. On this broader topic, see Adrian Johns, "Reading and Experiment in the Early Royal Society," in *Reading, Society, and Politics in Early Modern England*, ed. Kevin Sharpe and Steven N. Zwicker (Cambridge: Cambridge University Press, 2003), 256.

74. Joseph Addison and Richard Steele, *The Spectator*, March 1, 1711, in *The Spectator*, 4 vols., ed. Gregory Smith (London: Dent, 1964), 1:3. Translation of Horace mine, modified from Horace, *Satires. Epistles. The Art of Poetry*, trans. H. Rushton Fairclough (Cambridge, MA: Harvard University Press, 1926), 463. Some editions parse which contributions were Addison's and which were Steele's, but that is beyond the scope of our purposes here.

75. "Speculator" was also the name of an opinion-piece author in Providence and Boston in the early 1770s, and the Worcester Speculator was a section of Isaiah Thomas's *Worcester Magazine* in the mid-1780s. See Arthur M. Schlesinger, *Prelude to Independence: The Newspaper War on Britain, 1764–1776* (New York: Knopf, 1958), 132.

76. Addison and Steele, *The Spectator*, November 13, 1712, in Smith, *The Spectator*, 4:185. See also Peter Smithers, *The Life of Joseph Addison* (Oxford: Clarendon Press, 1968), 196–254; and Erin Mackie, *Market à la Mode: Fashion, Commodity, and Gender in "The Tatler" and "The Spectator"* (Baltimore, MD: Johns Hopkins University Press, 1997), 1–54. See also Sophia Rosenfeld, *Common Sense: A Political History* (Cambridge, MA: Harvard University Press, 2011), 30–33.

77. Addison and Steele, *The Spectator*, March 5, 1711, in Smith, *The Spectator*, 1:16.

78. Addison and Steele, *The Spectator*, October 30, 1711, in Smith, *The Spectator*, 2:123.

79. Addison and Steele, *The Spectator*, March 1, 1711, in Smith, *The Spectator*, 1:5. See Rebecca Bullard, *The Politics of Disclosure, 1674–1725: Secret History Narratives* (Abingdon, Oxon: Routledge, 2016), 116–120.

80. Addison and Steele, *The Spectator*, March 5, 1711, in Smith, *The Spectator*, 1:16. Addison later uses "Speculative Men," too, specifically to mean "spies," in the older sense of "speculative."

81. Addison and Steele, *The Spectator*, August 21, 1712, in Smith, *The Spectator*, 3:433.

82. Addison and Steele, *The Spectator*, July 28, 1712, in Smith, *The Spectator*, 3:365.

83. Addison and Steele, *The Spectator*, July 19, 1712, in Smith, *The Spectator*, 3:346. We see such language continue several years later in Addison's *Free-Holder* (1715–1716): "Bodies of Learned Men" need the "Indulgence" of the "Great and Powerful" in order to fund their "Pursuits of Knowledge," to "encourage" their work as "Speculative Persons, who have neither Opportunity nor a Turn of Mind to increase their own Fortunes" (Addison, *The Free-Holder; or, Political Essays* [London: D. Midwinter, 1716], 197, 198).
84. Jessica Richard notes that "the revenue from taxes was not enough to cover the annual payments to [the government-run] lottery participants, so the annuitants were given the opportunity to trade in their lottery claims for stock in the South Sea Company. Thus the South Sea scheme was literally based on the initial speculative ventures of lottery participants" (*The Romance of Gambling in the Eighteenth-Century British Novel* [New York: Palgrave Macmillan, 2011], 22).
85. For an accounting from within the moment, see Archibald Hutcheson, *Some Calculations Relating to the Proposals Made by the South-Sea Company...* (1720). See Paul, *The South Sea Bubble*, for a thorough forensic accounting from the present.
86. No one is sure how much Newton lost, if any at all. Newton's biographer Richard Westfall explains the possibility and the origin of the oft-quoted line attributed to Newton ("I can calculate the motions of heavenly bodies, but not the madness of people") in *Never at Rest*, 861–62. On Swift, see Leo Damrosch, *Jonathan Swift: His Life and His World* (New Haven, CT: Yale University Press, 2013), 339–40. For a general synopsis of philosopher-investors in the scheme, see Larry Stewart, "Measure for Measure: Projectors and the Manufacture of Enlightenment, 1770–1820," in Novak, *Age of Projects*, 370–89.
87. Quoted in Damrosch, *Jonathan Swift*, 339.
88. Edward Ward, "South-Sea Ballad," in *The Delights of the Bottle* (London: Sam. Briscoe, 1720), 55. Other writers such as Arthur Maynwaring and Thomas D'Urfey offered tunes on the South Sea stock, too. Incidentally, Ward used the phrase "Speculative Bubble" in his *Labour in Vain* (1700), but the phrase was not picked up for a number of decades at least.
89. "The South-Sea Ballad" (1720), quoted in Lewis Melville, *The South Sea Bubble* (Boston: Small, Maynard, 1923), 148.
90. Jonathan Swift, "The South-Sea Project" (1721), in *The Works of Jonathan Swift: Miscellaneous Poems* (Edinburgh: Archibald Constable, 1814), 147. This poem has a different title in other editions.
91. Jonathan Swift, *Gulliver's Travels* (New York: Signet Classics, 2008), xvi.
92. Swift, *Gulliver's Travels*, 183–84.
93. As many have noted, "Laputa" is likely a riff on Luther via Spanish: "la puta" is "the whore," and possibly therefore an oblique reference to Luther's characterization of reason as the devil's whore.
94. Swift, *Gulliver's Travels*, 161.
95. Swift, *Gulliver's Travels*, 168.
96. Swift, *Gulliver's Travels*, 182.

97. Swift, *Gulliver's Travels*, 188.
98. Swift, *Gulliver's Travels*, 188.
99. Swift, *Gulliver's Travels*, 183.
100. Swift, *Gulliver's Travels*, 183.
101. Defoe, *The Chimera*, 5–6.

3. GAMBLING ON A WORD

1. A *speculator* is "one who forms theories; ... an observer; a contemplator; ... a spy; a watcher." *Speculator*, for its part, had been in English at least since the 1500s, variously indicating "an abstruse thinker," "a lookout" or "sentry," and even (across the 1600s) "one who engages in occult observations or studies." *Speculator* (and sometimes *speculatist*) all the while remained a figurative term for a philosopher. *Speculation* is "examination by the eye; view," "mental view; intellectual examination; contemplation," and—as if defending the term in the contexts we just explored—"mental scheme not reduced to practice." To *speculate*, similarly, is "to meditate; to contemplate; to take a view of any thing with the mind," while *speculative* signals "contemplative ... theoretical, notional, ideal, not practical." Samuel Johnson, *A Dictionary of the English Language*, 2 vols. (London: W. Strahan, 1755), s.vv. "speculate," "speculation," "speculative."
2. *Journals of the House of Commons*, vol. 25 (1745–1750), 109, https://books.google.com/books?id=AwdDAAAAcAAJ. The purchasers are also said to "buy [tea] in a speculative way" (105).
3. See "The Meddler No. 3," *Royal Female Magazine*, May 1760, 194, Google Books; and various references in *The Herald; or, Patriot Proclaimer*, vol. 2 (1757–1758).
4. Josiah Tucker, "An Essay on Trade," in *A Brief Essay on the Advantages and Disadvantages...*, 3rd ed. (London: T. Trye, 1753), 123, Google Books.
5. Review of *Reasons for an Augmentation...*, by Mr. Hanway, *Monthly Review*, April 1759, 303, Google Books.
6. Thomas Mortimer, *Every Man His Own Broker* (London: S. Hooper, 1761), 40, accessed May 21, 2018, Eighteenth Century Collections Online.
7. Stephen Theodore Janssen, *Smuggling Laid Open...*, 2nd ed. (London: W. Owen, 1767), 28, accessed January 12, 2018, Eighteenth Century Collections Online.
8. Jacques Savary des Brûlons, *The Universal Dictionary of Trade and Commerce*, 2nd ed., 2 vols. (1757), 197, accessed December 8, 2017, Eighteenth Century Collections Online.
9. John Arbuthnot, *An Inquiry into the Connection between the Present Price of Provisions...* (London: T. Cadell, 1773), 16, accessed January 30, 2018, Eighteenth Century Collections Online.
10. Review of *An Enquiry into the Prices of Wheat, Malt, and Other Provisions...*, Review of the New Books, *Political Register, and Impartial Review of New Books* 3, no. 21 (1768): 384, Google Books.

11. "Extract of a Letter from a Principal House in London, to a Correspondent in Boston, Dated October 15, 1771," *Boston Evening-Post*, January 13, 1772, accessed May 4, 2018, America's Historical Newspapers.
12. For context, see Adam Sutcliffe, "Can a Jew Be a Philosophe? Isaac de Pinto, Voltaire, and Jewish Participation in the European Enlightenment," *Jewish Social Studies* 6, no. 3 (Spring/Summer 2000): 31–51.
13. Isaac de Pinto, *An Essay on Circulation and Credit*, trans. Rev. S. Baggs (London, 1774), 131, 1, https://books.google.com/books?id=_6JXAAAAMAAJ.
14. Pinto, *Essay on Circulation and Credit*, 39n24.
15. Richard Price, *Cursory Observations . . .* (London: T. Carnan, 1776), 14.
16. Carter v. Boehm (1766), 3 Burr 1905, 97 ER 1162, accessed August 18, 2018, HeinOnline Law Journal Library.
17. Carter v. Boehm. The Life Assurance Act of 1774, also known as the Gambling Act, or Gaming Act, was designed to stop insurance schemes from being used to evade existing anti-gambling laws.
18. Ian Baucom, *Specters of the Atlantic: Finance Capital, Slavery, and the Philosophy of History* (Durham, NC: Duke University Press, 2005), 95. See also Geoffrey Clark, *Betting on Lives: The Culture of Life Insurance in England, 1695–1775* (Manchester: Manchester University Press, 1999).
19. Baucom, *Specters of the Atlantic*, 95.
20. François Ewald, "Insurance and Risk," in *The Foucault Effect: Studies in Governmentality*, ed. Graham Burchell, Colin Gordon, and Peter Miller (Chicago: University of Chicago Press, 1991), 198.
21. See Michael McKeon, "Civic Humanism," in *The Political Imagination in History: Essays Concerning J. G. A. Pocock*, ed. D. N. DeLuna (Baltimore, MD: Owlworks, 2006), 81–84. See also John Ashton, *The History of Gambling in England* (Montclair, NJ: Patterson Smith, 1969); Donna Andrew, *Aristocratic Vice: The Attack on Duelling, Suicide, Adultery, and Gambling in Eighteenth-Century England* (New Haven, CT: Yale University Press, 2013). Thomas Kavanagh's, John M. Findlay's, and Ian Hacking's histories of chance in both general and nationally specific contexts bear on the broader arguments at play here, too.
22. Charles de Secondat, Baron de Montesquieu, *The Spirit of the Laws*, trans. Thomas Nugent, rev. J. V. Prichard, 2 vols. (New York: D. Appleton, 1900), 1:44, https://babel.hathitrust.org/cgi/pt?id=chi.39058570.
23. There is a great deal of scholarship on this; see Mark Valeri, *Heavenly Merchandize: How Religion Shaped Commerce in Puritan America* (Princeton, NJ: Princeton University Press, 2010); Stephen Innes, *Creating the Commonwealth: The Economic Culture of Puritan New England* (New York: W. W. Norton, 1995); and Jennifer J. Baker, *Securing the Commonwealth: Debt, Speculation, and Writing in the Making of Early America* (Baltimore, MD: Johns Hopkins University Press, 2005).
24. From around 1660 to 1740, the British passion for gambling was almost completely unrestrained. And after a generation or two of diminished ardor, the British

returned to it with a vengeance late in the eighteenth century. See David G. Schwartz, *Roll the Bones: The History of Gambling* (New York: Gotham, 2006), 111.
25. See Abraham de Moivre, *The Doctrine of Chances* (London: A. Millar, 1756), 188, 263, 277, 292, 329, Google Books.
26. Charles Cotton, *The Compleat Gamester* (London: Henry Broome, 1674), 1, 2, Google Books.
27. As Andrea Henderson observes, "Gambling and speculation, longtime recreations of the aristocracy, therefore became imbued with the spirit of a new age, linked to forms of political speculation that were, ironically enough, precisely opposed to aristocratic privilege" (*Romanticism and the Painful Pleasures of Modern Life* [New York: Cambridge University Press, 2008], 99).
28. Will Slauter, "Forward-Looking Statements: News and Speculation in the Age of the American Revolution," *Journal of Modern History* 81, no. 4 (December 2009): 775. Variations on the phrase "political speculation" became common in the mid-1700s, and as the phrase's senses broadened, it came to encompass anything from tracts on political economy to proposals on trade to mischievous corruption. Thus we find titles like John Almon's *Political Speculations* (1767) and the treatise *Political Speculations, Occasioned by the Progress of a Democratic Party in England* (1791). See also Christopher Castiglia, "Revolution Is a Fiction: The Way We Read (Early American Literature) Now," *Early American Literature* 51, no. 2 (2016): 397–418.
29. The Englishman Henry Fearon noted "a totally new character" to emigration to America in the late 1810s, when "it was no longer merely the poor, the idle, the profligate, or the wildly speculative, who were proposing to quit their native country," but also people "of sober habits and regular pursuits" (*Sketches of America*, 2nd ed. [London: Longman, 1818], vii, Google Books). See also James Chandler, *England in 1819: The Politics of Literary Culture and the Case of Romantic Historicism* (Chicago: University of Chicago Press, 1998), 462–63.
30. Ann Fabian has argued that speculative financial gain was the "negative analogue" of gambling, or "the one form of gain that made all other efforts to get rich appear normal, natural, and socially salubrious. To condemn gambling was to condone the speculative profits generated by the transfer of land and stock and by the sale of contracts for agricultural commodities" (*Card Sharps, Dream Books, and Bucket Shops: Gambling in Nineteenth-Century America* [Ithaca, NY: Cornell University Press, 1990], 4–5). See also David Itzkowitz, "Fair Enterprise or Extravagant Speculation: Investment, Speculation, and Gambling in Victorian England," in *Victorian Investments: New Perspectives on Finance and Culture*, ed. Nancy Henry and Cannon Schmitt (Bloomington: Indiana University Press, 2009), 101.
31. Henry Ward Beecher, *Lectures to Young Men* (London: Ward, 1851), 76, Google Books. See Reuven Brenner, with Gabrielle A. Brenner, *Gambling and Speculation: A Theory, a History, and a Future of Some Human Decisions* (Cambridge: Cambridge University Press, 1990), 7–18. When the English lottery was again ended in 1826, a newspaper columnist was relieved, for it had "corrupted the morals and encouraged

a spirit of speculation and gambling among the lower classes of people" (quoted in Schwartz, *Roll the Bones*, 129).

32. Jackson Lears, *Something for Nothing: Luck in America* (New York: Viking, 2003), 135.
33. "Extract of a Letter from Dantzick," *Pennsylvania Gazette*, June 2, 1772, accessed June 23, 2018, America's Historical Newspapers.
34. See Adam Smith, *An Inquiry into the Nature and Causes of the Wealth of Nations*, 2 vols., ed. R. H. Campbell, A. S. Skinner, and W. B. Todd (Oxford: Clarendon Press, 1979), 2:270–313. Tangentially: the bank's partners included the Duke of Buccleuch, from whom Nick Carraway claims descent in *The Great Gatsby*.
35. See Richard B. Sheridan, "The British Credit Crisis of 1772 and the American Colonies," *Journal of Economic History* 20, no. 2 (June 1960): 161–86.
36. D. [pseud.], "Remarks on an Address to the Douglas & Co. Bank," *Scots Magazine*, October 1772, 550.
37. "Remarks on an Address," 550.
38. "Remarks on an Address," 550.
39. Horace Walpole to Horace Mann, May 1, 1774, in *Horace Walpole's Correspondence with Sir Horace Mann*, vol. 7, *12 March 1768–1 May 1774*, ed. William Hunting Smith, vol. 23 of *The Yale Editions of Horace Walpole's Correspondence*, ed. W. S. Lewis, 48 vols. (New Haven, CT: Yale University Press, 1983), 23:569.
40. See John Brewer, *Pleasures of the Imagination: English Culture in the Eighteenth Century* (New York: Farrar, Straus and Giroux, 1997).
41. Hester Thrale, July 18, 1778, in *Thraliana: The Diary of Mrs. Hester Lynch Thrale, 1776–1809*, ed. Katharine C. Balderston, 2 vols. (Oxford: Clarendon Press, 1951), 1:335.
42. Thrale, July 18, 1778, in Balderston, *Thraliana*, 1:333, 1:334.
43. Adam Smith, *The Theory of Moral Sentiments*, ed. Knud Haakonssen (Cambridge: Cambridge University Press, 2004), 225, 28. See also Jonathan Sheehan and Dror Wahrman, *Invisible Hands: Self-Organization and the Eighteenth Century* (Chicago: University of Chicago Press, 2015); Jan Horst Keppler, *Adam Smith and the Economy of the Passions* (London: Routledge, 2013); and Robert Mitchell, *Sympathy and State in the Romantic Era: Systems, State Finance, and the Shadows of Futurity* (New York: Routledge, 2007).
44. Smith, *Wealth of Nations*, I.i.9. See also Alex Preda, *Framing Finance: The Boundaries of Markets and Modern Capitalism* (Chicago: University of Chicago Press, 2009), 33.
45. See Charles L. Griswold Jr., *Adam Smith and the Virtues of Enlightenment* (Cambridge: Cambridge University Press, 1999), 113–46.
46. Mike Hill and Warren Montag traces Smith's theories of contemplation of near and distant objects through his relationship with Lord Kames, in *The Other Adam Smith: Popular Contention, Commercial Society, and the Birth of Necro-Economics* (Stanford, CA: Stanford University Press, 2014), 214–15.
47. Adam Smith, "Early Draft of Part of *The Wealth of Nations*, Chap. 2," section 30, in *Lectures on Jurisprudence*, ed. R. L. Meek, D. D. Raphael, and P. G. Stein (Oxford: Clarendon Press, 1978), 574.

48. See Hill and Montag, *The Other Adam Smith*, 65.
49. Smith, "Early Draft," sections 19, 20, in Meek, Raphael, and Stein, *Lectures on Jurisprudence*, 570.
50. Smith, *Wealth of Nations*, II.iv.15. For a robust reappraisal of Smith's legacy, see the essays in *The Oxford Handbook of Adam Smith*, eds. Christopher J. Berry, Maria Pia Paganelli, and Craig Smith (Oxford: Oxford University Press, 2013).
51. Smith, *Wealth of Nations*, II.ii.57.
52. Smith, *Wealth of Nations*, I.xi.c.26.
53. Smith, *Wealth of Nations*, II.ii.78.
54. Smith, *Wealth of Nations*, II.ii.77.
55. Smith, *Wealth of Nations*, I.x.b.38.
56. On Smith's rhetorical devices here and elsewhere, see Samuel Fleishacker, *On Adam Smith's "Wealth of Nations": A Philosophical Companion* (Princeton, NJ: Princeton University Press, 2004), 20–31 passim. On the backgrounds of the mercantilist vocabulary, see Lars Magnusson, *Mercantilism: The Shaping of an Economic Language* (New York: Routledge, 1994).
57. Smith, *Wealth of Nations*, I.x.b.38.
58. *Niles' National Register*, December 12, 1818, 284.
59. Smith, *Wealth of Nations*, I.x.b.43; emphasis added. See also José R. Torre, *The Political Economy of Sentiment: Paper Credit and the Scottish Enlightenment in Early Republic Boston, 1780–1820* (London: Pickering & Chatto, 2007).
60. Smith, *Wealth of Nations*, I.x.b.38.
61. Smith, *Wealth of Nations*, II.ii.86.
62. Smith, *Wealth of Nations*, IV.v.b.26.
63. Smith, *Wealth of Nations*, V.i.g.14.
64. Smith, *Wealth of Nations*, V.i.e.33.
65. Smith, *Wealth of Nations*, V.i.f.26, V.iii.68.
66. Smith, *Wealth of Nations*, IV.ix.2.
67. Hill and Montag, *The Other Adam Smith*, 7. See also Susan Buck-Morss, "Envisioning Capital: Political Economy on Display," *Critical Inquiry* 21, no. 2 (Winter 1995), 434–67.
68. Appendix to *Monthly Review* 87 (1818): 529, Google Books.
69. "Speculative commerce" is used several times in the *Critical Review* in 1778; "speculation in trade" is a listing in John Trusler's *A Compendium of Useful Knowledge* (London: R. Baldwin, 1784).
70. "House of Commons," *The Times*, April 24, 1793, accessed July 27, 2018, *Times Digital Archive*.
71. Edmund Burke, *Reflections on the Revolution in France* (1790; New York: Cosimo Classics, 2007), 231.
72. A Practical Jobber [pseud.], *The Art of Stock-Jobbing Explained* (London: C. Chapple, 1816), Google Books.
73. Christopher Anstey, *Speculation; or, A Defence of Mankind* (London: J. Dodsley, 1780), 6, accessed May 29, 2016, Eighteenth Century Collections Online. For a sketch

of the history of the economic-literary language in which Anstey is writing, see the overview in Kurt Heinzelman, *The Economics of the Imagination* (Amherst: University of Massachusetts Press, 1980).

74. Anstey, *Speculation*, 4, 5.

75. Anstey, *Speculation*, 4. See also John C. Leffel, *Gambling on Empire: Colonial India and the Rhetoric of 'Speculation' in British Literature and Culture, c. 1769–1830* (Dissertation, University of Colorado at Boulder, 2013), 5.

76. Regulus [pseud.], "A Speculation on Paper-Wealth," *London Magazine: or, Gentleman's Monthly Intelligencer*, September 1776, 470, https://books.google.com/books?id=X1IDAAAAMAAJ.

77. See "Speculation, a Poem" (London: N. Conant, 1776), and Tasker's "Ode to Speculation" (1779), in which he calls speculation "Sister of Contemplation bright!" ("Ode to Speculation: A Poetical Amusement for Batheaston Villa" [Bath, 1779]), 5, accessed October 22, 2018, Eighteenth Century Collections Online.

78. *The Speculator*, March 27, 1790, 8. This short-lived journal was written and edited jointly by Nathan Drake and Edward Ash. Several decades later, the *Lady's Miscellany* featured a regular advice column called "The Speculator" in which "Mr. Speculator" answered questions.

79. *Speculation* also became a useful conceptual term in the versions of "conjectural history" that the philosopher Dugald Stewart charted.

80. In 1764, for instance, students at the University of Edinburgh founded the Speculative Society, of which Robert Louis Stevenson and Walter Scott would later become members during its long history. On the interplay of the speculative and the practical in Romanticism, see Richard Holmes, *The Age of Wonder: How the Romantic Generation Discovered the Beauty and Terror of Science* (New York: Pantheon, 2008); and Sarah Tindal Kareem, *Eighteenth-Century Fiction and the Reinvention of Wonder* (New York: Oxford University Press, 2014).

81. Mary Shelley, *Frankenstein*, 2nd ed., ed. J. Paul Hunter (New York: W. W. Norton, 2012), 89.

82. See also F. W. J. Schelling, *Neue Zeitschrift für speculative Physik* (1802).

83. Shelley, *Frankenstein*, 152.

84. In Jerome Christensen's reading, financial speculation violated the "sacred distinction between things and persons" that Coleridge, for one, cherished (*Lord Byron's Strength: Romantic Writing and Commercial Society* [Baltimore, MD: Johns Hopkins University Press, 1993], 158). Christensen is likely focusing too much on commodity speculation as *speculation* in general here, though, since *speculation* could also indicate an immaterial investment or idea for a venture in these contexts. See also Tilottama Rajan, *Romantic Narrative: Shelley, Hays, Godwin, Wollstonecraft* (Baltimore, MD: Johns Hopkins University Press, 2010), 144–73; and Robert Mitchell, *Experimental Life: Vitalism in Romantic Science and Literature* (Baltimore, MD: Johns Hopkins University Press, 2013).

85. John Keats to Benjamin Bailey, November 22, 1817, in *Selected Letters*, ed. Robert Gittings (Oxford: Oxford University Press, 2002), 36.

86. John Middleton Murry, *Studies in Keats* (London: Oxford University Press, 1930), 94, 96.
87. Murry, *Studies in Keats*, 97.
88. John Keats, "Gripus," in *Poetical Works*, ed. H. W. Garrod (Oxford: Oxford University Press, 1986), 456.
89. Samuel Taylor Coleridge, *Biographia Literaria*, in *The Collected Works of Samuel Taylor Coleridge*, ed. James Engell and W. Jackson Bate, 16 vols. (Princeton, NJ: Princeton University Press, 1983), 7.1:279. See also Alan R. White, *The Language of Imagination* (Cambridge, MA: Blackwell, 1990).
90. Percy Bysshe Shelley also retrieved a Keatsian and Shakespearean sense of *speculation* (through *Macbeth*, primarily) as penetrating vision in his "Ginevra," where the titular figure's dead body is noted to have "open eyes, whose fixed and glassy light / Mocked at the speculation they had owned" ("Ginevra: A Fragment," in *The Works of Percy Bysshe Shelley, with His Life*, 2 vols. [London: John Ascham, 1834], 1:175). In a letter to Thomas Jefferson Hogg, he argued furthermore that religion as purely "speculative" (without practice) is nothing but a "dry inactive knowledge of what really is, not influencing the conduct" (Shelley to Hogg, May 17, 1811, in *The Letters of Percy Bysshe Shelley*, ed. Roger Ingpen, 2 vols. [London: G. Bell and Sons, 1914], 1:82). On Shelley's and Robert Southey's opposition to "literary speculation," see Philip Connell, *Romanticism, Economics, and the Question of "Culture"* (Oxford: Oxford University Press, 2001), 228, 270. Like Keats, Shelley also penned "Speculations on Metaphysics" and "Speculations on Morals."
91. See M. H. Abrams, *The Mirror and the Lamp: Romantic Theory and the Critical Tradition* (New York: Oxford University Press, 1953).
92. For broader context, see Richard C. Sha, *Imagination and Science in Romanticism* (Baltimore, MD: Johns Hopkins University Press, 2018); Thomas H. Ford, *Wordsworth and the Poetics of Air: Atmospheric Romanticism in a Time of Change* (Cambridge: Cambridge University Press, 2018); and J. M. Cocking, *Imagination: A Study in the History of Ideas*, ed. Penelope Murray (London: Routledge, 1991), 268–81.
93. Samuel Johnson, *The History of Rasselas, Prince of Abyssinia*, ed. Thomas Keymer (Oxford: Oxford University Press, 2009), 93.
94. Percy Bysshe Shelley, "A Defence of Poetry," in *The Works of Percy Bysshe Shelley*, ed. Mary Shelley (London: Edward Moxon, 1847), 14.
95. See *Le dictionnaire de l'Académie française*, 4th ed. (1762) and 5th ed. (1798).
96. See *Diccionario de la lengua castellana* (Real Academia Española, 1780, 1803, 1817, 1822). In the first major ethnography of the Dutch bourse, an expatriate Jewish Spaniard, José de la Vega (who happens to have been born in a town named Espejo), published his *Confusión de confusiones* (1688). Here, he mentioned figures in the world of the stock exchange and finance such as the "gente de especulación" (speculative people) and called them "los especulativos." It is unclear how concretely he aims to tie them to certain economic practices, though, and regardless, the terms were not picked up in Spanish or other tongues at the time.

97. Jacob Grimm et al., *Deutches Wörterbuch*, 32 vols. (Leipzig, 1854–1961), s.v. "Spekulation," http://woerterbuchnetz.de/cgi-bin/WBNetz/wbgui_py?sigle=DWB&mode=Vernetzung&hitlist=&patternlist=&lemid=GS33808#XGS33808.
98. *An American Dictionary of the English Language*, ed. Noah Webster, 2 vols. (New York: S. Converse, 1828), s.v. "speculate." Later editions of Johnson's *Dictionary* did not update their senses of *speculate/speculation*.
99. *An American Dictionary*, s.v. "speculation." By the late 1820s, *speculator*, too, has no less than four distinct meanings for Webster, ranging from "an observer; a contemplator" to a "spy; a watcher," to the new commercial sense (*An American Dictionary*, s.v. "speculator.")

4. AMERICA THE SPECULATIVE

1. Nathanael Greene, quoted in Benjamin Rush, *A Memorial Containing the Travels Through Life or Sundry Incidents in the Life of Dr. Benjamin Rush* (Lanoraie, QC: Louis Alexander Biddle, 1905), 89. This characterization is repeated in *The Autobiography of Benjamin Rush*, ed. George W. Corner (Princeton, NJ: Princeton University Press, 1948), 119.
2. William Bingham to Silas Deane, February 28, 1777, in *Naval Documents of the American Revolution*, ed. William James Morgan, 12 vols. (Washington, DC: Department of the Navy, 1976), 7:1325.; Étienne Clavière to Jacques Pierre Brissot, May 22, 1788, in Brissot, *New Travels in the United States of America*, trans. Mara Soceanu Vamos and Durand Echeverria, ed. Echeverria (Cambridge, MA: Belknap Press of Harvard University Press, 1964), 47.
3. William Priest, *Travels in the United States of America* (London: J. Johnson, 1802), 132, Google Books; emphasis in original.
4. Benjamin Rush, *Medical Inquiries and Observations Upon the Diseases of the Mind* (1812), 4th ed. (Philadelphia: John Grigg, 1830), 66, Google Books. The Briton Charles Moore agreed; see *A Full Inquiry Into the Subject of Suicide*, 2 vols. (London: Rivington, 1790), 2:352–57.
5. Rush, *Memorial*, 134.
6. Burke, Carlyle, and Tocqueville are very much in the background here, but too far from the topic to merit fuller discussion. For an overview, see Stefan Jonsson, "The Invention of the Masses: The Crowd in French Culture from the Revolution to the Commune," in *Crowds*, ed. Jeffrey T. Schnapp and Matthew Tiews (Stanford, CA: Stanford University Press, 2006), 47–75.
7. Ralph Waldo Emerson, "The Young American," in *Essays and Lectures* (New York: Literary Classics, 1983), 217.
8. Adam Smith, *An Inquiry into the Nature and Causes of the Wealth of Nations*, 2 vols., ed. R. H. Campbell, A. S. Skinner, and W. B. Todd (Oxford: Clarendon Press, 1979), V.iii.92. Similarly, Elizabeth Fox-Genovese and Eugene Genovese record that Bordelais merchants in the 1780s took up the new sense of *speculation* that had come into

4. AMERICA THE SPECULATIVE 221

French and referred to "their operations in the [French Antilles] as 'speculations'" (*Fruits of Merchant Capital: Slavery and Bourgeois Property in the Rise and Expansion of Capitalism* [New York: Oxford University Press, 1983], 88). At least as early as 1743, Benjamin Franklin wanted more "men of speculation," in Smith's sense, to dream the impractical so that their ideas could eventually be translated into civic improvements ("A Proposal for Promoting Useful Knowledge Among the British Plantations in America," in *The Works of Benjamin Franklin*, ed. Jared Sparks, 9 vols. [Boston: Hilliard, Gray, 1840], 6:14).

9. Smith, *Wealth of Nations*, IV.vii.c.84. On Smith's views of the American Revolution, see Ian Simpson Ross, *The Life of Adam Smith*, 2nd ed. (New York: Oxford University Press, 2010), 265–84.

10. Charles Inglis, *The True Interest of America Impartially Stated . . .* (Philadelphia: James Humphreys, 1776), 69. Eighteenth Century Collections Online. Accessed August 12, 2018; Peter Oliver, *Peter Oliver's Origin and Progress of the American Rebellion: A Tory View*, ed. Douglass Adair and John. A. Schutz (Stanford, CA: Stanford University Press, 1961), 4. This language crops up in novels, too, like the English-Canadian Frances Brooke's *History of Emily Montague* (1769), where we find characters describing their "project[s]" of "setting out for America" (Letter 1) or "peopl[ing] the wilds of America" (Letter 3); repr., Toronto: McClelland & Stewart, 1995.

11. "Diary of John Adams," entry of March 22, 1773, Adams Family Papers: An Electronic Archive, Massachusetts Historical Society, https://www.masshist.org/digitaladams/archive/popup?id=D19&page=D19_17.

12. Thomas Jefferson to James Madison, February 5, 1795, in *The Works of Thomas Jefferson*, 12 vols. (New York: Cosimo Classics, 2009), 8:162. See Peter S. Onuf, *Jefferson's Empire: The Language of American Nationhood* (Charlottesville: University of Virginia Press, 2000).

13. See Perry Miller, *The New England Mind: From Colony to Province* (Cambridge, MA: Harvard University Press, 1953), 37; Mark Valeri, *Heavenly Merchandize: How Religion Shaped Commerce in Puritan America* (Princeton, NJ: Princeton University Press, 2010); and Stephen Innes, *Creating the Commonwealth: The Economic Culture of Puritan New England* (New York: W. W. Norton, 1995). See also John Samuel Ezell, *Fortune's Merry Wheel: The Lottery in America* (Cambridge, MA: Harvard University Press, 1960); and Charles T. Clotfelter and Philip J. Cook, *Selling Hope: State Lotteries in America* (Cambridge, MA: Harvard University Press, 1989). Most colonies and states had usury caps, but Robert E. Wright has shown that "person-to-person loans in the colonial period were generally high and usually exceeded the usury limit" because of ambiguities about the valuations of assets and collateral. (*The Wealth of Nations Rediscovered: Integration and Expansion in American Financial Markets* [Cambridge: Cambridge University Press, 2002], 29).

14. There is a great deal of scholarship on this topic. See, e.g., Howard Bodenhorn, *State Banking in Early America: A New Economic History* (New York: Oxford University Press, 2003); Bruce H. Mann, *Republic of Debtors: Bankruptcy in the Age of American Independence* (Cambridge, MA: Harvard University Press, 2002); Jeffrey Sklansky,

Sovereign of the Market: The Money Question in Early America (Chicago: University of Chicago Press, 2017); Stephen Mihm, *A Nation of Counterfeiters: Capitalists, Con Men, and the Making of the United States* (Cambridge, MA: Harvard University Press, 2007); Jennifer J. Baker, *Securing the Commonwealth: Debt, Speculation, and Writing in the Making of Early America* (Baltimore, MD: Johns Hopkins University Press, 2005), esp. 1–17; Stuart Banner, *Speculation: A History of the Fine Line Between Gambling and Investing* (Oxford: Oxford University Press, 2017); and Alex Preda, *Framing Finance: The Boundaries of Markets and Modern Capitalism* (Chicago: University of Chicago Press, 2009).

15. Robert Sobel, *The Money Manias: The Eras of Great Speculation in America, 1770–1790* (Washington, DC: Beard Books, 1973), 33; George Washington to Henry Laurens, November 5, 1779, in *The Writings of George Washington from the Original Manuscript Sources, 1745–1799*, ed. John C. Fitzpatrick, 39 vols. (Washington, DC: US Government Printing Office, 1944), 6:397. See also Arthur M. Schlesinger, *Prelude to Independence: The Newspaper War on Britain, 1764–1776* (New York: Alfred A. Knopf, 1958), 9n13.

16. George Washington to Lund Washington, May 29, 1779, in Fitzpatrick, *Writings*, 15:180.

17. Thomas Jefferson to Horatio Gates, May 30, 1797, in *The Writings of Thomas Jefferson*, ed. H. A. Washington, 9 vols. (Cambridge: Cambridge University Press, 2011), 4:178. See also Mark Peterson, *The City-State of Boston: The Rise and Fall of an Atlantic Power, 1630–1865* (Princeton, NJ: Princeton University Press, 2019).

18. The minister Orville Dewey attempted to clarify the issue. He held that, despite the present "rage for speculation . . . it is not against *speculation simply*, that I have anything to allege. . . . But this rage for speculation, this eagerness of many for sudden and stupendous accumulation, this spirit of gambling in trade, is a different thing. . . . It is drawing men's minds away from the healthful processes of sober industry and attention to business, and leading them to wait in a feverish excitement, as at the wheel of a lottery" ("On the Moral End of Business," in *Moral Views of Commerce, Society, and Politics* [London: Charles Fox, 1838], 58, Google Books); emphasis in original.

19. Quoted in Jeff Broadwater, *Jefferson, Madison, and the Making of the Constitution* (Chapel Hill: University of North Carolina Press, 2019), 147.

20. Adams quoted in Mihm, *Nation of Counterfeiters*, 74. On Hamilton's reports in their broader contexts, see Elizabeth Hewitt, *Speculative Fictions: Explaining the Economy in the Early United States* (Oxford: Oxford University Press, 2020). See also Drew R. McCoy, *The Elusive Republic: Political Economy in Jeffersonian America* (Chapel Hill: University of North Carolina Press, 1980), 136–84; and Joseph J. Ellis, *Founding Brothers: The Revolutionary Generation* (New York: Random House, 2000), 55–64. "Vain Speculations" and "imprudent and unfortunate Enterprises," as one clergyman put it in 1795, would "undermine and destroy our very Prosperity" (John Tyler, *The Blessing of Peace* [Norwich, CT: John Trumbull, 1795], 11).

21. "Autobiography of John Adams," part 1, p. 25, in Adams Family Papers, https://www.masshist.org/digitaladams/archive/popup?id=A1_25&page=A1_25_2; John Adams to Abigail Adams, August 12, 1776, in Adams Family Papers, https://www.masshist.org/digitaladams/archive/popup?id=L17760812ja&page=L17760812ja_1. See also Woody Holton, *Unruly Americans and the Origins of the Constitution* (New York: Farrar, Straus and Giroux, 2007), 106–7 and 121–22.
22. John Adams to Abigail Adams, August 19, 1777, in Adams Family Papers, https://www.masshist.org/digitaladams/archive/popup?id=L17770819ja&page=L17770819ja_2.
23. Abigail Adams to John Adams, July 21, 1783, in Adams Family Papers, https://www.masshist.org/digitaladams/archive/popup?id=L17830721aa&page=L17830721aa_2.
24. John Adams to Abigail Adams, March 29, 1796, in Adams Family Papers, https://www.masshist.org/digitaladams/archive/popup?id=L17960329ja&page=L17960329ja_1.
25. John Adams to Abigail Adams, December 13, 1795; Abigail Adams to John Adams, 27 December 1795, in Adams Family Papers, https://www.masshist.org/digitaladams/archive/popup?id=L17951213ja&page=L17951213ja_3.
26. See Woody Holton, *Abigail Adams: A Life* (New York: Free Press, 2009), esp. 213–15 and 275–77.
27. Henry Adams, *A History of the U.S.A. During the Administrations of Jefferson and Madison*, 2 vols. (New York: Library of America, 1986), 2:1345.
28. Mann, *Republic of Debtors*, 190.
29. See Karen A. Weyler, *Intricate Relations: Sexual and Economic Desire in American Fiction* (Iowa City: University of Iowa Press, 2004), 115. See also Joseph Fichtelberg, *Risk Culture: Performance and Danger in Early America* (Ann Arbor, MI: University of Michigan Press, 2010).
30. "Remarks on Manners, Government, Law, and the Domestic Debt of America—Addressed to the Citizens of the United States," *Pennsylvania Evening Herald*, February 28, 1787, 4.
31. James Sullivan, *The Path to Riches: An Inquiry Into the Origin and Use of Money* (Boston: J. Belcher, 1809), 35. On the gendered clash in the early republic between older and newer forms of commerce as civic participation—which the next chapter will address more fully—see Carroll Smith-Rosenberg, *This Violent Empire: The Birth of an American National Identity* (Chapel Hill: University of North Carolina Press, 2010), esp. 88–135.
32. Noah Webster, "The Grace of God in Dollars," *The Prompter; or, A Commentary on Common Sayings and Subjects* (Boston: I. Thomas and E. T. Andrews, 1792), 20, Google Books.
33. The rub here is the *means* by which one gains wealth, and how much of a role chance and fortune play in it. Mark Valeri explains, via a rereading of Weber's claims:

> Weber conceded that early Calvinists resisted the individualistic and materialistic implications of a market economy; yet he also claimed that Calvinist

teaching implicitly invested rationalized, bureaucratic regimes with divine purpose. He described the essence of Reformed belief to include the spiritual validity of secular vocations, the pursuit of wealth as an indication of otherwise mysterious divine favor, and the primacy of diligence, industriousness, and frugality as moral virtues. Such teaching, according to Weber, helped to create the ethos of early capitalism. It molded a truly modern economic personality, driven to prove itself through diligence and frugality in a rational system regardless of conventional notions of interpersonal obligation. Without a close reading of puritan texts, or an examination of transformations between early Reformers and late seventeenth century and early eighteenth-century puritans, Weber jumped to latter-day Protestants who embodied this personality even as they rejected Calvinist doctrine. Once shorn of its theological tenets and customary hedges on outright individualism, puritanism flowered into an economic culture of autonomy, rational discipline, entrepreneurialism, and specialization. (*Heavenly Merchandize*, 12)

See also Jackson Lears, *Something for Nothing: Luck in America* (New York: Viking, 2003), 70–135 passim.

34. "Foreign Intelligence," *London Magazine*, September 1785, 161.
35. Benjamin Franklin, "Advice to a Young Tradesman" (1748; Philadelphia: Daniel Humphreys, 1785), accessed August 2, 2018, Early American Imprints, series 1, no. 44684.
36. Quoted in Banner, *Speculation*, 8.
37. For example, we see phrases like "funding mania" and "scribbling mania" in the *Pennsylvania Packet* (Philadelphia) (May 24, 1790), and "commercial mania," "lottery mania," and "electioneering mania" in the *New-York Weekly Museum* (June 25, 1791).
38. See Alyn Brodsky, *Benjamin Rush: Patriot and Physician* (New York: St. Martin's Press, 2004), 47–58.
39. Sari Altschuler, *The Medical Imagination: Literature and Health in the Early United States* (Philadelphia: University of Pennsylvania Press, 2018), 25–32.
40. Benjamin Rush, "On the Different Species of Mania," in *Massachusetts Gazette*, February 20, 1787, 4, and *Massachusetts Gazette*, February 23, 1787, 4, accessed July 25, 2018, America's Historical Newspapers. Rush's article originally appeared in the *Columbian Magazine*, in December 1786, and was later reprinted in Scotland in the *Edinburgh Magazine*, August 1787, 86–91. See Stephen Fried, *Rush: Revolution, Madness, and the Visionary Doctor Who Became a Founding Father* (New York: Crown, 2018), 284–86.
41. Lisa M. Hermsen notes that "'Mania' until the nineteenth century described both a general form of madness and a unique variety of madness marked by rage, fury, excitement, delusions, and euphoria. Mania has always existed as madness, and it now exists in our contemporary diagnoses as an episode, a syndrome, a pole on the affective spectrum" (*Manic Minds: Mania's Mad History and Its Neuro-Future* [New

Brunswick, NJ: Rutgers University Press, 2011], 4). Physicians of the late 1700s and early 1800s who treated mental illnesses often referred to their patients as motivated by "fancy" and "speculation." The association of speculation with gambling does not in itself explain the fever or mania elements: that discourse was rarely used to describe gaming/gambling practices prior to the 1790s. This is not to elide the differences between fevers, manias, frenzies, and more, but for our purposes here, they belong to the same general category and taxonomy. For a fuller study, see David Healy, *Mania: A Short History of Bipolar Disorder* (Baltimore, MD: Johns Hopkins University Press, 2008). In 1835, the *United States Medical and Surgical Journal* classified "speculation" alongside "ambition" and "gambling" as a potential cause of "strife" and even death (see *United States Medical and Surgical Journal* 2 [1835]: 460.)

42. The *Oxford English Dictionary* dates the use of *mania* in English to around 1400, but its sense of "an obsessive enthusiasm for a particular thing" (like "tulip mania" and "lottery mania") only dates to 1776. *Oxford English Dictionary*, s.v. "mania," accessed December 24, 2018.

   There is an earlier, somewhat outlying listing for "Tulipæ Mania," or "Tulip-madness," in Nathan Bailey's *Universal Etymological English Dictionary*, 2 vols. (London: Thomas Cox, 1731), s.v. "tulip." I have not located substantive references elsewhere to confirm that this usage had much significance. Prior to the late 1770s, we find almost no correlations of *speculation*—in its older or newer senses—with frenzy, mania, disease, or any irrationality. A rare one exists in a catalog of portraits of Americans from 1777, when the English bookseller John Boosey looks ahead to much of the language we see here when he attributes the "REVOLT OF AMERICA" to a "frightful malady which fastens upon the brain of the speculator, who suffers himself to be led away by a party" (*Pictures of Men, Manners, and Times* [London: J. Boosey, 1779], 153).

43. William Gordon, *The History of the Rise, Progress, and Establishment of the Independence of the United States of America*, 4 vols. (London: John Woods,1788), 4:144, Google Books.

44. Rush, *Medical Inquiries and Observations*, 64.

45. "Scripomania," *General Advertiser* (Philadelphia), August 12, 1791, accessed September 10, 2018, Early American Imprints. This article and the term *scripomania* were reproduced in several other media, and it seems to have been the most powerful catalyst in the U.S. discourse.

46. See Scott Christopher Miller, "'Never Did I See So Universal a Frenzy': The Panic of 1791 and the Republicanization of Philadelphia," *Pennsylvania Magazine of History and Biography* 142, no. 1 (January 2018): 7–48. For context, see Thomas M. Doerflinger, *A Vigorous Spirit of Enterprise: Merchants and Economic Development in Revolutionary Philadelphia* (Chapel Hill: University of North Carolina Press, 1986).

47. "The Scripomania Is at Its Full Height," *General Advertiser* (Philadelphia), August 12, 1791, accessed September 3, 2018, Early American Imprints. See also Robert Sobel, *Panic on Wall Street: A History of America's Financial Disasters* (New York: Macmillan, 1968).

48. *Columbian Centinel*, August 13, 1791, accessed April 29, 2018, America's Historical Newspapers.
49. "Speculation," *New York Daily Gazette*, August 13, 1791, accessed January 24, 2018, America's Historical Newspapers.
50. Weyler, *Intricate Relations*, 124.
51. Freneau, "On a Travelling Speculator," in *Poems*, 3 vols. (Philadelphia: Lydia Bailey, 1809), 2:291.
52. "The Glass; or, Speculation: A Poem. Containing an Account of the Ancient, and Genius of the Modern, Speculators" (New York, 1791), n.p., accessed August 2, 2018, Early American Imprints, series 1, no. 23413. See also Colin Wells, *Poetry Wars: Verse and Politics in the American Revolution and Early Republic* (Philadelphia: University of Pennsylvania Press, 2018).
53. "The Glass," 3.
54. "The Glass," 7.
55. "The Glass," 11.
56. Quoted in Scott Reynolds Nelson, *A Nation of Deadbeats: An Uncommon History of America's Financial Disasters* (New York: Alfred A. Knopf, 2012), 32. See also Jane Kamensky, *The Exchange Artist: A Tale of High-Flying Speculation and America's First Banking Collapse* (New York: Viking, 2008). Amid the Panic of 1792, the state of New York passed "An Act to prevent the pernicious practice of stock jobbing, and for regulating sales at public auctions."
57. Stuart Banner offers a sampling of quotations in *Speculation*, 12–33 passim. See also William Barton, *Observations on the Nature and Use of Paper-Credit* (Philadelphia, 1781), 19.
58. "Extract of a Letter Dated Baltimore, December 6," *General Advertiser* (Philadelphia), December 20, 1793, accessed August 1, 2018, America's Historical Newspapers.
59. *Philadelphia Gazette*, May 25, 1795. See also *American Telegraphe*, March 16, 1796, accessed August 9, 2018, America's Historical Newspapers.
60. *American Mercury* (Hartford, CT), November 27, 1797, accessed August 1, 2018, America's Historical Newspapers.
61. *Some Considerations on the Late Mismanagement of the South-Sea Stock* (London: J. Roberts, 1720[?]), 2, accessed June 1, 2018, Eighteenth Century Collections Online. Other texts said the South Sea company "miscarried," and in the House of Lords, there was discussion of "villainous Projectors" and "unfair Management," which again suggests something different than irrationality (House of Lords, December 12, 1720, *The History and Proceedings of the House of Lords*, 8 vols. [London: Ebenezer Timberland, 1742], 3:128, Google Books).
62. Smith, *Wealth of Nations*, V.i.e.22.
63. William Coxe, *Memoirs of the Life and Administration of Robert Walpole, Earl of Oxford*, 3 vols. (London: T. Cadell Jr. and W. Davies, 1798), 1:133, Google Books. A writer for the *Pennsylvania Packet* noted in 1788 that the directors of the Bank of England "have awakened such a spirit of speculation as this country has not experienced since the year 1720" (May 20, 1788).

64. *Worchester Magazine*, April 1787, 3, accessed February 26, 2018, America's Historical Newspapers.
65. "Secretary of the Treasury's Report," January 28, 1790, in *Annals of Congress* (Washington: Gales and Seaton, 1834): 1:1135, 1136, Google Books.
66. "Secretary of the Treasury's Report," 1:1133, 1132.
67. Quoted in Mann, *Republic of Debtors*, 213.
68. *Republican Watch-Tower* (New York), January 23, 1807; *Washington Expositor* (Washington, DC), May 7, 1808, accessed June 4, 2018, America's Historical Newspapers. Many of these brief notices were reprinted and circulated in other newspapers.
69. "Our Foreign Relations," *Rutland (VT) Herald*, February 21, 1810, accessed June 15, 2018, America's Historical Newspapers.
70. *Danbury (CT) Gazette*, December 21, 1813, accessed January 31, 2018, America's Historical Newspapers.
71. *Poulson's American Daily Advertiser* (Philadelphia), May 10, 1814, accessed January 16, 2018, America's Historical Newspapers; letter to the editor, *Albany (NY) Gazette*, October 11, 1817, accessed January 16, 2018, America's Historical Newspapers.
72. See the various discussions of "manias" in the *Niles' Weekly Register* (Baltimore, MD) in 1835; and across the *North American Review* (Boston) in 1832.
73. See Donna T. Andrew, *Aristocratic Vice: The Attack on Duelling, Suicide, Adultery, and Gambling in Eighteenth-Century England* (New Haven, CT: Yale University Press, 2013), 100–101, 175–217.
74. William Leggett, "Causes of Financial Distress" (1836), in *A Collection of the Political Writings of William Leggett*, ed. Theodore Sedgwick, 2 vols. (New York: Taylor & Dodd, 1840), 2:96, Google Books.
75. Andrew Jackson to Roger Brooke Taney, October 13, 1836, Andrew Jackson papers, Library of Congress, accessed December 23, 2018, https://www.loc.gov/resource/maj.01096_0174_0177/?st=text.
76. Andrew Jackson, Farewell Address, American Presidency Project, accessed December 26, 2018, https://www.presidency.ucsb.edu/documents/farewell-address-0. See Charles Sellers, *The Market Revolution: Jacksonian America, 1815–1846* (New York: Oxford University Press, 1991), esp. 345–48.
77. John Tyler, State of the Union address (1842), quoted in Lyle Nelson, *John Tyler: A Rare Career* (New York: Nova Science, 2008), 79. See also Scott A. Sandage, *Born Losers: A History of Failure in America* (Cambridge, MA: Harvard University Press, 2005), 89–92.
78. John Tyler, State of the Union address (1844), quoted in Nelson, *John Tyler*, 132. See also David Anthony, *Paper Money Men: Commerce, Manhood, and the Sensational Public Sphere in Antebellum America* (Columbus: Ohio State University Press, 2009).
79. *Oxford English Dictionary Online*, s.v. "panic," accessed January 8, 2018.
80. Mary Templin has identified the minigenre of "panic fiction": "Between 1836 and 1840 alone—the period spanning the peak of the speculative boom of the 1830s to the

beginnings of the depression that followed the Panic of 1837—women had written and published dozens, perhaps hundreds, of novels and stories that were ... centered on economic themes, ... responding directly to the panic but within a domestic context" (*Panic Fiction: Women and Antebellum Economic Crisis* [Tuscaloosa: University of Alabama Press, 2014], 2). See also David A. Zimmerman, *Panic! Markets, Crowds, and Crises in American Fiction* (Chapel Hill: University of North Carolina Press, 2006).

81. See Jessica M. Lepler, *The Many Panics of 1837: People, Politics, and the Creation of a Transatlantic Financial Crisis* (New York: Cambridge University Press, 2013), 71. Harriet Martineau's much-reprinted *Society in America* (1837) appeared in the same moment and addressed the "wild speculation" that she saw in her travels as nearly synonymous with the panic itself (*Society in America*, 2 vols. [New York: Saunders and Otley, 1837], 2:75).

82. Charles Mackay, *The Hope of the World, and Other Poems* (London: Richard Bentley, 1840), 12, 2, 12.

83. Charles Mackay, *Memoirs of Extraordinary Popular Delusions*, 3 vols. (London: Richard Bentley, 1841), 3:3.

84. Mackay, *Memoirs of Extraordinary Popular Delusions and the Madness of Crowds*, 2 vols. (London: Office of the National Illustrated Library, 1852), 1:220. Because the timing of Mackay's first edition is important here, I will quote primarily from it in the following.

85. Mackay, *Memoirs of Extraordinary Popular Delusions* (1841), 1:1.

86. Mackay, *Memoirs of Extraordinary Popular Delusions* (1841), 1:1.

87. Mackay, *Memoirs of Extraordinary Popular Delusions* (1841), 1:78.

88. Mackay, *Memoirs of Extraordinary Popular Delusions* (1841), 2:1.

89. As Peter Garber notes, Mackay relies on "a pair of anecdotes" that include highly "implausib[le]" details, and then cites a speculative frenzy based on an influx of foreign funds directed at tulips—but gives no evidence of this, and no evidence of the price collapses he says ensued (*Famous First Bubbles: The Fundamentals of Early Manias* [Cambridge, MA: MIT Press, 2000], 26).

90. Ralph Waldo Emerson, entry of December 13, 1829, in *Journals of Ralph Waldo Emerson*, 10 vols., ed. Edward Waldo Emerson and Waldo Emerson Forbes (Boston: Houghton and Mifflin, 1909), 2:278.

91. Ralph Waldo Emerson, "The American Scholar," in *Essays and Lectures* (New York: Library of America, 1983), 60.

92. Ralph Waldo Emerson, "Self-Reliance," in *Essays and Lectures*, 275–76.

93. Ralph Waldo Emerson, "Wealth," in *The Complete Essays and Other Writings of Ralph Waldo Emerson*, ed. Brooks Atkinson (New York: Modern Library, 1940), 694. This essay "Wealth," from *Conduct of Life* (1860), is distinct from "Wealth" in *English Traits* (1856). Edgar Allan Poe's story "The Gold-Bug" is a valuable intertext here that I do not have space to treat.

94. Ralph Waldo Emerson, "Compensation," in *Essays and Lectures*, 289.

95. Emerson, "Wealth," in *Complete Essays*, 698–99.

96. Henry David Thoreau, entry of December 7, 1838, in *Journal*, 8 vols., ed. John C. Broderick et al. (Princeton, NJ: Princeton University Press, 1981), 1:58. Maurice Lee notes that Thoreau was especially wary of speculation as a get-rich-quick scheme (*Uncertain Chances: Science, Skepticism, and Belief in Nineteenth-Century American Literature* [New York: Oxford University Press, 2012], 134).
97. Baker, *Securing the Commonwealth*, 166.
98. Henry David Thoreau, *A Yankee in Canada, with Anti-Slavery and Reform Papers* (New York: Haskell House, 1969), 77.
99. John Sergeant, *Select Speeches of John Sergeant* (Philadelphia: E. L. Carey & A. Hart, 1832), 164.
100. Aaron M. Sakolski, *The Great American Land Bubble* (New York: Harper, 1932), 1.
101. Thoreau, *Yankee in Canada*, 77.

5. SPECULITIS, OR THE TECHNOLOGIES OF PROPHECY

1. The financial speculation that took place during this period has been studied intensely. A brief bibliographic overview would include Charles P. Kindleberger, *Manias, Panics, and Crashes: A History of Financial Crises* (New York: Palgrave Macmillan, 2011); Lawrence Mitchell, *The Speculation Economy: How Finance Triumphed Over Industry* (New York: Barrett-Koehler, 2009); and John Kenneth Galbraith, *The Great Crash of 1929* (Boston: Houghton Mifflin, 1997); in addition to the works cited below and in the introduction's note 12. Numbers on stock ownership are notoriously difficult to pin down here, but for well-researched estimates, see Walter A. Friedman, *Fortune Tellers: The Story of America's First Economic Forecasters* (Princeton, NJ: Princeton University Press, 2013), 8; and Julia C. Ott, *When Wall Street Met Main Street: The Quest for an Investors' Democracy* (Cambridge, MA: Harvard University Press, 2011), 2–4. Urs Stäheli bafflingly claims that "the death of the speculator at the hands of the ticker tape symbolized the uncanny combination of economic subjectivity and mediality. The ticker, the medium that reliably represented the life and pulse of the market even in times of crises, strangled the once-successful speculator," but even without exact numbers, it's not hard to contradict this and observe that speculation thrived through the ticker (*Spectacular Speculation: Thrills, the Economy, and Popular Discourse*, trans. Eric Savoth [Stanford, CA: Stanford University Press, 2013], 237).
2. Reyam Ora, "Speculitis," *The Ticker*, August 1908, 161, Google Books.
3. I borrow this term from Richard R. John, "Recasting the Information Infrastructure for the Industrial Age," in *A Nation Transformed by Information: How Information Has Shaped the United States from Colonial Times to the Present*, ed. Alfred D. Chandler Jr. and James W. Cortada (New York: Oxford University Press, 200), 56. There is a great deal of work on the topic of information economies and media archaeology, with significant influence from figures like Friedrich Kittler, that I do not have the

space to address fully here. Niklas Luhmann and Karl Polanyi are very much in the background of this chapter, too.

4. See Murat Halstead, "The Varieties of Journalism," *The Cosmopolitan*, December 1892, 205.
5. David Hochfelder, *Telegraph in America,1832–1920* (Baltimore, MD: Johns Hopkins University Press, 2013), 111, table 4.2.
6. Peter Knight adds a further irony: "The machine that supposedly promoted anonymity and abstraction in the market was itself often personified, just as the investment guides that sought to introduce seemingly scientific, technical analyses to ordinary speculators continued to invoke more-mystical forms of interpretation" (*Reading the Market: Genres of Financial Capitalism in Gilded Age America* [Baltimore, MD: Johns Hopkins University Press, 2016], 22).
7. Sereno S. Pratt, *The Work of Wall Street* (New York: D. Appleton, 1903), 340.
8. I borrow this phrase from Alan Liu, *The Laws of Cool: Knowledge Work and the Culture of Information* (Chicago: University of Chicago Press, 2004), 1.
9. Alex Preda, *Framing Finance: The Boundaries of Markets and Modern Capitalism* (Chicago: University of Chicago Press, 2009), 131; Hochfelder, *Telegraph in America*, 102; emphasis in original. On the more embodied and racialized components of the telegraph, see Paul Gilmore, "The Telegraph in Black and White," *ELH* 69, no. 3 (Fall 2002): 805–833.
10. See David Hochfelder, "'Where the Common People Could Speculate': The Ticker, Bucket Shops, and the Origins of Popular Participation in Financial Markets, 1880–1920," *Journal of American History*, 93, no. 2 (September 2006): 335–58; and more generally, *Victorian Investments: New Perspectives on Finance and Culture*, ed. Nancy Henry and Cannon Schmitt (Bloomington: Indiana University Press, 2008); and Ann Fabian, *Card Sharps, Dream Books, and Bucket Shops: Gambling in Nineteenth-Century America* (Ithaca, NY: Cornell University Press, 1990).
11. Julius Chambers, *On a Margin* (New York: Fords, Howard, and Hulbert, 1884), 190, 191.
12. Chambers, *On a Margin*, 356.
13. George Parsons Lathrop, *Would You Kill Him?* (1889; Upper Saddle River, NJ: Literature House, 1970), 41.
14. Edwin Lefèvre, *Reminiscences of a Stock Operator* (New York: George H. Doran, 1923), 31.
15. George Rutledge Gibson, *The Stock Exchanges of London, Paris, and New York: A Comparison* (New York: G. P. Putnam's Sons, 1889), 83–84.
16. *The Chronicle: A Weekly Insurance Journal*, September 21, 1882, 1, https://books.google.com/books?id=Yz3YxSlgzcsC&pg=PA177#v=onepage&q&f=false.
17. Joaquin Miller, "The New Napoleon," *The Californian: A Western Monthly Magazine*, November 1880, 389, Google Books.
18. Miller, "The New Napoleon," 390.
19. Robert Grant, *The Lambs: A Tragedy* (Boston: James R. Osgood, 1883), 7.

20. Grant, *The Lambs*, 10–11.
21. Charles Dudley Warner, *A Little Journey in the World* (New York: Harper and Brothers, 1889), 82–83.
22. Warner, *Little Journey*, 84.
23. The Chicago Board of Trade earned its corporate charter from Illinois in 1859, while the first futures contracts codified under what we would now recognize as modern norms were traded in 1865.
24. *Report of the Federal Trade Commission on the Grain Trade* (Washington, DC: Government Printing Office, 1920), 226. Compare a journal from 1893: "In a word, in exchanging present for future goods, the employing producer not only discounts future values *qua* future, but he endeavors to deduct an ample rate of insurance on the risks of the speculation" (Franklin H. Giddings, "The Relation of Recent Economic Theory to Profit Sharing," *Employer and Employed* 1, no. 4 [July 1893]: 62, Google Books).
25. Scott A. Sandage, *Born Losers: A History of Failure in America* (Cambridge, MA: Harvard University Press, 2005), 88.
26. Samuel Butler, *Erewhon; or, Over the Range*, 6th ed. (London: David Bogue, 1880), 211.
27. William Stanley Jevons, *The Theory of Political Economy*, 3rd ed. (London: Macmillan, 1888), 34, 35.
28. Jevons, *Theory of Political Economy*, 35; emphasis in original.
29. Jevons, *Theory of Political Economy*, 111.
30. Jevons, *Political Economy* (London: Macmillan, 1892), 115.
31. See Jason Puskar, *Accident Society: Fiction, Collectivity, and the Production of Chance* (Stanford, CA: Stanford University Press, 2012). See also Kevin Rozario, *The Culture of Calamity: Disaster and the Making of Modern America* (Chicago: University of Chicago Press, 2007).
32. Caitlin Zaloom, *Out of the Pits: Traders and Technology from Chicago to London* (Chicago: University of Chicago Press, 2006), 105.
33. Thomas Gibson, *The Cycles of Speculation* (New York: Moody's Magazine, 1907), 4, 22.
34. Jamie L. Pietruska, *Looking Forward: Prediction and Uncertainty in Modern America* (Chicago: University of Chicago Press, 2017), 6. A valuable source text here is Louis Bachelier's *Théorie de la speculation* (1900). See also Martin van Creveld, *Seeing Into the Future: A Short History of Prediction* (London: Reaktion Books, 2020).
35. Pietruska, *Looking Forward*, 8. See also Katharine Anderson, *Predicting the Weather: Victorians and the Science of Meteorology* (Chicago: University of Chicago Press, 2005), 180.
36. See George Macloskie, "Scientific Speculation," *Presbyterian Review* 8 (1887): 617–25. See also Audrey Jaffe, *The Affective Life of the Average Man: The Victorian Novel and the Stock-Market Graph* (Columbus: Ohio State University Press, 2010); Regenia Gagnier, *The Insatiability of Human Wants: Economics and Aesthetics in Market Society* (Chicago: University of Chicago Press, 2000); and Theodore M. Porter, *The*

Rise of Statistical Thinking, 1820–1900 (Princeton, NJ: Princeton University Press, 2000).

37. See I. Bernard Cohen, "Newton and the Social Sciences, with Special Reference to Economics, or, the Case of the Missing Paradigm," in *Natural Images in Economic Thought: "Markets Read in Tooth and Claw"*, ed. Philip Mirowski, 55–90 (Cambridge: Cambridge University Press, 1994).

38. Lawrence Chamberlain, *The Principles of Bond Investment*, 3rd ed. (New York: Henry Holt, 1913), 11. This came through in titles like Philip L. Carret's *The Art of Speculation* (1930), too.

39. Lisi Schoenbach, *Pragmatic Modernism* (New York: Oxford University Press, 2011), 88.

40. See Max Weber, "Science as a Vocation," in *The Vocation Lectures*, ed. David Owen and Tracy B. Strong, trans. Rodney Livingstone (Indianapolis, IN: Hackett, 2004), 1–31.

41. See Aaron M. Sakolski, "American Speculative Mania," *Current History* 30 (August 1929): 860–68.

42. See Ian Hacking, *The Taming of Chance* (Cambridge: Cambridge University Press, 1990), 1–2.

43. See Jackson Lears, *Something for Nothing: Luck in America* (New York: Viking, 2003), 4, 135, 200.

44. Cf. William James: "Truth lives, in fact, for the most part on a credit system. Our thoughts and beliefs 'pass,' so long as nothing challenges them, just as bank-notes pass so long as nobody refuses them. But this all points to direct face-to-face verifications somewhere, without which the fabric of truth collapses like a financial system with no cash-basis whatever. You accept my verification of one thing, I yours of another. We trade on each other's truth. But beliefs verified concretely by somebody are the posts of the whole superstructure" (*Pragmatism: A New Name for Some Old Ways of Thinking* [London: Longmans, Green, 1907], 207).

45. See Stuart Banner, *Speculation: A History of the Fine Line Between Gambling and Investing* (New York: Oxford University Press, 2017); and Banner, *Anglo-American Securities Regulation: Cultural and Political Roots, 1690–1860* (Cambridge: Cambridge University Press, 2002) on some of the history here.

46. Oliver Wendell Holmes Jr., "The Path of the Law," *Harvard Law Review* 10, no. 8 (March 1897): 458. See also Paul Halpern, *The Pursuit of Destiny: A History of Prediction* (Cambridge, MA: Perseus, 2000).

47. Board of Trade v. Christie Grain & Stock Co., 198 U.S. 236, 247 (1905). See John Stuart Mill, *Principles of Political Economy*, 2 vols. (London: John W. Parker, 1848), 2:257–59, on speculation and equilibrium.

48. *Board of Trade*, 198 U.S. at 247.

49. Theodore Roosevelt, State of the Union address, December 3, 1906, Office of the Historian, United States Department of State, accessed November 7, 2019, https://history.state.gov/historicaldocuments/frus1906p1/annual.

50. *Board of Trade*, 198 U.S. at 249.

51. Quoted in Cedric B. Cowing, *Populists, Plungers, and Progressives: A Social History of Stock and Commodity Speculation, 1868–1932* (Princeton, NJ: Princeton University Press, 1965), 107.
52. "The Speculator in War Time," *The Outlook*, August 22, 1917, 630.
53. See *Saturday Evening Post*, May 2, 1908, 6–10.
54. "No speculation" (advertisement), *Saturday Evening Post*, May 16, 1908.
55. J. Thomas Reinhardt, "As the 'Curb' Sees It," *Saturday Evening Post*, May 16, 1908.
56. Reinhardt, "As the 'Curb' Sees It," 11.
57. Henry Clews, "No Speculation Would Mean Socialism," *Saturday Evening Post*, May 16, 1908.
58. Mark Twain and Charles Dudley Warner, *The Gilded Age: A Tale of To-Day*, ed. Bryant Morey French (New York: Bobbs-Merrill, 1972), 74, 20, 54, 60, 67.
59. Twain and Warner, *Gilded Age*, 186.
60. Mark Twain, *Following the Equator: A Journey Around the World* (Hartford, CT: American Publishing, 1898), 535. On Twain's speculations, see Peter Krass, *Ignorance, Confidence, and Filthy Rich Friends: The Business Adventures of Mark Twain, Chronic Speculator and Entrepreneur* (Hoboken, NJ: John Wiley, 2007); and Alan Pell Crawford, *How Not to Get Rich: The Financial Misadventures of Mark Twain* (New York: Houghton Mifflin Harcourt, 2017).
61. R. H. Mottram, *A History of Financial Speculation* (Boston: Little, Brown, 1929), 3. See also Lisle Abbott Rose, "A Bibliographical Survey of Economic and Political Writings, 1865–1900," *American Literature* 15 (January 1944): 381–410; and Nathan Leahy, "Finance Fictions: Crises, Value, and Nationalism in American Literature" (PhD diss., Northwestern University, 2015).
62. See Walter Fuller Taylor, *The Economic Novel in America* (Chapel Hill: University of North Carolina Press, 1942), 58–59.
63. See Knight, *Reading the Market*, for a fuller treatment of this literature.
64. Of course, this trend continued and continues: we could point to the speculators and discussions of speculations in Wilde's *An Ideal Husband* (1895), Conrad's *Chance* (1913), Joyce's *Ulysses* (1922), Toomer's *Cane* (1923), Dos Passos's *Manhattan Transfer* (1925), and any number of other modernist texts. Woolf's *Three Guineas* (1938) and Pound's *Cantos* (1917–1969) take up the questions of monetary value at length, in very different veins, with speculative abstraction often surfacing in their diametrically opposed discussions.
65. On the tension between the type and the particular in realism, for instance, see Alex Woloch, *The One vs. the Many: Minor Characters and the Space of the Protagonist in the Novel* (Princeton, NJ: Princeton University Press, 2003).
66. Cowing, *Populists, Plungers, and Progressives*, 5.
67. In a similar vein, as Peter Knight writes, "one of the most common modes of allegorizing the market in the Gilded Age and Progressive Era was anthropomorphization, with the individuals, generic types, or even abstract traits of speculative capitalism appearing in the guise of animals. Many nineteenth-century depictions of financial

panics focus on the herd-like behavior of market crowds, in which the violence of the struggle for financial survival on the floor of the exchange resembles the Darwinian jungle." "Representations of Capital in the Gilded Age and Progressive Era," in *American Capitalism: New Histories*, ed. Sven Beckert and Christine Desan (New York: Columbia University Press, 2018), 238.

68. On the term, see Karen Halttunen, *Confidence Men and Painted Ladies: A Study of Middle-Class Culture in America, 1830–1870* (New Haven, CT: Yale University Press, 1982), 6; and Gary H. Lindberg, *The Confidence Man in American Literature* (Oxford: Oxford University Press, 1982).

69. See Sandage, *Born Losers*.

70. For more on this trend, see Donald Worster, *Dust Bowl: The Southern Plains in the 1930s* (New York: Oxford University Press, 1979).

71. See Jaffe, *Affective Life*, 5; and Knight, *Reading the Market*, 11.

72. Jonathan Levy, *Freaks of Fortune: The Emerging World of Capitalism and Risk in America* (Cambridge, MA: Harvard University Press, 2012), 238. See Karl Marx, *Grundrisse: Foundations of the Critique of Political Economy*, trans. Martin Nicolaus (New York: Vintage, 1973), 168. Marx, of course, confessed himself a speculator in 1864. The prominent financial writer Alexander Dana Noyes notes in his *Forty Years of American Finance* (New York: Putnam, 1909) the huge spikes in cereal grain production from 1866 to 1878 and the "iron bubble" in 1879–1880 as two similarly functioning phenomena in the moment, too (60–61). See also Zaloom, *Out of the Pits*, 96–97; and for stories of individual commodities, see Emily Lambert, *The Futures: The Rise of the Speculator and the Origins of the World's Biggest Markets* (New York: Basic Books, 2012).

73. Frank Norris, *The Pit: A Story of Chicago* (London: Thomas Nelson, 1930), 14. See Christophe den Tandt, *The Urban Sublime in American Literary Naturalism* (Urbana: University of Illinois Press, 1998), 85–87.

74. We can see this articulated neatly in John Thomas Flynn's *Security Speculation* (1934), which draws on Henry Crosby Emery's work to argue that speculation "involves the purchase and sale of property, while gambling does not"; that risk is "inherent in business and ... exists whether the speculator assumes it or not," whereas "in gambling it is an artificial [risk]"; that speculative "buying and selling affect the forces of supply and demand and tend to bring about the very change in price for which he hopes," while gambling has "no effect" on an outcome; and that in "gambling the winner takes what the loser loses. But in speculation, ... there are occasions where practically everyone profits and where everyone loses" (*Security Speculation: Its Economic Effects* [New York: Harcourt, Brace, 1934], 13).

75. "Have you idle money?" (advertisement), *McClure's Magazine*, March 1905, 75, https://modjourn.org/issue/bdr534433/

76. See Walter Benn Michaels, *The Gold Standard and the Logic of Naturalism* (Berkeley: University of California Press, 1987), esp. 48–80. See also Alison Shonkwiler, *The Financial Imaginary: Economic Mystification and the Limits of Realist Fiction* (Minneapolis: University of Minnesota Press, 2017), 1–29.

77. Stäheli, *Spectacular Speculation*, 2, 20.

78. Georg Simmel, Fredric Jameson, and Giovanni Arrighi are perhaps the best-known figures to comment on this.
79. See Jesse Matz, *Lasting Impressions: The Legacies of Impressionism in Contemporary Culture* (New York: Columbia University Press, 2016), on this process from the late 1800s to its continuation in the present.
80. Laura Meixner, "'Gambling with Bread': Money, Speculation, and the Marketplace," *Modernism/modernity* 17, no. 1 (January 2010): 180.
81. "Modernism and Politics Play Havoc with Art: Part II," editorial, *Art World* 1, no. 3 (December 1916): 152.
82. Quoted in Andrew Stephenson, "'Strategies of Situation': British Modernism and the Slump c.1929–1934," *Oxford Art Journal* 14, no. 2 (1991), 30–51. William Carlos Williams's dogged materialism may be the counterclaim here.
83. Claude McKay, *Harlem: Negro Metropolis* (New York: E. P. Dutton, 1940), 26. My thanks to Benjy Kahan for this one. For context on McKay's notion, see Booker T. Washington and W. E. B. DuBois's *The Negro in the South* (1907). Longer studies came in Sterling D. Spero and Abram L. Harris, *The Black Worker: The Negro and the Labor Movement* (1931; New York: Columbia University Press, 1959); and St. Clair Drake and Horace R. Cayton, *Black Metropolis: A Study of Negro Life in a Northern City* (1945; Chicago: University of Chicago Press, 2015). More recently, see Kevin McGruder, *Race and Real Estate: Conflict and Cooperation in Harlem, 1890–1920* (New York: Columbia University Press, 2015).
84. Richard Ellmann writes that the young Joyce failed in his venture to found an early movie theater in Dublin, then attempted to "turn himself into a joint-stock company and sell shares, which would increase spectacularly in value as his books began to appear" (*James Joyce* [New York: Oxford University Press, 1982], 164). Proust, too, "squander[ed] about a third of his fortune on stocks," writes Hannah Freed-Thall, then eventually came to believe that "speculation and writing practices [were] two sides of the same coin" ("Speculative Modernism: Proust and the Stock Market," *Modernist Cultures* 12, no. 2 [2017]: 153, 154).
85. *Oxford English Dictionary Online*, s.v. "speculative fiction," accessed December 31, 2019. Robert Heinlein used the term at least as early as 1947. Hugo Gernsback influentially charted the science fiction tradition through Poe, Wells, and Verne. On Wells in particular, see Sarah Cole, *Inventing Tomorrow: H. G. Wells and the Twentieth Century* (New York: Columbia University Press, 2019).
86. "Literary Notes," *Mosher's Magazine*, August 1902, 298. Philosophical poetry is labeled "speculative" as early as 1823, if not before, and "speculative literature" comes up in searches dating back to the 1740s. Thomas Bellamy, editor of *Bellamy's Picturesque Magazine, and Literary Museum*, published in his own journal a short piece, "What May Be: A Speculative Fiction" (1793), set in the year 1799 and concerning political intrigue among English and French nobles; see "What May Be," *Bellamy's . . .*, no. 1 (1793): 51–52 accessed December 4, 2019, Eighteenth Century Collections Online.
87. "Books and Authors," *Living Age*, January 29, 1910, 319.

88. Nicky Marsh, *Money, Speculation, and Finance in Contemporary British Fiction* (London: Continuum, 2007), 14.
89. H. G. Wells, *The Time Machine: An Invention* (New York: Henry Holt, 1895), 206. See also John Plotz, "Speculative Naturalism and the Problem of Scale: Richard Jefferies's *After London*, After Darwin," *Modern Language Quarterly* 76, no. 1 (March 2015): 31–56; and more generally, David F. Noble, *America by Design: Science, Technology, and the Rise of Corporate Capitalism* (New York: Alfred A. Knopf, 1977).
90. Edward Bulwer-Lytton, *The Coming Race* (London: Routledge, 1900), 36, 53.
91. See Mark Seltzer, *Bodies and Machines* (New York: Routledge, 1992).
92. The ticker joined other machines in inspiring what Alan Trachtenberg characterized as a proliferation of novels, especially in the 1880s, in the twin genres of "popular romance and utopian speculation fastened on science and the machine as a hope for rationality, for the control so wanted in present affairs" (*The Incorporation of America: Culture and Society in the Gilded Age* [New York: Hill and Wang, 1982], 49).
93. Stephen Ross, "Speculative Modernism," in *Reconnecting Aestheticism and Modernism: Continuities, Revisions, Speculations*, ed. Bénédicte Coste, Catherine Delyfer, and Christine Reynier (New York: Routledge, 2017), 141.
94. Albert Einstein, foreword to *Dialogue Concerning the Two Chief World Systems: Ptolemaic and Copernican*, by Galileo Galilei, trans. Stillman Drake (New York: Modern Library, 2001), xxviii.
95. Max Planck, *Eight Lectures on Theoretical Physics*, trans. A. P. Wills (Minneola, NY: Dover, 1998), 120; translation modified. Some transcriptions of this lecture read "speculative natural phenomena," but the original German seems to have been *Naturforschung*.
96. Moses Smith, *Plain Truths About Stock Speculation* (Brooklyn, NY: E. V. Smith, 1887), 103, 136.
97. Quoted in Thomas A. Hieronymus, *Economics of Futures Trading: For Commercial and Personal Profit* (New York: Commodity Research Bureau, 1971), 89.
98. Hieronymus, *Economics of Futures Trading*, 89.
99. Hieronymus, *Economics of Futures Trading*, 90. See Thomas C. Jepsen, *My Sisters Telegraphic: Women in the Telegraph Office, 1846–1950* (Athens: Ohio University Press, 2000). Jepsen notes the irony here: telegraph offices were mostly staffed and operated by women.
100. "Women as Gamblers," *New York World*, reprinted in *Youngtown Daily Vindicator*, June 10, 1895, Google Books.
101. Eunice Fuller Barnard, "Ladies of the Ticker," *North American Review* 227, no. 4 (April 1929): 406.

6. THE LADY SPECULATOR

1. The classic study of this pattern is Elaine Showalter, *Hystories: Hysterical Epidemics and Modern Media* (New York: Columbia University Press, 1997).

2. Daniel Defoe, "Of Credit in Trade," *Review of the State of the English Nation*, January 8, 1706, 18. See Sandra Sherman, *Finance and Fictionality in the Early Eighteenth Century: Accounting for Defoe* (Cambridge: Cambridge University Press, 1996), 156–78.
3. J. G. A. Pocock, "Mobility of Property," in *Virtue, Commerce, and History: Essays on Political Thought and History, Chiefly in the Eighteenth Century* (New York: Cambridge University Press, 1985), 114. See also Terry Mulcaire, "Public Credit; or, The Feminization of Virtue in the Marketplace," *PMLA* 114, no. 5 (October 1999): 1029–42; Marieke de Goede, *Virtue, Fortune and Faith: A Genealogy of Finance* (Minneapolis: University of Minnesota Press, 2005), 24–45; and Catherine Ingrassia, *Authorship, Commerce, and Gender in Early Eighteenth-Century England: A Culture of Paper Credit* (Cambridge: Cambridge University Press, 1998).
4. Charles Mackay, *Memoirs of Extraordinary Popular Delusions*, 3 vols. (London: Richard Bentley, 1841), 1:161, 3:284, 3:305. Here we might also recall that Nathaniel Hawthorne lashed out in a famous letter not at a single female author or a small group of them, but rather claimed that "America is now wholly given over to a d—d mob of scribbling women" (Hawthorne to William Ticknor, January 19, 1855, in *The Centenary Edition of the Works of Nathaniel Hawthorne*, ed. William Charvat et al., 23 vols. [Columbus: Ohio State University Press, 1962–97], 17:304).
5. Gustave Le Bon, *The Crowd: A Study of the Popular Mind* (New York: Macmillan, 1897), 20.
6. Ralph Waldo Emerson, "The American Scholar," in *Essays and Lectures* (New York: Library of America, 1983), 60.
7. Another way of structuring this book would have been to interweave female speculators into the historical periods in which they were situated, but I have followed the traditions of feminist thought and authorship that this chapter reconstructs as a means of understanding a semiautonomous tradition—and as a process of character construction in which male and female writers were battling for authority.
8. See Mimi Abramovitz, *Regulating the Lives of Women: Social Welfare Policy from Colonial Times to the Present* (Boston: South End Press, 1996), 86.
9. Bathsua Makin, *An Essay to Revive the Antient Education of Gentlewomen* (London: J. D., 1673; Ann Arbor, MI: Text Creation Partnership, 2011), 26 http://name.umdl.umich.edu/A51611.0001.001.
10. Damaris Masham *Occasional Thoughts in Reference to a Vertuous and Christian Life* (London: A. and J. Churchil, 1705), 228, Google Books; Hannah Woolley, *The Gentlewomans Companion* (London: A. Maxwell, 1675; Ann Arbor, MI: Text Creation Partnership, 2003), 107–8, http://name.umdl.umich.edu/A66844.0001.001. Woolley's authorship has been disputed by some, but that is not a topic I can address here.
11. See Laura Brown, *Ends of Empire: Women and Ideology in Early Eighteenth-Century English Literature* (Ithaca, NY: Cornell University Press, 1993), esp. 96–119; and Edward Copeland, *Women Writing About Money: Women's Fiction in England, 1790–1820* (New York: Cambridge University Press, 1995).
12. Allan Ramsay, "The Rise and Fall of Stocks," in *The Poems of Allan Ramsay*, rev. ed., 2 vols. (Leith, Scotland: A. Allardice, 1814), 1:182, 184, Google Books.

13. Joseph Addison, *Spectator*, March 3, 1711, in *The Works of Joseph Addison*, 3 vols. (New York: Harper and Brothers, 1837), 1:21, Google Books.
14. See Jehanne Wake, *Sisters of Fortune: America's Caton Sisters at Home and Abroad* (New York: Simon & Schuster, 2010), 276.
15. Jonathan Swift, "The Journal of a Modern Lady," in *The Works of Jonathan Swift: Miscellaneous Poems* (Edinburgh: Archibald Constable, 1814), 220.
16. Alexander Pope, *Imitations of Horace*, in *The Poems of Alexander Pope*, ed. John Butt. 6 vols. (London: Methuen, 1939), 4:77; Pope to John Caryll, April/May 1720, in *The Works of Alexander Pope*, ed. John Wilson Croker, 10 vols. (London: John Murray, 1871), 6:272; Pope, "Epistle II: To a Lady. Of the Characters of Women," in *Pope: Selected Poems*, ed. Douglas Grant (Oxford: Oxford University Press, 1965), 154.
17. *The Adventures of a Turk*, 2 vols. (Dublin: Dillon Chamberlaine, 1760), 1:51, accessed June 16, 2019, Eighteenth Century Collections Online; William Dodd, "Sermon 13: On Gaming" (1771), in *Discourses to Young Men* (Philadelphia: W. A. Leary, 1848), 335, Google Books.
18. Nancy Henry and Cannon Schmitt, "Introduction: Finance, Capital, Culture," in *Victorian Investments: New Perspectives on Finance and Culture*, ed. Henry and Schmitt (Bloomington: Indiana University Press, 2008), 7–8. See also Leonore Davidoff and Catherine Hall, *Family Fortunes: Men and Women of the English Middle Class, 1780–1850*, rev. ed. (Abingdon: Routledge, 2002), esp. 277–79; and Catherine Gallagher, *Nobody's Story: The Vanishing Acts of Women Writers in the Marketplace, 1670–1820* (Berkeley: University of California Press, 1994).
19. Ingrassia, *Authorship, Commerce, and Gender*, 2. John Carswell, *South Sea Bubble* (Dover, NH: Alan Sutton, 1993), 8. See also P. G. M Dickson, *The Financial Revolution in England: A Study in the Development of Public Credit, 1688–1756* (London: Macmillan, 1967), 282, table 38; and Alastair Owens, "'Making Some Provision for the Contingencies': Women and Investment in Early Nineteenth-Century England," in *Women, Business, and Finance in Nineteenth-Century Europe: Rethinking Separate Spheres*, ed. Robert Beachy, Béatrice Craig, and Alastair Owens (Oxford: Berg, 2006), 20–35.
20. Ingrassia, *Authorship, Commerce, and Gender*, 30. See also George Robb, *Ladies of the Ticker: Women and Wall Street from the Gilded Age to the Great Depression* (Champaign: University of Illinois Press, 2017), 9; Robert E. Wright, *Hamilton Unbound: Finance and the Creation of the American Republic* (Westport, CT: Greenwood Press, 2002), 26; and more generally, Linda K. Kerber, *Women of the Republic: Intellect and Ideology in Revolutionary America* (Chapel Hill: University of North Carolina Press, 1980); Seth Rockman, *Scraping By: Wage Labor, Slavery, and Survival in Early Baltimore* (Baltimore, MD: Johns Hopkins University Press, 2009), 100–131; Rachel Bowlby, *Carried Away: The Invention of Modern Shopping* (London: Faber, 2001); Rita Felski, *The Gender of Modernity* (Cambridge, MA: Harvard University Press, 1995).
21. David R. Green and Alastair Owens, "Gentlewomanly Capitalism? Spinsters, Widows, and Wealth Holdings in England and Wales, c. 1800–1860," *Economic History Review* 56, no. 3 (2003): 524.

22. See Scott Christopher Miller, "'Never Did I See So Universal a Frenzy': The Panic of 1791 and the Republicanization of Philadelphia," *Pennsylvania Magazine of History and Biography* 142, no. 1 (January 2018): 27. See also Ellen Hartigan-O'Connor, *The Ties That Buy: Women and Commerce in Revolutionary America* (Philadelphia: University of Pennsylvania Press, 2009); Rosemarie Zagarri, *Revolutionary Backlash: Women and Politics in the Early American Republic* (Philadelphia: University of Pennsylvania Press, 2007).
23. See Robert E. Wright, *Wealth of Nations Rediscovered: Integration and Expansion in American Financial Markets, 1780–1850* (Cambridge: Cambridge University Press, 2002), 68–70. See also Janette Rutterford et al., "Who Comprised the Nation of Shareholders? Gender and Investment in Great Britain, c. 1870–1935," *Economic History Review* 64, no. 1 (February 2011): 157–87; Sheri J. Caplan, *Petticoats and Pinstripes: Portraits of Women in Wall Street's History* (Santa Barbara, CA: Praeger, 2013); and more generally, Joseph Fichtelberg, *Critical Fictions: Sentiment and the American Market, 1780–1870* (Athens: University of Georgia Press, 2003).
24. William Findley, *A Review of the Revenue System...* (Philadelphia: T. Dobson, 1794), 56, accessed January 12, 2019, Eighteenth Century Collections Online. Kathleen D. McCarthy has also pointed to the wide array of investing practices among women's philanthropic societies, widows' societies, and woman-directed funds beginning in the late 1700s (*American Creed: Philanthropy and the Rise of Civil Society, 1700–1865* [Chicago: University of Chicago Press, 2003]).
25. Louis-Sébastien Mercier, *New Picture of Paris*, 2 vols. (London: C. Whittingham, 1800), 1:319.
26. See Mary Astell, *Some Reflections Upon Marriage* (1700; Champaign: University of Illinois Press, 2015). See also Jacqueline Broad and Karen Green, *A History of Women's Political Thought in Europe, 1400–1700* (Cambridge: Cambridge University Press, 2009), 199–287.
27. Joseph Addison and Richard Steele, *The Guardian*, July 29, 1713, in *The Guardian*, 2 vols. (London: Jacob and Richard Tonson, 1740): 2:202–3.
28. Thomas Mortimer, *Every Man His Own Broker*, 9th ed. (London: G. Robinson, 1782), xx, Google Books. Charles Pigott's *The Female Jockey Club* (1794) furthermore describes lady gamblers as drawn by the "distractions of a gaming house" in a "fervent" effort at "labour[ing] indefatigably" to "fill up the wrinkled deformities of nature," only to discover that "the remedy [is] worse than the disease" (*The Female Jockey Club* [London: D. I. Eaton, 1794], 104, 105, Google Books).
29. Addison and Steele, *The Guardian*, July 29, 1713, in *The Guardian*, 2 vols. (London: Jacob and Richard Tonson, 1740): 2:203.
30. See Carol F. Karlsen, *The Devil in the Shape of a Woman: Witchcraft in Colonial New England* (New York: W. W. Norton, 1998), 77–116.
31. See Ingrid H. Tague, *Women of Quality: Accepting and Contesting Ideals of Femininity in England, 1690–1760* (Rochester, NY: Boydell Press, 2002), 60.
32. Mary Wollstonecraft, *A Vindication of the Rights of Women* (New York: Cosimo Classics, 2008), 155.

33. Eliza Leslie, *The Behaviour Book: A Manual for Ladies* (Philadelphia: W. P. Hazard, 1853), 252.
34. Harriet Arbuthnot, entry of March 1825, in *The Journal of Mrs. Arbuthnot, 1820–1832*, eds. Francis Bamford and the Duke of Wellington, 2 vols. (London: Macmillan, 1950), 1:381–82.
35. A similar set of overlapping concerns and fields operate in Sarah Fielding's *The Governess* (1749): Mrs. Teachum loses both her husband and her children to a "violent Fever that then raged in the Country"; in the same sentence, we learn that "about the same time, by the unforeseen Breaking of a Banker, in whose Hands almost all her Fortune was just then placed, she was bereft of the Means of her future Support" (*The Governess*, ed. Candace Ward [Peterborough, ON: Broadview, 2005], 49).
36. See Gillian Russell, "'Faro's Daughters': Female Gamesters, Politics, and the Discourse of Finance in 1790s Britain," *Eighteenth-Century Studies* 33, no. 4 (Summer 2000): 481–504.
37. Mary Poovey's *Genres of the Credit Economy: Mediating Value in Eighteenth- and Nineteenth-Century Britain* (Chicago: University of Chicago Press, 2008), including its bibliography, is a valuable resource here.
38. See Catherine Gallagher, "The Rise of Fictionality," in *The Novel*, ed. Franco Moretti, 2 vols. (Princeton, NJ: Princeton University Press, 2006), 1:336–63.
39. There is more scholarship on this topic than I could address here; Liz Bellamy, Patrick Brantlinger, Dorrit Cohn, Margaret Doody, Catherine Gallagher, Deidre Lynch Michael McKeon, Mona Scheuermann, Sandra Sherman, Janet Todd, and James Thompson are among those who have published on this topic with a particular focus on gender.
40. See Janet Todd, *The Sign of Angellica: Women, Writing, and Fiction, 1660–1800* (London: Virago, 1989), 36.
41. Jessica Richard, *The Romance of Gambling in the Eighteenth-Century British Novel* (New York: Palgrave Macmillan, 2011), 111, 112.
42. Daniel Defoe, *Moll Flanders*, ed. David Blewett (New York: Penguin Classics, 1989), 128. Moll herself notes that she "has a Project for *Virginia*" (217), or that, in one scene, a "Captain's Lady" managed to put a "Project into my Head" (123).
43. Sarah Fielding, *The Adventures of David Simple*, ed. Linda Bree (New York: Penguin Classics, 2002), 264, 265, 266.
44. Daniel Defoe, *Roxana: The Fortunate Mistress*, ed. David Blewett (New York: Penguin Classics, 1987), 183, 37, 183–84. See also Christina L. Healey, "'A Perfect Retreat Indeed': Speculation, Surveillance, and Space in Defoe's *Roxana*," *Eighteenth Century Fiction* 21, no. 4 (Summer 2009): 493–512.
45. Defoe, *Roxana*, 110.
46. Eliza Haywood, *The Female Spectator*, 4 vols. (London: T. Gardner, 1755), 1:11, Google Books.
47. Haywood, *Female Spectator*, 1:189.
48. Haywood, *Female Spectator*, 1:166, 164.

49. Margaret Cavendish, Letter 75, in *Sociable Letters*, ed. James Fitzmaurice (Peterborough, ON: Broadview, 2004), 130.
50. Eliza Haywood, *The History of Betsy Thoughtless*, ed. Christine Blouch (Peterborough, ON: Broadview, 1998), 210.
51. Haywood, *History of Betsy Thoughtless*, 221.
52. Anne Radcliffe, *The Mysteries of Udolpho: A Romance*, 4 vols. (London: G. G. and J. Robinson, 1794), 3:170.
53. Andrea Henderson, *Romanticism and the Painful Pleasures of Modern Life* (Cambridge: Cambridge University Press, 2011), 101.
54. Frances Burney, *Camilla: A Picture of Youth* (Auckland, NZ: Floating Press, 2009), 510.
55. Burney, *Camilla*, 511.
56. Gallagher, "Rise of Fictionality," in Moretti, *The Novel*, 1:346.
57. Maria Edgeworth and R. L. Edgeworth, *Essays on Practical Education*, 2 vols. (London: J. Johnson, 1811), 2:182, 183 Google Books. See also Maria Edgeworth, *Belinda*, in *The Works of Maria Edgeworth*, 12 vols. (Boston: Samuel H. Parker, 1824), 3:8–9, Google Books. Edgeworth's *Castle Rackrent* (1800) also features several minor plays on *speculation*.
58. Edgeworth and Edgeworth, *Practical Education*, 2:405.
59. Maria Eliza Rundell, *A New System of Domestic Cookery* (New York: Robert M'Dermut, 1817), xii, Google Books.
60. Jane Austen, *Mansfield Park*, ed. John Lucas (London: Oxford University Press, 1970), 216. Whist, which would be immortalized as the card game that prompts the wager central to Verne's *Around the World in Eighty Days* (1873), was widely played because it did not require risking money at casinos, only wagers within the controlled environment of the game. It would evolve into bridge, a staple of the American leisure class. I owe Amy Murray Twyning deeply for pointing me to the many connections across this novel and *Daniel Deronda* (below).
61. Edmond Hoyle, *Hoyle's Games Improved* (London: M. Ritchie, 1800), iv, https://books.google.com/books?id=GABeAAAAcAAJ.
62. Thomas Hudson, *Comic Songs* (London: Thomas Hudson, 1820), 7, Google Books.
63. Austen, *Mansfield Park*, 216. See also Lynda A. Hall, *Women and "Value" in Jane Austen's Novels: Settling, Speculating, and Superfluity* (New York: Palgrave Macmillan, 2017), 115–58; Regulus Allen, "Speculation in *Mansfield Park*," in *Approaches to Teaching Jane Austen's "Mansfield Park"*, ed. Marcia McClintock Folsom and John Wiltshire (New York: MLA, 2014), 97–104.
64. Austen, *Mansfield Park*, 216. See also Peter Knox-Shaw, *Jane Austen and the Enlightenment* (Cambridge: Cambridge University Press, 2004), 243–54; and for a brief reading of the scene through game theory, see Michael Suk-Young Chew, *Jane Austen, Game Theorist* (Princeton, NJ: Princeton University Press, 2013), 139–40. See also Margaret Doody, *Jane Austen's Names: Riddles, Persons, Places* (Chicago: University of Chicago Press, 2015), 200–201.
65. Austen, *Mansfield Park*, 224.

66. Austen, *Mansfield Park*, 221, 219.
67. Austen, *Mansfield Park*, 224–25.
68. Austen, *Mansfield Park*, 341, 429, 430.
69. Julia Pardoe, *Speculation*, 2 vols. (New York: Harper & Brothers, 1837), 1:227–28.
70. Anna Bartlett Warner [Amy Lothrop, pseud.], *Speculation; or, The Glen Luna Family* (London: Routledge, 1854), 2, accessed June 21, 2019, HathiTrust. See Andre Lawson, *Downwardly Mobile: The Changing Fortunes of American Realism* (Oxford: Oxford University Press, 2012), 1–18.
71. Charles Dickens, *Nicholas Nickleby*, ed. Paul Schlicke (Oxford: Oxford University Press, 2008), 4. Speculation motivates the plot of Harriet Beecher Stowe's *Uncle Tom's Cabin* (1852), too, and the novel features discussions of the slave speculator as the most evil of his type.
72. Dickens, *Nicholas Nickleby*, 5.
73. Anna Kornbluh, *Realizing Capital: Financial and Psychic Economies in Victorian Form* (New York: Fordham University Press, 2014), 95. Balzac's comedy *Mercadet* was also translated as *The Game of Speculation*. See also Gail Turley Houston, *From Dickens to "Dracula": Gothic, Economics, and Victorian Fiction* (Cambridge: Cambridge University Press, 2009).
74. For an overview of the literature on this topic, see Tamara Wagner, *Financial Speculation in Victorian Fiction: Plotting Money and the Novel Genre, 1815-1901* (Columbus: Ohio State University Press, 2010); and *The Financial System in Victorian Britain*, ed. Mary Poovey (New York: Oxford University Press, 2002). By Elizabeth Gaskell, see esp. *North and South* (1854–55). See also Barbara Weiss, *The Hell of the English: Bankruptcy and the Victorian Novel* (Lewisburg, PA: Bucknell University Press, 1986).
75. George Eliot, *Daniel Deronda* (Ware: Wordsworth Classics, 2003), 10.
76. Eliot, *Daniel Deronda*, 42.
77. Eliot, *Daniel Deronda*, 75.
78. Eliot, *Daniel Deronda*, 73.
79. Eliot, *Daniel Deronda*, 193.
80. Eliot, *Daniel Deronda*, 296.
81. Just to point to some texts from the same moment: Thomas Hardy would again align "whist for love," being "unduly speculative," and modern marriage markets (*Far from the Madding Crowd* [London: Macmillan, 1958], 104). And a short story published in *Godey's Lady's Book*, F. M. Bickell's "A Trap to Catch an Heiress" (1879), opens with two men meditating upon the same question in similar language: "I think it as honorable to get a fortune by marriage as by speculation or gambling in stocks." Bickell, "A Trap to Catch an Heiress," *Godey's Lady's Book*, May 1879, 488, Google Books.
82. Kate Chopin, *The Awakening* (Chicago: Stone, 1899), 9.
83. Chopin, *Awakening*, 269–70.
84. Edith Wharton, *The House of Mirth* (New York: Penguin, 1990), 3.
85. William Worthington Fowler, *Ten Years in Wall Street; or, Revelations of Inside Life and Experience on 'Change* (Hartford, CT: Worthington, Dustin, 1870), 450.

86. "The Bewitching Brokers.—Women on 'Change" (cartoon), *Harper's*, March 5, 1870, https://www.harpweek.com/09Cartoon/BrowseByDateCartoon-Large.asp?Month=March&Date=5.
87. See "Wall-Street Aroused," *New York Times*, February 6, 1870.
88. See, e.g., "Speculating Women," *New York Times*, January 17, 1875.
89. Gordon Thomas and Max Morgan-Witts, *The Day the Bubble Burst: A Social History of the Wall Street Crash of 1929* (London: H. Hamilton, 1979), 73.
90. Antoinette Brown Blackwell, "Industrial Reconstruction," *Women's Advocate*, January 1869, 42, Abolition, Freedom, and Rights Collection, accessed April 15, 2019, http://womenwriters.digitalscholarship.emory.edu/abolition/content.php?level=div&id=advocate1_120&document=advocate1. David C. Itzkowitz notes that "speculation was, by the 1880s at the latest, also becoming a form of entertainment and was entering into the same raffish bohemian world that was described by sporting and theatrical journalists" ("Fair Enterprise or Extravagant Speculation: Investment, Speculation, and Gambling in Victorian England," *Victorian Studies* 45, no. 1 [Autumn 2002]: 137).
91. Advertisement in *Twenty Years a Detective in the Wickedest City in the World*, by Clifton R. Woolridge (1908), 535.
92. Caroline H. Dall, *The College, The Market, and the Court* (Boston: Lee and Shepard, 1868), 496. George Robb notes that "the most remarkable literary defense of the stock market and women investors is James Blanchard Clews's *Fortuna: A Story of Wall Street* (1898)" (*Ladies of the Ticker*, 32).
93. Ouida [Maria Louise Ramé], *Friendship: A Story of Society* (Toronto: Rose-Belford Publishing, 1878), 242.
94. "Wall Street Shaken to Foundation by Wild Panic in the Stock Market," *Morning Herald* (Lexington, KY), May 10, 1901.
95. Reproduced in *Life History of the United States*, part 44 (New York: Time Life Books/Marshall Cavendish, 1973), 1226.
96. S. A. Nelson, "Wall Street as It Is," *World's Work*, February 1905, 5822.
97. Laura Meixner, "'Gambling with Bread': Money, Speculation, and the Marketplace," *Modernism/modernity* 17, no. 1 (January 2010): 188.
98. E. V. Smith, *Plain Truths About Stock Speculation* (Brooklyn, New York, 1887), 136, https://books.google.com/books?id=vrdGAAAAIAAJ.
99. E. C. Spitzka, *Insanity: Its Classification, Diagnosis, and Treatment* (New York: Bermingham, 1883), 188.
100. Spitzka, *Insanity*, 398, 399.
101. Meixner, "Gambling with Bread," 192.
102. Asquith made this comment, often repeated by Emmeline Pankhurst, Bertrand Russell, and others, to the House of Commons on May 26, 1908. Quoted in Martin Pugh, *The Pankhursts: The History of One Radical Family* (London: Vintage Books, 2008), 176.
103. See "Speculations on Sex War," *The Freewoman*, December 14, 1911, 65.
104. Avrom Barnett, *Foundations of Feminism: A Critique* (New York: Robert M. McBride, 1921), 71.
105. Mabel Dodge, "Speculations," *Camera Work*, June 1913, 9.

106. Virginia Woolf, *Orlando: A Biography* (New York: Harcourt, 1956), 119.
107. See Jeremy Braddock, *Collecting as Modernist Practice* (Baltimore, MD: Johns Hopkins University Press, 2012); and Lawrence Rainey, *Institutions of Modernism: Literary Elites and Public Culture* (New Haven, CT: Yale University Press, 1998).
108. See Glenn Willmott, *Modernist Goods: Primitivism, the Market, and the Gift* (Toronto: University of Toronto Press, 2008), 3.
109. Adrienne Monnier, *The Very Rich Hours of Adrienne Monnier*, ed. and trans. Richard McDougall (Lincoln: University of Nebraska Press, 1996), 141; emphasis in original. Monnier adds, "Let me be clearly understood, I am speaking here of speculation and not of business in general. I do not call someone a speculator who possesses a just appreciation of the value of things and who knows how to fix their price. I call someone a speculator who does not love to begin with, someone who sees only the possible material profit, who exploits the creator and the amateur at one and the same time" (141).
110. Gabriella Friedman, "The Social Life of Speculation," *American Quarterly* 71, no. 1 (March 2019): 205–6.
111. Friedman, "The Social Life of Speculation," 205. Continuing such invocations of the term, the Speculative Futures Research Group across the University of California system similarly seeks to understand the alternative worlds of speculative fictions as "strategies for world-making" in which scholars and critics participate (Shelley Streeby et al., Speculative Futures grant synopsis, accessed November 25, 2019, https://app.dimensions.ai/details/grant/grant.7925754). A special issue of the journal *ASAP* promises to examine "New Worlds of Speculation" by exploring the ties between "speculation and identity" through the fantastic, strange, horrifying, and otherwise non-"real" (call for papers, *ASAP/Journal* special issue, accessed March 3, 2020, http://asapjournal.com/call-for-papers/). See also Alexis Lothian, *Old Futures: Speculative Fiction and Queer Possibility* (New York: New York University Press, 2018); John Pfeiffer, "Black American Speculative Fiction," *Extrapolation: A Journal of Science Fiction and Fantasy* 17, no. 1 (1975): 35–43; Isaiah Lavender III, *Race in American Science Fiction* (Bloomington: Indiana University Press, 2011); André M. Carrington, *Speculative Blackness: The Future of Race in Science Fiction* (Minneapolis: University of Minnesota Press, 2016); and Alex Zamalin, *Black Utopia: The History of an Idea from Black Nationalism to Afrofuturism* (New York: Columbia University Press, 2019). Speculation has become a staple of the contemporary critical vocabulary in academic circles especially: recent collections and titles like *Speculations on Speculation* (2005), *Speculative Everything* (2013), *Speculation, Now* (2015), *Genealogies of Speculation* (2016), *After the "Speculative Turn"* (2016), *Speculation as a Mode of Production* (2018), *Speculative Aesthetics* (2019), and *Speculation: Politics, Ideology, Event* (2019) address these matters with essays largely from the art world, philosophy, and literary aesthetics on the intersections of speculative finance, abstract thought, and multimedia creations. The term *speculative realism*, too, has generated controversy for its attempt to think of objects in and of themselves, without and/or against the definitionally anthropocentric

perceptions of human minds. Quentin Meillassoux is the figure most often identified with this strand of thought. For an overview, see Rebekah C. Sheldon, "Speculative Realism Is Speculative Aesthetics (Three New Books on Speculative Realism)," *Configurations* 23, no. 3 (2015): 403–7. See also *Genealogies of Speculation: Materialism and Subjectivity Since Structuralism*, ed. Suhail Malik and Armen Avanessian (London: Bloomsbury, 2016). Rob Nixon has recently written of the impending catastrophes captured by "speculative nonfiction" ("All Tomorrow's Warnings," *Public Books*, August 13, 2020, https://www.publicbooks.org/all-tomorrows-warnings/).

112. Stefano Harney and Fred Moten, *The Undercommons: Fugitive Planning and Black Study* (Minor Compositions, 2013), 110; Aimee Bahng, *Migrant Futures: Decolonizing Speculation in Financial Times* (Durham, NC: Duke University Press, 2017); Saidiya Hartman, "An Unnamed Girl, a Speculative History," NewYorker.com, February 9, 2019, https://www.newyorker.com/culture/culture-desk/an-unnamed-girl-a-speculative-history. Hartman's essay is drawn from her book *Wayward Lives, Beautiful Experiments: Intimate Histories of Social Upheaval* (New York: W. W. Norton, 2019).

113. uncertain commons, *Speculate This!* (Durham, NC: Duke University Press, 2013), n.p., https://speculatethis.pressbooks.com/.

114. uncertain commons, *Speculate This!*

115. Jens Beckert, *Imagined Futures: Fictional Expectations and Capitalist Dynamics* (Harvard University Press, 2016); Gert Verschraegen, *Imagined Futures in Science, Technology, and Society* (New York, Routledge, 2017); Julia Cook, *Imagined Futures: Hope, Risk, and Uncertainty* (Basingstoke: Palgrave Macmillan, 2017); Max Saunders, *Imagined Futures: Writing, Science, and Modernity in the To-Day and To-Morrow Book Series, 1923–1931* (Oxford: Oxford University Press, 2019).

CONCLUSION

1. "Social Insurance," *Studies in Social Christianity*, September 1914, 134. See Viviana A. Rotman Zelizer, *Morals and Markets: The Development of Life Insurance in the United States* (New York: Columbia University Press, 2017); Paul Virilio, *The Original Accident*, trans. Rose Julie (Cambridge: Polity, 2007); Eric Wertheimer, *Underwriting: The Poetics of Insurance in America, 1722–1872* (Stanford, CA: Stanford University Press, 2006); David A. Moss, *When All Else Fails: Government as the Ultimate Risk Manager* (Cambridge, MA: Harvard University Press, 2004).
2. Wyndham Lewis, "A Super-Krupp—or War's End," *Blast*, no. 2 (July 1915): 14.
3. Ulrich Beck, *World at Risk*, trans. Ciaran Cronin (Malden, MA: Polity, 2009), 110. As critics have noted, Beck's early formulations of "risk society" did not adequately distinguish "risk" from "hazard" or "peril," but that discussion requires more space to treat. There is an extensive bibliography on this topic in Deborah Lupton, *Risk* (New York: Routledge, 2013), 245–58.

4. Hannah Arendt, *The Origins of Totalitarianism* (New York: Harcourt, Brace & World, 1966), xxix.
5. Lisi Schoenbach sees this, in part, as a reactionary formation: "The characteristically modernist representation of radical contingency and unpredictability cannot be understood apart from modernity's thoroughly systematized, newly bureaucratic understanding of time as a medium for managing workforces and stabilizing institutions" (*Pragmatic Modernism* (New York: Oxford University Press, 2011), 84). On other contexts, see the special issues of *Victorian Review* on risk (vol. 40, no. 2 [2014]) and of *Amerikastudien/American Studies* on risk and security (vol. 60, no. 4 [2015]).
6. Beck, *World at Risk*, 114. Beck is drawing on Zygmunt Bauman's work here.
7. John Maynard Keynes, "Speculation in the Mark and German's Balances Abroad" (1922), in *The Collected Writings of John Maynard Keynes*, 30 vols., ed. Elizabeth Johnson (Cambridge: Macmillan / Cambridge University Press, 1978), 18:49–50.
8. See "Risk: A Dossier," ed. Gayle Rogers, *Critical Quarterly* 62, no. 1 (April 2020).
9. Anthony Giddens, quoted in Giddens and Christopher Pierson, *Conversations with Anthony Giddens: Making Sense of Modernity* (Stanford, CA: Stanford University Press, 1998), 100, 101. Or, risk asks, in Peter L. Bernstein's words, "how to put the future at the service of the present" (*Against the Gods: The Remarkable Story of Risk* [New York: John Wiley and Sons, 1998], 1).
10. Elaine Freedgood, *Victorian Writing About Risk: Imagining a Safe England in a Dangerous World* (Cambridge: Cambridge University Press, 2000), 1. See also Justin Fox, *The Myth of the Rational Market: A History of Risk, Reward, and Delusion on Wall Street* (New York: HarperCollins, 2009); and John Cassidy, *How Markets Fail: The Logic of Economic Calamities* (New York: Farrar, Straus and Giroux, 2009).
11. Beck, *World at Risk*, 8, 9.
12. Frank H. Knight, *Risk, Uncertainty, and Profit* (New York: Augustus M. Kelley, 1964), 255. For more context, see George G. Szpiro, *Risk, Choice, and Uncertainty: Three Centuries of Economic Decision-Making* (New York: Columbia University Press, 2020).
13. Alan Turing, "Computing Machinery and Intelligence," *Mind: A Quarterly Review of Psychology and Philosophy* 59, no. 236 (October 1950): 433.
14. Turing, "Computing Machinery and Intelligence," 434, 443.
15. On the implications of such questions for humanistic studies, see Annette Vee, *Coding Literacy: How Computer Programming Is Changing Writing* (Cambridge, MA: MIT Press, 2017); Marcus Du Sautoy, *The Creativity Code: Art and Innovation in the Age of AI* (Cambridge, MA: Belknap Press of Harvard University Press, 2019); and Susan Schneider, *Artificial You: AI and the Future of Your Mind* (Princeton, NJ: Princeton University Press, 2019).
16. Translator's notes to L. F. Menabrea, "Sketch of the Analytical Engine Invented by Charles Babbage Esq.," trans. Ada Lovelace, *Scientific Memoirs*, vol. 3 (London: Richard and John E. Taylor, 1843), 699.
17. Lovelace, translator's notes to Menabrea, "Sketch of the Analytical Engine," 700.

18. Lovelace, translator's notes to Menabrea, "Sketch of the Analytical Engine," 722.
19. See, e.g., Donna Haraway, *Simians, Cyborgs, and Women: The Reinvention of Nature* (New York: Routledge, 1991); N. Katherine Hayles, *Writing Machines* (Cambridge, MA: MIT Press, 2002). See also R. John Williams, *The Buddha in the Machine: Art, Technology, and the Meeting of East and West* (New Haven, CT: Yale University Press, 2014).
20. Peter Knight, "Speculation," in *The Routledge Companion to Literature and Economics*, ed. Michelle Chihara and Matt Seybold (New York: Routledge, 2018), 353.
21. See Mark Maremont and Leslie Scism, "Odds Skew Against Investors in Bets on Strangers' Lives," *Wall Street Journal*, December 21, 2010, https://www.wsj.com/articles/SB10001424052748704694004576019344291967866.
22. Michael Lewis, *Flash Boys: A Wall Street Revolt* (New York: W. W. Norton, 2014), 3.
23. "The Stockmarket Is Now Run by Computers, Algorithms and Passive Managers," *The Economist*, October 5, 2019, https://www.economist.com/briefing/2019/10/05/the-stockmarket-is-now-run-by-computers-algorithms-and-passive-managers.
24. See Safiya Noble, *Algorithms of Oppression: How Search Engines Reinforce Racism* (New York: New York University Press, 2018); and Sun-ha Hong, *Technologies of Speculation: The Limits of Knowledge in a Data-Driven Society* (New York: New York University Press, 2020).
25. Maggie Koerth, "Every Decision Is a Risk. Every Risk Is a Decision," *FiveThirtyEight*, https://fivethirtyeight.com/features/every-decision-is-a-risk-every-risk-is-a-decision/.
26. Tom McCarthy, *Remainder* (New York: Vintage, 2007), 46, 47.
27. McCarthy, *Remainder*, 123–24. *Speculation* is one of several words that capture the narrator's sensibilities and curiosities; others include *accrued*, *settlement*, *resolution*, *enlist*, and *recidual* (which he insists is distinct from *residual*), and more elliptically, *vaporize* and *escape*.
28. McCarthy, *Remainder*, 307. *Remainder* refuses both the stability of material reality that traditional realism promised and the complete detachment from it that high-theory postmodernism offered, as Zadie Smith pointed out in an essay that brought wider attention to the novel ("Two Paths for the Novel," *New York Review of Books*, November 20, 2008, https://www.nybooks.com/articles/2008/11/20/two-paths-for-the-novel/). McCarthy is dramatizing, in effect, what Alison Shonkwiler has described as the logic of financialization since the early 1970s, in which "risk replaces money as the most abstract form of value and works to produce value through 'compounding' of abstractions" (*The Financial Imaginary: Economic Mystification and the Limits of Realist Fiction* [Minneapolis: University of Minnesota Press, 2017], 7). There is much more to say here about what Shonkwiler has called "financialization," and more broadly about the widening field of critical finance studies. In addition to the studies already cited, see Annie McClanahan, *Dead Pledges: Debt, Crisis, and Twenty-First-Century Culture* (Stanford, CA: Stanford University Press, 2017); Leigh Claire La Berge, *Scandals and Abstraction: Financial Fiction of the Long 1980s* (New York: Oxford University Press, 2014); Kevin R. Brine and Mary Poovey, *Finance in*

America: An Unfinished Story (Chicago: University of Chicago Press, 2017); Katy Shaw, *Crunch Lit* (London: Bloomsbury Academic, 2015); and Thomas Bay and Christophe Schinckus, "Critical Finance Studies: An Interdisciplinary Manifesto," *Journal of Interdisciplinary Economics* 24, no. 1 (2012): 1–6; Benjamin Lee and Edward LiPuma, *Financial Derivatives and the Globalization of Risk* (Durham, NC: Duke University Press, 2004); Sherryl Vint, "Promissory Futures: Reality and Imagination in Finance and Fiction," *CR: The New Centennial Review* 19, no. 1 (Spring 2019): 11–36; and Dan Sinykin, *American Literature and the Long Downturn: Neoliberal Apocalypse* (New York: Oxford University Press, 2020).

29. Vladimir Nabokov, *Transparent Things* (New York: Vintage, 1989), 1.
30. Ben Levisohn, "The Stock Market Keeps Rising No Matter What. Time to Call It a Bubble?" *Barron's*, September 2, 2020, https://www.barrons.com/articles/can-we-call-it-a-stock-market-bubble-yet-51598998768.

INDEX

abstraction: and aesthetics, 136–37, 139–40; in Bacon, 41, 43; in Boethius, 15, 18, 20–21; in Calvin, 29–30; in Chaucer, 21; and cognition, 11, 28–29, 36, 46–47, 170, 181; and computation, 177; and futurity, 3, 38, 123, 125, 182–83; of speculators, 133–34, 167; of wealth, 51–52, 62, 69, 97, 107, 117–18, 125, 135, 182
activism, 169–71
Adams, Abigail, 96–97
Adams, John, 94, 96–97, 108
addiction, 2, 76, 92, 115–16, 122, 144, 148, 168
Addison, Joseph, 39, 56–58, 69, 147–48, 153, 212n83
adventurers, 75–76, 79–81, 148, 151
"air-money," 52, 135, 152, 183
algorithms, 4, 5, 178–80, 182
Anstey, Christopher, 7, 65, 67, 83–85, 89, 93, 102, 155
anticipation, 5; of catastrophe, 171, 175–76; and finance, 49, 70, 125; as literary topic, 85, 138; and the scientific revolution, 38, 40, 48
Aquinas, Thomas, 22, 30, 42, 72, 193n1, 197n38
Arbuthnot, Harriet, 149–51

Arendt, Hannah, 16, 174, 194n10
Aristotle: and Platonism, 13, 16–17, 23, 42; and *theōria*, 15–18, 21; translations of, 4, 15–21, 23, 26, 195n10
Armitage, David, 6, 190n6
artificial intelligence, 176
art speculators, 137, 170
Asquith, H. H., 169, 243n102
augury. *See* divination
Augustine (Saint): and Bacon, 42; *De trinitate* by, 9–10, 12–15, 17, 193n1; and Luther, 30
Austen, Jane, 2, 144, 157–59, 161, 163–64
avarice, 72, 87, 158
Awakening, The (Chopin), 162–63

Babbage, Charles, 177
Babson, Roger, 126
Bacon, Francis, 2, 38–39, 46, 53, 72; and the new science, 40, 45–46, 49; *Novum organum* by, 43; and "speculative prudence," 40–44; speculator figure in, 58
banking: crises in, 75, 79; federal, 96; regulation of, 82; and speculation, 51, 70, 75–76, 79, 82, 98, 106, 132, 147–49, 167

Bank of England, 50, 143, 147, 149, 226n63
Bank of the United States, 95, 101, 148
Banner, Stuart, 5, 99
Baucom, Ian, 71
Beck, Ulrich, 174–75
Beecher, Henry Ward, 74
behavior: of crowds, 106, 109, 143, 234n67; gendering of, 143–44, 146–47, 150, 170; speculation as, 18, 67, 92, 104, 111, 116, 126–27, 144, 150, 170
Bible: King James version of, 9–10, 13, 35, 194n6; Latin Vulgate version of, 10, 13, 193n1, 194n6–7, 195n11; and speculation, 31, 34, 203n93; and translational questions, 4, 9, 13, 31, 35
Board of Trade of Chicago v. Christie Grain & Stock Co., 129
Boethius: *Consolation of Philosophy* (*De consolatione philosophiae*) by, 17–20, 24–25, 199n50; *De institutione musica* by, 17; *De trinitate* by, 17; modernizations of, 122, 134, 176, 180; and Porphyry, 16, 195n11; and *speculatio*, 11, 15–26, 41, 83, 88, 93; and *theōria*, 15–19; as transitional figure, 21; translation by Chaucer of, 21, 23–27; as translator of Aristotle, 11, 15–19, 21, 26, 195n11–13; Wheel of Fortune of, 122
Boyle, Robert, 46, 52
Browne, Thomas, 46
Bulwer-Lytton, Edward, 139
Burney, Frances, 151, 154–55
Butler, Samuel, 125, 178

Calvin, John, 9, 145; and anti-chance theology, 72–74, 128, 162, 223n33; and "idle speculation," 5, 11, 29–42, 57, 63, 68
capitalism: Defoe on, 52; early modern, 38–39, 58, 224n33; and finance, 2, 66–67, 71, 106, 108, 180; and futurity, 124, 145, 171; and madness, 111; Smith on, 68, 78, 80–83, 94. *See also* economics

Carter v. Boehm, 70–71
Catholicism, 33, 36, 50, 202n77. *See also* Aquinas; Augustine; scholasticism; theology
Cavendish, Margaret, 151, 154
Chambers, Julius, 119–20
chance: in Calvinist theology, 72–74, 128, 162, 223n33; in capitalism, 66, 71–72, 168; conceptual histories of, 5; and free will, 20; and gambling, 73–74, 150, 156–57, 168; and idleness, 34; and predictability, 126–28; and speculative fiction, 140. *See also* fortune; gambling
Chaucer, Geoffrey: *Boece* by, 18, 23–26, 199n50–52; and Calvin, 31, 33, 35, 40; influence of, 27, 198n45; as translator, 4, 9, 11, 18, 21, 23–26; *Troilus and Criseyde* by, 26
Chimera, The (Defoe), 63–64
Chopin, Kate, 162–63
Christianity. *See* Aquinas; Augustine; Bible; Boethius; Calvin; Catholicism; Jerome; Paul; philosophy; Protestantism; Puritans; scholasticism; theology
Claflin sisters, the, 165–66
cognition: and computers, 176; as contemplation, 5, 20, 136, 153–54; and data, 118; as evidence, 46; and imagination, 87; philological history of, 3, 11, 83, 88; as pointless labor, 30, 33, 36; projective, 49, 54
Coleridge, Samuel Taylor, 87–88, 111
Columbus, Christopher, 79, 114
commodity speculation, 2, 115–19, 124, 126, 133–37, 156, 175
computation, 3, 124, 171, 173, 176–80
concepts. *See* intellectual history
conduct manuals (for women), 149, 157
Confidence-Man, The (Melville), 133
conjecture, 38, 45–46, 71, 77, 91, 103, 109, 176
Conrad, Joseph, 127, 132
Consolation of Philosophy (Boethius), 17–20, 24–25

INDEX 251

contemplation: in aesthetic production, 136; in Bacon, 42–43; creativity of, 1; divine, 15, 20–22, 57, 86, 153, 197n38; and finance, 109, 112, 123; and futurity, 182; gendering of, 153–55, 159; as *katoptrizō*, 10; in linguistic history, 12–13, 15, 16, 20–29, 31, 42, 193n1, 194n10, 195n10, 197n38; as method, 40, 42–43, 46, 48, 55, 58; in romanticism, 86–90; and *speculacioun*, 24, 26–27, 31; and *speculatio*, 13, 15–17, 20–22, 24–25, 197n39; stakes of, 8; and *theōria*, 16, 195n10; as visual observation, 27, 55, 58, 86–87, 153
Cotton, Charles, 74
Coulter, Dale, 197n32, 198n43
creativity, 1, 23, 37, 86, 170
credit instruments: crises and, 107–8; effect on language of, 84–85; emergence of, 6; as fictions, 50–51, 107; and futurity, 50–51, 66, 85, 95; and gambling, 74–75, 95, 150; personifications of, 54, 143, 147, 151–52, 156, 165
critical finance studies, 247n28
critique, 5, 7, 141, 144, 164, 170–71
crowds: and confidence men, 133; psychology of, 109, 111, 143, 233n67

Dall, Caroline H., 167
Daniel Deronda (Eliot), 161–64
Darwin, Charles, 48, 178
Daston, Lorraine, 202n77
debt: personal, 64, 97–98, 146, 149, 151–52, 159, 169; public, 50–51, 53, 59, 64, 69–70, 84, 95
deception, 54–55, 59, 61, 67, 74. *See also* trust
Declaration of Independence of the United States, the, 91, 94, 96
Defoe, Daniel, 39; on "air money," 135, 152, 183; *Anatomy of Exchange-Alley* by, 51–52; *The Chimera* by, 63–64; *Essay Upon Projects* by, 53, 55; and Haywood, 154; and Lady Credit, 143, 151–52; and the "Projecting Age," 52–56, 59; *Roxana* by, 152; and Swift, 61
Descartes, René, 46
De trinitate (Augustine), 9–10, 12–15, 17, 193n1
Dickens, Charles, 160–61
Dickson, P.G.M., 49
dictionaries, 5, 25–26, 28, 67, 89–90, 125, 182
Dictionary of the English Language (Johnson), 3, 35, 65–66, 69, 213n1
disease: speculation as, 5, 74, 100, 106, 147, 165
divination, 1, 109–10, 113, 123, 126, 165
divinity, 2, 11, 13–15, 18, 20–23, 26–27, 32–33, 35, 40, 44, 86, 128, 144, 153
Duer, William, 103, 148

economics: and gambling, 51–52, 67–69, 73, 75–76, 79, 82, 95, 124; in literature, 83–85, 102, 132–35, 138–40, 152, 159, 161, 228n80; manias in, 101–2, 104–8, 112, 129; projects in, 56, 59, 68, 79, 94, 102; risks in, 66, 117, 127, 130, 192n11; and science, 51–52, 56, 79, 137; and states, 51–52; theories of, 66, 78–79, 82, 84, 125–27; vocabularies of, 49, 67, 69, 79, 82–85, 87, 89, 104, 106, 108, 125, 159; and women, 2, 143–44, 147, 152, 159, 161, 164, 170. *See also* banking; capitalism; commodity speculation; credit instruments; debt; futures contracts; gambling; insurance; investment; lotteries; political economy
Edgeworth, Maria, 155–56
Edwards, Jonathan, 35
Einstein, Albert, 140, 174
Eliot, George, 144, 161–64
Elizabeth I (Queen), 26, 73
Elyot, Thomas, 28, 200n61
embodiment, 20, 25, 104–5, 114, 117, 131, 142, 144–45, 148, 154, 162, 167, 180, 182

Emerson, Ralph Waldo, 93, 111–13, 143, 150, 156
Emery, Henry Crosby, 129, 234n74
empiricism, 11, 13, 39, 46, 49, 57, 111
engrossing, 81, 94–95
epistemology, 10–11, 18, 51, 56
etymology, 5. *See also* philology
Evans, Gillian Rosemary, 21–22
evidence: interpretation of, 39, 56, 58, 63, 70, 79, 81, 116; nature of, 46, 55–56, 63; and prediction, 1–2, 55–56, 63, 70, 72, 75–76; visual, 55, 58
Ewald, François, 72
experience, 181, 183; of the market, 118; and scientific inquiry, 44–48, 55, 206n21; and speculitis, 116
experiment: America as, 91–93, 95, 105, 111, 113; computational, 177; on money, 49–52; and Mr. Spectator, 58, 78; and projects, 53, 55–56, 62–63, 79, 89; proof by, 71; scientific, 5, 39–40, 43–49, 51–52, 62–63, 66, 72, 109, 116, 206n21; in Smith, 78–79; thought, 48, 57, 77, 87
expertise: and hunches, 121; and information, 116–17, 125, 130, 145, 167; politics of, 116, 119, 129–31, 137, 145, 149, 165, 167, 170

Fabian, Ann, 5, 74, 215n30
fancy, 34, 51, 54–55, 79, 87, 142–43, 153–54, 225n41
faro, 150
Female Spectator, The (Haywood), 153
feminism, 148–49, 164, 169–70, 237n7
fever, 5, 8, 61, 92, 105–6, 111, 141–42, 150, 225n41. *See also* addiction; disease; gender; madness; mania; medical history
Fielding, Sarah, 152, 240n35
financialization, 145, 247n28
financial revolution, the, 5, 49, 53, 72, 143, 146, 150, 152, 155
Florio, John, 28
fortune, 5, 174; in Boethius, 20, 122; in Calvinism, 30–31, 34, 73, 223n33; in finance, 55, 58–59, 72–75, 79–81, 104, 122, 141, 150; and gaming, 34, 73–75, 79–81, 141, 150, 157–58, 162; and idleness, 34, 110; of nations, 74, 93, 144; personifications of, 84, 152
fortune-telling, 8, 109, 119
Fowler, William Worthington, 142–43, 165
Frankenstein (Shelley), 86–87
Franklin, Benjamin, 99, 221n8
Freneau, Philip, 101–2
futurity: abstract, 11; and Bacon, 44; and Calvinism, 31; early modern debates about, 63; fictions of, 124, 139–40; and insurance contracts, 70; narratives of, 6; and projects, 53–54, 114; and risk, 175, 182; and the state, 51; technological, 2, 117, 120, 123, 137; and women, 145, 153, 164, 169
futures contracts, 117, 124–25, 135–36, 231n23

Gallagher, Catherine, 151, 155
gambling, 2–3, 5, 88; in Calvinism, 73; and computers, 177; as contagion, 92, 103, 105; financial, 8, 38, 51–52, 66, 71–73, 75, 79–83, 92, 95, 97, 106, 109, 115, 119, 124, 135, 148–49, 215n30; philology of, 73–75; and women, 141, 143–45, 147–51, 154–55, 157, 161–65; writing against, 73–76, 92, 98–100, 102–3, 105, 136, 141, 147, 150, 165. *See also* addiction; disease; lotteries; madness
gender: and embodied passions, 142–44; and expertise, 129, 137; and futurity, 164. *See also* feminism; women; women's writing
Gibson, Thomas, 126–27
Giddens, Anthony, 174–75
Gilded Age, the, 131, 136
Goethe, Johann Wolfgang von, 86, 89
Gordon, William, 100, 105–6
Greek (language), 10, 12–14, 16, 18–19, 25, 36, 193n1, 194n6, 195n12

Green, Hetty, 168
Gulliver's Travels (Swift), 61–63

Habermas, Jürgen, 56
Hacking, Ian, 5, 214n21
Hamilton, Alexander, 96–97, 105
Haraway, Donna J., 178
Hardy, Thomas, 132, 151, 242n81
Hawthorne, Nathaniel, 237n4
Haywood, Eliza, 144, 149, 153–54, 159
Hebrew (language), 14, 194n9, 197n39
Heinlein, Robert, 137–38
Henderson, Andrea, 154, 215n27
history of the novel, 56, 132, 136, 138, 144–45, 151–53, 156–57, 162, 236n92
Hobbes, Thomas, 48–49, 82, 202n77
Hogarth, William, 59–60
Holmes, Oliver Wendell, 129–30
Hoyle, Edmond, 157
Hoyne, Thomas Temple, 139
Hume, David, 49, 53, 208n45
Hurston, Zora Neale, 170

ideas: and concepts, 190n3; of context, 193n13; formation of, 18; history in, 6; and hypotheses, 47; as technologies, 139; trade in, 135. *See also* intellectual history
idleness, 7–8; and Bacon, 40; and Boethius, 18; and Calvinism, 5, 11, 31–34, 40, 63, 145; disruptive power of, 39; and finance, 51, 96, 98–99, 135; and gaming, 73–74, 165; and projects, 54; and women, 145–48, 165, 167
imagination, 5, 66; American, 96; in Bacon, 42; Boethian, 33; in Calvinism, 32; in Coleridge, 87–88, 111; collective, 3, 128, 181–82; and credit, 54, 59, 64; in early Christianity, 13; in Emerson, 111; and gambling, 76, 135; and science, 42, 46–47; and women, 146, 148, 169. *See also* fancy
Impressionism, 136

information: cultural history of, 1–3, 70–71, 115–30, 176–77
insurance, 2, 83, 178; contracts of, 70–73; and science, 66; social, 172
intellectual history, 15, 33, 36, 53, 134
investment, 127, 135–37, 148, 151, 167, 179–80, 181–83
irrationality, 3, 109, 150, 165, 168, 225n42
Isagōgē (Porphyry), 16, 195n11

Jackson, Andrew, 107–8
James, William, 128, 232n44
Janssen, Stephen Theodore, 68
Jefferson, Thomas, 95
Jevons, William Stanley, 125–26
Jerome (Saint), 14, 197n39
Johnson, Samuel, 3, 35, 55, 65–66, 69, 88–89
Jonson, Ben, 53
Joyce, James, 137, 170, 233n64, 235n84

Keats, John, 87
Keynes, John Maynard, 174
Knight, Frank, 175
Knox, John, 32, 45
Koselleck, Reinhart, 191n9

"Lady Credit" (Defoe), 143, 151–52, 156, 165
Latin (language), 9–14, 16–17, 19, 23–29, 31, 36, 41–43, 53, 57, 64, 88–89, 193–95
Law, John, 63, 79, 109. *See also* Mississippi Bubble
Lears, T. J. Jackson, 5, 75, 128
Le Bon, Gustave, 143
Levy, Jonathan, 5, 134
Locke, John, 39, 49, 207n45
Lord Mansfield, 70–71, 104
lotteries, 51, 59–60, 71, 73–74, 79–80, 84, 95, 101, 125, 154, 212n84, 215n31
Lovelace, Ada, 4, 177
luck. *See* chance
Luther, Martin, 30, 212n93

Mace, Daniel, 35
machines, 78; cognition of, 176–80; and information, 116–20, 123; and risk, 173, 176, 181, 183; and speculative fiction, 139–40
Mackay, Charles, 81–82, 93, 104, 109–11, 113, 118, 143, 157–58, 165
Madison, James, 96, 103
madness, 93, 99, 101, 104, 110–13, 115, 156, 224n41. *See also* mania
Makin, Bathsua, 145–46
mania, 61, 92–93, 99–114, 149–50, 159–62. *See also* crowds; disease
Mansfield Park (Austen), 157–59, 241n60
Marx, Karl, 64, 134, 136
McCarthy, Tom, 180–83, 247n28
McKay, Claude, 137, 235n83
medical history, 92, 99–100, 105, 108, 169, 224n41
Meixner, Laura, 136, 168–69
Melville, Herman, 133
Memoirs of Extraordinary Popular Delusions and the Madness of Crowds (Mackay), 93, 109–11, 143
mercantilism, 24, 80, 217n56
mint. *See* money
Mississippi Bubble, the, 63, 79, 101, 103, 109–10
mobs. *See* crowds
modernism, 136–37, 233n64, 264n5
modernity, 1, 36, 83, 117, 145, 174, 246n5
Moivre, Abraham de, 73
money: 7–8, 39, 49–56, 69–70, 73, 79, 98–99, 135, 148–49, 180–82. *See also* "air money"; banking; capitalism; commodity speculation; credit instruments; debt; economics; futures contracts; gambling; insurance; investment; lotteries; political economy
Mortimer, Thomas, 68, 148–49
Murray, William. *See* Lord Mansfield

natural philosophy, 5, 10, 35, 38–39, 41–46, 48, 52, 58, 75, 140
nature: as book, 40; of collective agency, 175; of divinity, 14, 22, 40, 112; in Emerson, 112; history of, 41; human, 15, 131, 208n45; of the United States, 94; of value, 39
New Capitalist Studies, 192n11
New Negro Movement, the, 137, 235n83
Newton, Isaac, 39, 45, 59, 212n86
Norris, Frank, 132, 134–35
Novum organum (Bacon), 43, 205n12

Ora, Reyam, 115–16
Ouida [Maria Louisa Ramé], 167
Oxford English Dictionary, the, 108, 137, 192n10, 200n57, 225n42

panics, 108–9, 123, 142, 149, 168, 227n80, 234n67
Paul (Saint), 9–10, 13–14, 40, 202n80
perception: and comprehension, 27–28; Greek and Latin theories of, 9, 193n2; and imagination, 88; insufficiency of, 3; and *speculatio*, 14, 17, 23; visual, 3, 17, 23, 27, 193n2
philology, 4, 6, 191n7
philosophy: Aristotelian, 13, 16, 23; Baconian, 40–46; Boethian, 15–22, 41, 83, 195; of chance, 128; Christian, 15, 21, 23; empiricist, 11, 13, 39, 46, 49, 57, 111; figures of, 18–19, 21, 77–78, 110; history of, 4–6, 9–10, 15–16, 38, 46, 86, 194n10; idealist, 86–87, 106; medieval, 10, 21, 23; and mirrors, 14; moral, 45, 85; natural, 5, 10, 35, 38–39, 41–46, 48, 52, 58, 75, 140; Platonic, 15–18, 23, 42, 87, 202n77; practical, 6, 16, 35, 45–48, 78, 85, 194n10; speculative, 6, 16, 18, 35, 45–48, 86; and women, 159
physiocrats, 51, 77, 82, 98, 133
Picciotto, Joanna, 204n2, 206n17
Pietruska, Jamie, 5, 127

Pinto, Isaac de, 69–70, 81
Planck, Max, 140
Platonism, 15–18, 23, 42, 87, 202n77
Pocock, J.G.A., 50, 70, 143, 152
political economy, 53, 67, 73, 78, 82–83, 125
Poovey, Mary, 45–46, 203n85
Pope, Alexander, 59, 147
Porphyry of Tyre, 16, 195n11
practice/practical, 6, 11; and finance capitalism, 81–83, 90; 112, 131, 171, 190n3; and speculation/speculative experimentation, 38–49, 54, 57–58, 62–63; and speculation/speculative philosophy, 15–37
prediction, 5; in capitalism, 80, 127; by computers, 177–79; data-driven, 1, 117, 126, 128, 178; hypothetical, 72; languages of, 137; legal study of, 129; and the new science, 39; and the ticker, 117, 120, 123, 125
probability, 75, 125, 128, 175
Projecting Age, the, 53–54, 56, 152
projects, 5; debates about, 39, 52–56, 59–63
Protestantism, 2, 31, 33, 36, 75, 195n10, 224n33. *See also* Calvin; Reformation; theology
Proust, Marcel, 137, 179, 235n84
psychoanalysis, 140
Puritans, 34, 95, 98, 204n98, 224n33

Ramsay, Allan, 146–47
reason, 8, 13, 29, 43, 45, 66, 88, 154, 212n93
Reformation, the, 30, 73
Remainder (McCarthy), 180–83, 247n28
Richard, Jessica, 151, 212n84
risk, 2–5, 181; condemnation of, 7; and futurity, 175–77; and machines, 178, 183; management of, 127, 182; manufactured, 174, 176; monetary, 39, 56, 63, 66–67, 69, 73–74, 76, 81–82, 106, 111, 117, 129–31, 135, 144, 148–49, 165, 168, 234n74; technologies of, 72; as value, 247n28

risk society, 172, 174, 176, 245n3
romanticism, 67, 85–88, 90, 111, 179, 218n80
Rosenfeld, Sophia, 190n6
Royal Society, 39, 45–48, 53, 58, 62
Rush, Benjamin, 92, 99–101, 108, 113, 115, 134

Sakolski, Aaron M., 114, 128
Sandage, Scott, 5, 124
Schoenbach, Lisi, 127–28, 246n5
scholasticism, 21, 24, 27–28, 30, 40
Schwartz, David G., 5, 215n24, 216n31
science: history of, 1, 29, 36, 38–56, 63–64, 82–83, 109, 124–27, 137–40, 174–79. *See also* philosophy; reason; technology
scientific revolution, 2, 5, 38, 49, 53, 140, 169, 195n10
Scots Magazine, 75–76
scripomania, 101, 148, 225n45
Shakespeare, William, 32, 53, 126, 219n90
Shelley, Mary, 86–87
Shonkwiler, Alison, 247n28
Sidney, Sir Philip, 32, 202n84
sight. *See* vision
Smith, Adam, 5, 66, 72–73, 77–83, 88–89, 92–94, 104, 109, 131, 134
smuggling, 67–68, 72–73, 89
South Sea Bubble, the, 6, 39, 51, 59–63, 74, 101, 103–4, 109–10, 147, 149, 152, 156, 173
Spectator, The, 56–58, 78, 147, 153. *See also* Joseph Addison; Richard Steele
specula (Latin), 10, 14, 20, 28, 43, 88, 182
speculatio (Latin), 10–26, 27, 28, 30, 43
Speculation; Or, A Defence of Mankind (Anstey), 7, 65, 83–85
speculum (Latin), 10–15, 20–26, 30–34, 102
speculation: as chimera, 4, 54, 191n7; as contagion 7, 92, 100, 102–8; divine, 11, 13–15, 20–21, 26–27, 32–33, 47, 86, 197n38; female, 142–45, 148, 153–54, 159, 161, 168–70; financial, 2, 4–5, 7–8, 34, 49–56, 59, 63–64, 69–73, 82–83, 87, 92–93, 95–97, 104, 110–11, 114–20, 125, 130, 132, 135–36, 138, 143–50, 172, 174–75, 178–82, 192n11,

speculation (*continued*)
200n61, 215n30, 218n84; idle, 5, 7, 11, 18, 27–34, 40, 49, 51, 63, 67, 73–74, 96, 135, 145, 155; marriage, 2, 145, 155–64; as mastery, 116–17, 119, 129–30, 142, 145, 170; mechanized, 125, 180; political, 74, 94, 101, 215n28; romantic, 67, 83–88, 90, 111; scientific, 4, 44–49, 52–53, 59, 62; as sin, 30, 32, 41, 135
speculation (card game), 157–59
speculative execution (computation), 179
speculative fiction, 2, 6, 85, 137–40
Sprat, Thomas, 47, 55
Stäheli, Urs, 5, 135, 234n77
statistics, 125, 128
Steele, Richard, 56–58, 69, 148, 153. See also Joseph Addison
stockjobbers, 51–52, 79, 83, 95, 97, 103–4, 107, 146, 149–50
stock tickers: and futures markets, 123–25, 134–35, 229n1; as information infrastructure, 117–18, 123–25, 140; invention of, 5, 116; as literary object, 122–23, 236n92; and magic, 118–20; and women, 141
superstition, 5, 82, 99, 109, 147
Swift, Jonathan, 39, 66, 94, 147; and the South Sea Bubble, 59–62

technology: and futurity, 117, 123–24, 137; and risk, 72, 174–76; and speculative fiction, 6, 139–40; and war, 173; and women, 145
telegraphy, 118
theology: Augustinian, 12–14; and Bacon, 40, 42; Boethian, 18, 21–26; Calvinist, 29–30, 32–33, 35, 40, 162, 223n33; speculative, 21, 29–30, 32–33, 35, 139, 197n32
theōria, 15–19, 21, 23, 25, 28, 195n10. See also *speculatio*
Theory of Moral Sentiments, The (Smith), 77–78

Thoreau, Henry David, 91, 113–14, 142, 163
Thrale, Hester, 76–77
Ticker, The (magazine), 115
transcendentalism, 111
translation: and Augustine, 9–10, 13–14, 193n1; of Aristotle, 4, 15–18, 195n10; of the Bible, 10, 13, 35, 193n1, 194n6; and Boethius, 15–19, 21, 23–24, 26–27, 195n11–13; and Calvin, 31–32, 69, 201n72; and Chaucer, 21, 23–24, 26–27, 199n46; in early modern English dictionaries, 27–28; networks of, 11, 199n50
trust, 71, 74, 150
tulip mania, 109, 225n42, 228n89
Turing, Alan, 176–77
Twain, Mark, 131–32
Tyler, John, 107–8, 129

uncertain commons, 171
United States of America, the: colonies of, 33, 94; contemporary life in, 5, 180; discovery of, 119, 130; founding of, 6, 91–92; information infrastructure of, 117; manias in, 100–111, 115; as a speculation, 91–96, 99, 111–14, 130
usury, 72, 99, 101, 130, 221n13

Verne, Jules, 138, 241n60
vision: abstraction of, 118; contemplative, 22; as etymological root, 6, 26, 82; female, 153; imperfection of, 3, 13–15, 18, 41; of machines, 173; and money, 61; physical, 87; and romanticism, 86. See also perception

Wall Street: and women, 141–43, 145, 163–66, 168, 170; writing on, 126, 130–31. See also stock tickers; investment
Warner, Charles Dudley, 122–23, 131
Washington, George, 95, 108
Wealth of Nations, The (Smith), 66, 75, 77–82, 93–94
Weber, Max, 33, 99, 128, 233n33

Webster, Noah, 90, 98, 220n99
Wells, H. G., 138–39, 235n85
Weyler, Karen, 101
Wharton, Edith, 132, 163
whist, 157, 241n60
whiteness, 114, 119, 130
Williams, Raymond, 6–7
Wilson, Woodrow, 7
witchcraft, 81, 149, 165

Wollstonecraft, Mary, 149, 154
women: as gamblers, 141, 143–45, 147–51, 157, 161–65; as investors, 143, 147–48, 151, 167, 170; as speculators, 2, 7, 22, 142–44, 146–71
women's writing, 5, 144–46, 149–64, 167, 169, 237n4
Woolf, Virginia, 154, 164, 169, 233n64
Wycliffe, John, 29

GPSR Authorized Representative: Easy Access System Europe, Mustamäe tee
50, 10621 Tallinn, Estonia, gpsr.requests@easproject.com

www.ingramcontent.com/pod-product-compliance
Lightning Source LLC
Chambersburg PA
CBHW021940290426
44108CB00012B/913